The British Dyslexia Association –
Teaching Dyslexic Students

of related interest

Parenting a Dyslexic Child
Edited by Gillian Ashley for the BDA
Foreword by Gavin Reid
ISBN 978 1 78775 426 3
eISBN 978 1 78775 427 0

Maths Learning Difficulties, Dyslexia and Dyscalculia
Second Edition
Steve Chinn
ISBN 978 1 78592 579 5
eISBN 978 1 78450 989 7

The Big Book of Dyslexia Activities for Kids and Teens
100+ Creative, Fun, Multi-sensory and Inclusive Ideas for Successful Learning
Gavin Reid, Nick Guise and Jennie Guise
ISBN 978 1 78592 377 7
eISBN 978 1 78450 725 1

GCSE Maths for Neurodivergent Learners
Build Your Confidence in Number, Proportion and Algebra
Judy Hornigold and Rose Jewell
Illustrated by Sophie Kennedy
ISBN 978 1 78775 700 4
eISBN 978 1 78775 701 1

The Dyslexia, ADHD and DCD Friendly Study Skills Guide
Tips and Strategies for Exam Success
Ann-Marie McNicholas
ISBN 978 1 78775 177 4
eISBN 978 1 78775 178 1

The Memory and Processing Guide for Neurodiverse Learners
Strategies for Success
Alison Patrick
Illustrated by Matthew Patrick
ISBN 978 1 78775 072 2
eISBN 978 1 78775 073 9

The British Dyslexia Association – Teaching Dyslexic Students

THEORY AND PRACTICE

British Dyslexia Association

Edited by Lynn Lovell

Foreword by Dr. Helen Ross

Jessica Kingsley Publishers
London and Philadelphia

First published in Great Britain in 2023 by Jessica Kingsley Publishers
An imprint of John Murray Press

3

A CIP catalogue record for this title is available from the British Library and the Library of Congress

ISBN 978 1 78775 745 5
eISBN 978 1 78775 746 2

Printed and bound by CPI Group (UK) Ltd, Croydon, CR0 4YY

Jessica Kingsley Publishers' policy is to use papers that are natural, renewable and recyclable products and made from wood grown in sustainable forests. The logging and manufacturing processes are expected to conform to the environmental regulations of the country of origin.

Jessica Kingsley Publishers
Carmelite House
50 Victoria Embankment
London EC4Y 0DZ

www.jkp.com

John Murray Press
Part of Hodder & Stoughton Limited
An Hachette UK Company

Contents

Contents . . . 5

Foreword by Dr Helen Ross . . . 7

Introduction by Michelle Catterson and Sarah Young . . . 9

1. What is Dyslexia? . . . 19
Lynn Lovell

2. Theories of Dyslexia . . . 29
Lynn Lovell

3. Other Specific Learning Difficulties Explained . . . 43
Implications for Specialist Interventions and Classroom Practice
Rachel Burn and Kayleigh Chang

4. Reading and Spelling . . . 59
Brenda Ferrie and Suzy Sheppard

5. How to Support Learners with Dyslexia in the Classroom and During Intervention . . 89
General Strategies/Principles
Sara Watts and Karen Bartlett

6. Identifying Strengths and Areas for Development for One-to-One/Small Group/ Class Work. . . . 105
What to Assess/Screen For and How – Individual and Group Screening and Analysing Results
Rachel Burn and Kayleigh Chang

7. Principles of Specialist Teaching . . . 123
Lucy Fletcher, Jill Hudson and Sarah Young

8. How to Support Learners with Dyslexia in the Classroom and During Intervention . . 135
Lynn Lovell, Lucy Fletcher, Humara Abidi and Sarah Hayman

9. Specialist Teaching 147
Brenda Ferrie, Suzy Sheppard and Sarah Young

10. Specialist Teaching for Older Learners 161
Alison Fairfax and Lynn Lovell

11. Planning a Specialist Teaching Programme 179
Lynn Lovell and Samantha Maylor-Wrout

12. Materials for Teaching 191
Resources and Methods for Specialist Teaching and Classroom Practice
Anna Sutton

13. Evaluation of Teaching 211
Lynn Lovell

14. Dyslexia-Friendly Practice 219
Alison Fairfax

Subject Index 231

Author Index 237

Foreword

DR HELEN ROSS, Vice Chair of the British Dyslexia Association Board of Trustees, Owner and Founder, Helen's Place Education Consultancy

Writing a foreword for a book is a privilege, but in starting to draft this piece of writing, the importance of dyslexia-friendly teaching was brought home to me; I am dyslexic and reading is a process that I find excruciatingly difficult. I had to think very hard about how to write the word 'foreword'. English is a complex language, full of diverse and sometimes almost nonsensical spelling and reading rules, which are often more like broad suggestions. I used the etymology of the word, breaking it into its constituent parts.

The process of using morphology, etymology and context to help discern words exemplifies the broad range of approaches that the specialist teacher needs when working with dyslexic learners. Spelling, reading and writing in English are complex beasts. This book provides the most wonderful foundation for specialist teacher trainees to develop their understanding of dyslexia and its effects, while delving into causal models, and exploring models of reading and spelling acquisition. The consideration of co-occurring difficulties included in this book provides vital insight into the challenges which are often experienced by young people with dyslexia; the intersection of learning difficulties presents diverse and complex challenges for which the specialist teacher must be prepared. This book gives pragmatic suggestions to support young people, but grounds them in solid, evidence-based strategies.

Structured, cumulative and multisensory approaches are at the heart of all good, dyslexia-friendly practice. Reflection and evaluation of progress are vital in supporting learners effectively in the classroom. This book embodies these principles perfectly for trainee Level 5 teachers: they are given structured information about dyslexia and its impacts (Chapters 1–5), supported to develop programmes of intervention for young people through rigorous assessment (Chapters 6–12) and then taken full-circle back to evaluation of progress against students' targets.

This book is a must-have resource for the trainee specialist teacher and experienced veteran alike! I am certainly grateful for having had the opportunity to read it!

Introduction

MICHELLE CATTERSON, Head of the Board of Trustees, and
SARAH YOUNG, Professional Level Tutor with the British Dyslexia Association

The role of a specialist teacher is one of immense value. The potential you will have, when you qualify, in meeting a dyslexic person's needs, can be transformational.

Dyslexia is thought to affect one in ten of the population. As you embark on training to become a specialist teacher – specifically to achieve accredited teacher or practitioner status (ATS/APS) on a Level 5 course – you are a committed educator who wishes to increase their knowledge of literacy difficulties. You also wish to develop the necessary skills to support children and young people to reach their full potential, guiding them to harness support, such as assistive technology, at each stage of their lifelong learning journey.

This book is produced by the British Dyslexia Association (BDA) to guide you through this process. At the BDA, we strive to raise awareness in schools, workplaces and communities in order to support learners and promote a better understanding of the needs of dyslexic individuals, thus ensuring a successful future for all. The BDA is the leading UK charity for those with dyslexia. As a charity, our work in outreach and in supporting the dyslexic community, and our impact on practical research and policy in the field of dyslexia, are second to none. We already offer the Level 5 training, and this textbook for specialist teachers is designed to support all those undertaking that training. It enables the BDA to reach a far wider audience with our top-quality teaching programmes and our expertise, and ensure that many more dyslexics benefit from the expertise of qualified Level 5 individuals.

We hope that all those reading this book feel equipped as specialist teachers to deliver dyslexia-friendly strategies and interventions that enable all those they are working with to feel empowered, understood and able to achieve their very best.

This go-to guide was developed by experienced professional course tutors at the British Dyslexia Association to support individuals undertaking a Level 5 course to become specialist teachers of learners with literacy difficulties and/or dyslexia. However, while the book is closely connected to our Level 5 course, the content is applicable much more broadly to all those who work with learners whose literacy difficulties are impacting their access to the curriculum of study. All the content in this book, including the research analysis and the theoretical framework surrounding literacy acquisition, and the multisensory methods of teaching discussed in each chapter, is applicable to all dyslexic learners in a full range of contexts, and comes from a place of profound knowledge and understanding, developed over the years of the BDA's work.

This book should be considered an introduction to the Level 5 specialist teaching course, and it should be used as a resource alongside the reader's individual, independent research and review of seminal works and more recent research sources.

This publication is designed to inform practice by providing a theoretical foundation to understanding dyslexia in the first chapters, then moving on to describe current effective teaching strategies rooted in this pedagogical context. Chapter 1 discusses the definition of dyslexia as a specific learning difficulty as outlined by the Rose Report (2009), affecting efficient and effortless word reading and spelling. There is additional guidance from the BDA (2010), which acknowledges possible visual and auditory processing difficulties as well as the many strengths exhibited by an individual with dyslexia. As in all areas of teaching, it is important to determine and understand the areas of difficulty as well as acknowledge and utilize the individual strengths of the learner, so that there is a clear rationale for the methods of support chosen. In this chapter, the characteristic features of dyslexia are explained within the context of its complex nature, and reference is made to co-occurring difficulties that may be experienced by some learners.

Chapter 2 introduces many of the underpinning theories of dyslexia as well as the possible causal theories from a historical perspective. Theories discussed include the phonological deficit theory (Bradley & Bryant, 1983; Liberman *et al.*, 1974; Ramus, n.d.; Stanovich, 1986; Snowling *et al.*, 2019; Vellutino *et al.*, 2004), double deficit theory (Wolf & Bowers, 1999), magnocellular theory (Stein, 2001), temporal sampling theory (Goswami *et al.*, 2012) and cerebellar theory (Nicolson & Fawcett, 1999). The multi deficit model (Pennington, 2006) is explained, which attempts to unify the causal theories and the variety of possible difficulties and challenges experienced by the learner with dyslexia. The purpose here is to inform your knowledge base and justify the later suggested methods of multisensory, structured and cumulative support which link to these possible causes of dyslexia and the impact on areas of cognitive function related to literacy acquisition. Morton and

Frith's (1995) three-level framework is also discussed with reference to the likely biological origins of dyslexia, the cognitive, behavioural and environmental impacts, alongside other characteristics of dyslexia such as working memory and genetic research. This elucidates the myriad of interacting factors described by researchers and seeks to acknowledge the individual profiles of the nature of dyslexia.

Research tells us that the co-existence of specific learning difficulties (SpLDs) is common and it is unlikely that any SpLD exist in isolation (Snowling, 2009). This is discussed in Chapter 3, which outlines other specific learning difficulties and developmental conditions that dyslexia may overlap with, to enable practitioners to derive a general overview of the variety of individual learner profiles in order to plan appropriate support. Links are again made to multiple risk factors (Pennington, 2006) as well as protective factors and the commonly co-occurring neurodiverse conditions. These may include attention-related disorders described as attention deficit hyperactivity disorder (ADHD) or attention deficit disorder (ADD), developmental language disorder (DLD), dyscalculia, developmental coordination disorder (DCD, dyspraxia) and autism (ASD), as well as anxiety and visual difficulties. A short discussion of each is included with suggested approaches for supportive strategies in the learning environment.

In order to support understanding of how literacy skills develop and the difficulty with these processes for the learner with dyslexia, Chapter 4 is divided into two sections to explain the models of reading and spelling. In part 1, reading is considered as a product of both decoding words and linguistic comprehension (Gough & Tunmer, 1986). Rose (2006) emphasized how Gough and Tunmer's 'Simple View of Reading' identifies the good reader who has good decoding and language comprehension as opposed to a learner with dyslexia who may have good language comprehension but poor decoding skills. An outline of further models is also included, such as Scarborough's rope model (2001), the phonological and orthographic routes to reading and spelling (Milne, 2005), the connectionist model (Seidenberg & McClelland, 1989) and the dual route cascaded model (Coltheart, 2005) with lexical and non-lexical routes to reading. These models are included in this chapter to support understanding of the semantic lexical processes and the complex task of reading which informs teaching of regular words (phonological non-lexical route) and irregular words through a lexical whole-word route as described by Milne (2005). Reference to teaching methods is included here to specifically identify the need for good oral language skills to teach phonological awareness and then word reading separately from prose reading.

Part 2 of this chapter is dedicated to defining spelling and the processes involved in making links between written letters and spoken sounds which can cause difficulties for the learner with dyslexia. Spelling English words is a complex process as English is an opaque language having been derived from our rich and diverse cultural heritage. Helping learners understand this etymology can also support learning. In this section, spelling is discussed with reference to authors such as Milne (2005), who describes the brain's upper circuit for encoding and the lower circuit for direct recall of whole words as the processes used for spelling regular or irregular words. An introduction to the staged/phased models of Ehri (2002) and Gentry (1982) is included, and morphological awareness is described in relation to the work of researchers such as Bowers *et al.* (2010). Links to the English National Curriculum (Department for Education, 2013), expectations and possible support strategies are also found in this chapter.

Didactic approaches to supporting the learner with dyslexia will relate to the impact of difficulties in areas such as phonological awareness, verbal memory (working memory and phonological memory) and verbal processing speed as well as attention, motor skills, organization and visual/auditory processing. An introduction to suggested further support for these areas and reasonable adjustments in the classroom and in individual interventions is discussed in Chapter 5, where general teaching strategies are outlined relating to a learner's needs. The specialist teacher needs to consider the areas of difficulty in order to enable access to learning and support reading and spelling skills and automaticity. This chapter explains how targeted intervention needs to be structured, cumulative, sequential and multisensory, with opportunities for overlearning (Rose, 2009). Multisensory teaching involves two or more senses being used simultaneously, resulting in a stronger memory being formed. Therefore, activities that combine visual, auditory, tactile and kinaesthetic actions are multisensory and will lead to more successful learning (Kelly & Phillips, 2022), and this is why we advocate using a programme such as the Conquering Literacy Programme by Kelly and Phillips (2022) to support literacy difficulties. It is widely acknowledged that early identification of difficulties and targeted intervention are key to success.

In order to support learners effectively, there must be a robust initial screening to identify those who may need support, followed by an assessment process to establish individual strengths and learning requirements. These are outlined in Chapter 6, which is designed to support the assessment part of the specialist teaching phase of the Level 5 course. The primary focus of initial assessment is to inform planning and teaching, but teachers will continue to monitor and evaluate their learner's responses and ongoing needs as they teach their programme of support, while personalizing any programme with the recognition of the learner's strengths and interests. The requirements of the Level 5 course with regard to assessment are explained throughout this chapter.

Chapter 7 explains the principles of specialist teaching and what is meant by the terms multisensory, structured and cumulative, while outlining why overlearning is essential for the learner with dyslexia. Aspects of memory are described with reference to Baddeley and Hitch's (1974) multicomponent working memory model so that the reasons for the multisensory approach are clarified. In addition, the importance of teaching to foster metacognition so that a learner understands how they learn is woven into the advocated teaching approaches, with a clear explanation of why this is required before it is discussed in more detail in the next chapter.

Although approaches to supporting learners with dyslexia are discussed in Chapter 5, in Chapter 8 this is developed further to focus on specific 'tools' to empower the learner. A crucial consideration here is to support self-esteem and confidence, as research has identified the impact of low self-esteem on learner motivation and engagement (Alexander-Passe, 2015). An important aspect, as discussed earlier, is developing learner metacognition, which requires the learner to be aware of their own thought processes and therefore their most effective learning strategies (Education Endowment Foundation, 2011). This is further explained in this chapter within the context of how to foster metacognition within your lessons, supporting study skills and the importance of enabling the learner's voice.

Many learners with dyslexia and literacy difficulties require specialist teaching to develop distinct skills. Although synthetic phonics is the current method of teaching letter-sound knowledge, the most effective approach is likely to be one that teaches children to identify sounds (phonemes) in spoken language first (phonological awareness) before teaching how these are represented by letters and letter combinations (graphemes), as advocated by Rose (2006). The importance of analytic phonics, morphology and whole language also needs to be considered (Muter, 2021). This approach is presented in Chapter 9 with reference to the historical philosophy that underpins the Conquering Literacy Programme (Kelly & Phillips, 2022), which is the multisensory intervention recommended on the BDA's Level 5 course. This programme of support is based on recent research on dyslexia and is rooted in the principles of structured, cumulative and multisensory learning. An overview is presented here of a specialist literacy lesson with structured alphabet work, phonological awareness training, discovery learning, reading and spelling cards, whole-word reading and spelling, prose reading, writing skills and the use of ICT and games to support and consolidate learning according to the learner's needs. Review and routines are interspersed throughout a lesson to provide opportunities for overlearning and developing metacognition, which is further encouraged with a structured plenary.

As dyslexia can be considered as a lifelong learning difficulty (Rose, 2009), strategies for teaching older learners are presented in Chapter 10. As difficulties with literacy may remain, the far-reaching impacts are discussed, and, again, the importance of the unique learner profile is explained because experiences and compensatory strategies will differ for each individual, as established through relevant assessment. Therefore, individualized programmes of support which maintain the principles of specialist teaching need to be developed relating to the type of educational setting or workplace, the learner's needs and the priorities of the individual. In addition, the common areas of difficulty with study skills will also be addressed relating to reading, writing, organization and memory (Reid, 2020). Encouraging access to assistive technology and appropriate resources also needs to be a key element.

Chapter 11 expands on how to plan a specialist teaching programme of support based on the results of assessment outlined in Chapter 6, which allows creation of a scheme of work related to the learner's needs. How to formulate SMART targets, using a graduated approach, is explained in this chapter in more detail. These enable ongoing monitoring of progress and the teaching programme as a whole. Although you are planning a scheme of work, you also need to evaluate the effectiveness of this while teaching, and review this regularly, indicating where adjustments may be needed in the light of, for example, the learner's changing needs, mastery of concepts, pace of work and motivation. It may be that specialist teaching is targeted at the individual, small group or classroom level, but regular reflection and review are still essential and any intervention should focus on transferable skills that link to the classroom and wider life.

Resources and methods for specialist teaching and classroom practice are considered in Chapter 12, signposting the specialist teacher to some materials that are available and that highlight quality-first teaching practices. This is not an exhaustive list of dyslexia-friendly approaches and resources but is gathered from a range of suggestions from experienced specialist teachers. Trainee specialist teachers will need to choose engaging resources relevant to the needs, strengths and interests of their learners, and remember the principle of multisensory teaching, accessibility and individual learning styles. The chapter is organized into skills-based sections for ease of reference and you are encouraged to make your own list/toolkit and add to it over time. As available technology is updated frequently, the specialist must make their own judgement before investing in programmes or subscriptions, but current websites, assistive technology and games are included that reflect the time of publication of this book. You are advised to keep up to date with short courses, conferences and webinars.

Evaluation of teaching at regular intervals is a crucial aspect of any teaching programme of support to ensure that the learner is making progress and to identify the next steps of support required. In order to become a reflective practitioner, who maintains the focus on the learner's ongoing needs in planning and teaching, regular review is required, as discussed in Chapter 13. When and how to evaluate progress is explained, as is the importance of discussing effective approaches with others involved in the individual's learning as well as the learners themselves to ensure continued support and ongoing success. In addition, professionals must maintain and extend their own level of knowledge with regular access to sources enabling continued professional development.

The final chapter considers a whole-school approach to supporting those with dyslexia and literacy difficulties by outlining dyslexia-friendly schools/organizations good practice and how to achieve this. A dyslexia-friendly organization requires the involvement and commitment of all those involved. The BDA website provides access to the BDA Dyslexia Friendly Quality Mark for settings to aspire to and achieve. This covers four standards: leadership and management, the quality of learning, the climate for learning, and the partnerships with parents, carers, governors and stakeholders (BDA, n.d.). This provides a framework of support and understanding of dyslexia and literacy difficulties.

We trust that this book will inform and guide you on the path to becoming a specialist teacher who will maintain the principles of structured, cumulative and multisensory teaching to support learners with dyslexia, while empowering them to achieve success and independence.

BDA

References

Alexander-Passe, N. (2015) *Dyslexia and Mental Health: Helping People Identify Destructive Behaviours and Find Positive Ways to Cope*. London: Jessica Kingsley Publishers.

Baddeley, A.D. & Hitch, G. (1974) Working Memory. In G.H. Bower (ed.), *Psychology of Learning and Motivation*, 8, pp.47–89. New York, NY: Elsevier.

Bowers, P.N., Kirby, J.R. & Deacon, S.H. (2010) The effects of morphological instruction on literacy skills: A systematic review of the literature. *Review of Educational Research*, 80, 144–179.

Bradley, L. & Bryant, P.E. (1983) Categorizing sounds and learning to read – a causal connection. *Nature*, 301(5899), 419–421.

British Dyslexia Association (n.d.) *Dyslexia Friendly Quality Mark*. Available at: www.bdadyslexia.org.uk/services/dyslexia-friendly-awards/dyslexia-friendly-quality-mark-awards [Accessed 24 August 2022].

British Dyslexia Association (2010) *What is Dyslexia?* Available at: www.bdadyslexia.org.uk/dyslexia/about-dyslexia/what-is-dyslexia [Accessed 22 August 2022].

Coltheart, M. (2005) Modelling Reading: The Dual-Route Approach. In M.J. Snowling & C. Hulme (eds), *The Science of Reading: A Handbook*, pp.6–23. Oxford: Blackwell.

Department for Education (DfE) (2013) *The National Curriculum in England*. Available at: https://assets.publishing.service.gov.uk/government/uploads/system/uploads/attachment_data/file/425601/PRIMARY_national_curriculum.pdf [Accessed 24 August 2022].

Education Endowment Foundation (EEF) (2011) *Metacognition and Self-Regulation*. Available at: https://educationendowmentfoundation.org.uk/education-evidence/teaching-learning-toolkit/metacognition-and-self-regulation?utm_source=/education-evidence/teaching-learning-toolkit/metacognition-and-self-regulation&utm_medium=search&utm_campaign=site_search&search_term=metacognition [Accessed 24 August 2022].

Ehri, L.C. (2002) Phases of acquisition in learning to read words and implications for teaching. *British Journal of Educational Psychology: Monograph Series*, 1, 7–28.

Gentry, J.R. (1982) An analysis of developmental spelling in GNYS AT WRK. *The Reading Teacher*, 36, 192–200.

Gough, P.B. & Tunmer, W.E. (1986) Decoding, reading, and reading disability. *Remedial and Special Education*, 7, 6–10.

Goswami, U., Gerson, D., Astruc, L., Huss, M. & Mead, N. (2012) Dyslexia – in tune but out of time. *Trends in Cognitive Sciences*, 15, 3–10.

Kelly, K. & Phillips, S. (2022) *Teaching Literacy to Learners with Dyslexia: A Multisensory Approach*, third edition. London: Corwin.

Liberman, I.Y., Shankweiler, D., Fischer, F.W. & Carter, B. (1974) Explicit syllable and phoneme segmentation in the young child. *Journal of Experimental Child Psychology*, 18(2), 201–212.

Milne, D. (2005) *Teaching the Brain to Read*. Hungerford: Smart Kids Publishing.

Morton, J. & Frith, U. (1995) Causal Modelling: A Structured Approach to Developmental Psychopathology. In D. Cicchetti & D.J. Cohen (eds), *Manual of Developmental Psychopathology*, pp.357–390. New York, NY: Wiley.

Muter, V. (2021) *Understanding and Supporting Children with Literacy Difficulties*. London: Jessica Kingsley Publishers.

Nicolson, R.I. & Fawcett, A.J. (1999) Developmental Dyslexia: The Role of the Cerebellum. In *Dyslexia: Advances in Theory and Practice*, pp.173–196. New York, NY: Springer.

Pennington, B.F. (2006) From single to multiple deficit models of developmental disorders. *Cognition*, 101(2), 385–413.

Ramus, F. (n.d.) Dyslexia, Phonological Processing. In H. Pashler (ed.), *Encyclopedia of the Mind*, pp.1–3. Thousand Oaks, CA: Sage.

Reid, G. (2020) *The Dyslexia Workbook for Adults*. Emeryville, CA: Rockridge Press.

Rose, J. (2006) *Independent Review of the Teaching of Early Reading*. London: Department for Education and Skills.

Rose, J. (2009) *Identifying and Teaching Children and Young People with Dyslexia and Literacy Difficulties: An Independent Report from Sir Jim Rose to the Secretary of State for Children, Schools and Families.* London: Department for Children, Schools and Families.

Scarborough, H. (2001) Connecting Early Language and Literacy to Later Reading (Dis)abilities: Evidence, Theory, and Practice. In S.B. Neuman & D.K. Dickinson (eds), *Handbook of Early Literacy*, pp.97–110. New York, NY: Guilford Press.

Seidenberg, M.S. & McClelland, J.L. (1989) A distributed developmental model of word recognition and naming. *The American Psychologist: Psychological Review*, 96(4), 523–568.

Snowling, M.J. (2009) Changing concepts of dyslexia: Nature, treatment and co-morbidity. *Journal of Child Psychology and Psychiatry*, 48, 609–618.

Snowling, M.J., Hayiou-Thomas, M.E., Nash, H.M. & Hulme, C. (2019) Dyslexia and developmental language disorder: Comorbid disorders with distinct effects on reading comprehension. *Journal of Child Psychology and Psychiatry*, 61(6), 672–680.

Stanovich, K.E. (1986) Matthew effects in reading – some consequences of individual differences in the acquisition of literacy. *Reading Research Quarterly*, 21(4), 360–407.

Stein, J. (2001) The magnocellular theory of developmental dyslexia. *Dyslexia*, 7(1), 12–36.

Velluntino, F., Fletcher, J., Snowling, M. & Scanlon, D. (2004) Specific reading disability (dyslexia): What have we learned in the past four decades? *Journal of Child Psychology and Psychiatry*, 45(1), 2–40.

Wolf, M. & Bowers, P.G. (1999) The double-deficit hypothesis for developmental dyslexia. *Journal of Educational Psychology*, 91(3), 415–438.

Chapter 1

What is Dyslexia?

LYNN LOVELL

To begin to understand how to support learners with dyslexia, we must first understand what dyslexia is. While we will explore causal factors of dyslexia in Chapter 2, the key focus here is on the definition or definitions of dyslexia. While there are various definitions, the most widely utilized and accepted one comes from *Identifying and Teaching Children and Young People with Dyslexia and Literacy Difficulties* (2009), that is, the Rose Report. This report was commissioned by the then Secretary of State for Children, Families and Schools, Ed Balls MP, to 'make recommendations on the identification and teaching of children with dyslexia' (Rose, 2009: 8). In liaison with the expert advisory group that informed the report, the following definition of dyslexia was given:

- Dyslexia is a learning difficulty that primarily affects the skills involved in accurate and fluent word reading and spelling.
- Characteristic features of dyslexia are difficulties in phonological awareness, verbal memory and verbal processing speed.
- Dyslexia occurs across the range of intellectual abilities.
- It is best thought of as a continuum, not a distinct category, and there are no clear cut-off points.
- Co-occurring difficulties may be seen in aspects of language, motor coordination, mental calculation, concentration and personal organization, but these are not, by themselves, markers of dyslexia.
- A good indication of the severity and persistence of dyslexic difficulties can be gained by examining how the individual responds or has responded to well founded intervention.

(Rose, 2009: 9–10)

Another definition to consider is that given by the British Dyslexia Association, which acknowledges 'that there are positives to thinking differently' (BDA, 2020 [online]) and not solely negative outcomes. It also adds the following to the Rose Report's definition of dyslexia:

> The British Dyslexia Association (BDA) acknowledges the visual and auditory processing difficulties that some individuals with dyslexia can experience, and points out that dyslexic readers can show a combination of abilities and difficulties that affect the learning process. Some also have strengths in other areas, such as design, problem solving, creative skills, interactive skills and oral skills. (BDA, 2010 [online])

In order to understand these definitions, it is important to understand the meaning of key terms within them. So, we will now dissect and define each key term to ensure a clear understanding of these definitions.

From the Rose Report (2009)

Accurate and fluent word reading and spelling: This phrasing acknowledges that dyslexia does not just affect the ability to read and spell accurately but also the ability to do these *fluently* – with ease and at a good speed. Such skills are 'key to success in education and an essential "life skill"' (Rose, 2009: 1). If an individual cannot read accurately and fluently, they may not be able to access everyday materials such as class handouts and reading books in childhood, or documents such as formal letters and emails in adulthood.

Phonological awareness: This is the ability to know the structure of words in terms of their sounds. The skills required for good phonological awareness include the abilities to:

- identify the syllables in words
- know the initial sound of a word (onset) and the end of a word (rime), e.g. c (onset), at (rime) = cat
- produce rhymes
- manipulate sounds in words by:
  - deleting sounds: what is snowball without snow? Ball. What is ball without b? All
  - blending sounds: bed-room = bedroom, or b-e-d = bed
  - swapping sounds (spoonerisms): bad cat – swapping the first letters of each word, it becomes cad bat.

Phonological awareness skills allow individuals to access novel but phonetically regular words (words that can be sounded out). Coupled with vocabulary knowledge, this enables individuals to read unknown words. In childhood, such skills will be the foundation on which they learn to read; in adulthood, this ability can expand word knowledge continuously.

Verbal memory: In simple terms, this is the ability to retain information given verbally. This may be verbal instructions in the classroom or information in the workplace. An inability to do so effectively may mean that tasks are not fully completed, as only some aspects of instructions are remembered. However, this refers to short-term memory only, and the Rose Report (2009) also refers to working memory in its definition.

Working memory is the ability to complete an action with information held in memory. This is key in tasks such as mental maths, where the individual may have to hold two numbers in memory and add these numbers together, for example. In adulthood, poor working memory may affect the ability to multitask, such as writing a note while talking on the phone.

Verbal processing speed: This aspect of the definition of dyslexia is linked to long-term memory. If an individual has good verbal processing speed, they are able to retrieve known information efficiently from their memory store. As an example, if asked to name a random series of numbers quickly, they would be able to do so at a good speed. This requires the stages of reading the numbers, recognizing the information, pulling information from memory about the names of the numbers and saying that information aloud.

Difficulties with processing often result in an individual being slow to respond to verbal information, which could be misconstrued as the individual not knowing the answer, when in fact it is the efficient retrieval of the information that is the difficulty, not the knowledge itself. In general, tasks such as reading and writing take longer to complete for someone with processing speed difficulties than they would for others.

Intellectual ability: This term is difficult to explain as it is used in various ways, but it is most generically described as the 'ability to think and understand things, especially complicated ideas' (Cambridge Dictionary, n.d.). Intellectual ability has also been referred to as intelligence (Glutting *et al.*, 2000).

Glutting, Adams and Sheslow's widely used test, the Wide Range Intelligence Test (2000), is believed to quantifiably measure intelligence by testing the ability to complete tasks based on prior knowledge (crystallized ability (verbal)) and the ability to perform novel tasks (fluid ability (non-verbal)). These skills are required to access learning, build on prior knowledge and develop new skills.

Rose (2009) states that dyslexia has no relationship to intellectual ability and thus that the specific areas associated with dyslexia are not related to crystallized or fluid ability. It is important to note here that while intelligence tests are widely used when assessing individuals for dyslexia, assessors are not primarily concerned with intelligence but are more focused on the individual's 'potential to learn'. Thus they would use the term 'underlying ability' rather than 'intelligence' or 'intellectual ability'.

From the BDA

Visual processing difficulties: Visual processing difficulties are not related to eyesight; it is the processing of visual information within the brain that is a difficulty. This may mean that the individual is unable to accurately or effectively identify incoming visual information, such as letters when reading. This can affect reading speed and accuracy. Visual processing difficulties may also help to explain why some learners reverse letters when reading or writing or see them out of sequence. These tendencies can make it hard to identify words. The problem may be further compounded by difficulties with tracking lines of text, which may mean that words or lines are omitted when reading.

It is important to note here that although the use of coloured overlays/paper and so on may be seen as helpful for those with visual difficulties, we are advised not to use terms such as 'visual stress'. Diagnosing and managing visual stress are the remit of qualified optometrists (Gilchrist *et al.*, 2018), and the term has a different meaning from that which has previously been applied by educators and dyslexia assessors. This is not to say that we should not provide overlays and so on if they are helpful to individuals; when doing so, however, we must advise those individuals to report any visual difficulties to their optometrist.

Auditory processing difficulties: Similar to visual processing difficulties, poor auditory processing is not a hearing difficulty. It is again about the way the brain processes information, in this case auditory information. This affects the abilities to understand verbal information, discriminate between sounds and filter out background noise. This can mean that instructions given by teachers or colleagues cannot be followed accurately or completely. The inability to discriminate between sounds can cause difficulties that look like poor phonological awareness, impacting on the ability to decode words for reading and encode words for spelling. The additional interference of background noise will make it hard for key information to be identified and may impact on the individual's ability to concentrate.

Rose also highlights other areas that those with dyslexia may struggle with, including 'language, motor coordination, mental calculation, concentration and personal organization' (2009: 10). These are not characteristics of dyslexia but are usually caused by dyslexia. For example, learners who struggle to read may not gain the same level of vocabulary that competent readers gain from books, and thus their written or spoken language may be more limited than others. Conversely, however, their spoken communication may be very well developed if they are in a language-rich environment.

Motor coordination: As you will discover in Chapter 2, some researchers have found connections between dyslexia and motor coordination, which is linked to the cerebellar area of the brain (Nicolson & Fawcett, 2007). This would suggest that those with dyslexia may also have motor coordination difficulties. We also need to consider the fact that dyslexia can co-occur with other specific learning difficulties (SpLDs), such as dyspraxia, which affects fine and gross motor skills, including coordination (Kaplan *et al.*, 1998). Difficulties in this area can affect the ability to participate in sport/exercise (gross motor) or to manipulate small tools and use a pen (fine motor), for example.

Mental calculation: As we have seen previously, dyslexia can be characterized by difficulties with memory and verbal processing speed. If an individual has poor short-term memory, they may not be able to recall mathematical information or the order in which to carry out sums. In addition, difficulties with working memory will make it hard to hold on to numerical information while performing calculations. This, coupled with the inability to retrieve information from long-term memory effectively, will impact on an individual's mathematical ability.

Concentration: The ability to concentrate can be impacted by dyslexia for a number of reasons. If an individual struggles to process or retain verbal information, this may make it very hard to maintain focus when spoken information is given. If they struggle to access text or to write, the ability to continue with such tasks for a sustained period of time will be affected. In addition, the extra energy needed to carry out everyday tasks that others may find straightforward will inevitably make an individual tired, which again impacts on concentration. Every individual is different, so the reasons for poor concentration will vary widely, and thus these are just some examples.

Personal organization: Memory and processing difficulties also impact on organizational skills. Individuals may forget items needed for school or work or for a particular task.

Difficulties may also impact on their written organization, and work may lack a logical structure or omit key points. Organization may also be affected in individuals who display 'non-linear' thinking and therefore do not follow the traditional route through a task or written assignment from A to Z. There is an additional impact when an individual is unable to read an analogue clock or has a poor concept of time, as this may mean that they are late for appointments or do not complete tasks in good time.

So, we can see that dyslexia has certain characteristics that distinguish it from other learning difficulties. Dyslexia is in a category of needs known as SpLDs; other SpLDs include dyspraxia and dyscalculia, which will be discussed in Chapter 3. They are specific because they have characteristic features that centre on certain areas, such as memory or processing speed. This distinguishes them from moderate or general learning difficulties, which occur across the range of cognitive abilities, including underlying ability. Any individual displaying difficulties that impact on their education and employment should, of course, be supported, regardless of the root cause.

Why is it important?

It is important to know what dyslexia is and how to support those with dyslexia because an estimated 10% of the population may have this specific learning difficulty (BDA, n.d.). In a classroom, lecture hall or workplace of 30 people, this means that around three people may have dyslexia, which will affect them in differing ways. In the UK, which has a population of around 66 million (Office for National Statistics, 2019), this equates to approximately 6.6 million people. In a worldwide population of 7.7 billion (United Nations, 2019), this could be up to 770 million people. These numbers highlight the need for greater understanding of dyslexia among educators, employers and individuals.

Another point to consider here in order to obtain a well-rounded understanding of dyslexia is the impact of this SpLD, which can vary from positive to negative. The Dispel Project (Klein, 1998) found that 38% of a sample of people in the prison system showed signs of dyslexia, though figures from different studies vary, with some higher and others lower than this (Kirk & Reid, 2001). The figure of 38% is higher than the 10% of people that are believed to have dyslexia in the general population and may thus indicate a causal link between dyslexia-related difficulties and offending.

In addition, the Westminster AchieveAbility Commission Report, *Neurodiverse Voices: Opening Doors to Employment*, found that 'there is a significant gap between the percentage of dyslexic and neurodivergent people in employment, and the rest of the population'

(AchieveAbility, 2018: 5). The report highlights difficulties experienced by individuals with dyslexia from the recruitment stage to employment and career progression that may have a negative impact on their ability to obtain, retain and progress in suitable employment.

The reasons for the apparent disadvantages in employment and the high proportion of those with dyslexia in the prison system are likely to be wide ranging, varied and interconnected. One reason may be that those with dyslexia may be disadvantaged from an early age. The attainment gap between those with special educational needs (SEN), including those with dyslexia, and other pupils is already evident before pupils go to school and increases at each subsequent stage of education (Education Endowment Foundation, 2017). More recent evidence has shown that 'pupils with SEN perform markedly worse than pupils with no identified SEN across all headline measures of attainment' (Department for Education, 2019: 12). This was the same as the previous year's results, showing a historic gap in attainment. These early disadvantages are likely to impact on the individual's future life opportunities.

Conversely, it has been reported that 40% of millionaires may have dyslexia, and this has been attributed to the positive traits of determination and self-belief that some with dyslexia display (Flanagan, 2003). These traits mean that those with dyslexia may persevere and succeed where others may give up, though this is a generalization and individual cases will vary.

The BDA also highlights strengths in reasoning and in visual and creative areas. These could be due to the fact that those with dyslexia think differently from other people (2020). This is highlighted by a number of well-known individuals who have dyslexia and are successful in their chosen careers, including actors, singers and inventors (Davis & Braun, 2011).

Some research goes further and suggests that having dyslexia or another 'neurodiverse' condition was historically, and still is, an evolutionary advantage and that this is why such differences have survived in the population (Armstrong, 2015). It is important to highlight that the term 'neurodiverse' here stemmed from a speech by the autism activist Jim Sinclair, who highlighted that those who think differently should not be viewed as lacking in value in society just because they may be different in some ways to others (2012). This is not to imply that all those with dyslexia are advantaged over others, just that every person has a unique skill set due to their varying needs and abilities.

These points are important to remember as you work through this book and discover more about dyslexia and how to support learners with dyslexia in educational settings and as part of specialist teaching. Learners are not one-dimensional: it is not simply the case that an individual struggles with reading, writing or spelling. Learners are multifaceted, with skills, knowledge and experience that we can utilize to overcome challenges and that we can learn from every day.

References

AchieveAbility (2018) *Neurodiverse Voices: Opening Doors to Employment*. The Westminster AchieveAbility Commission interactive report. Available at: www.achieveability.org.uk/main/policy/wac-report-is-released-and-presentation-at-bda-conference-2018 [Accessed 14 April 2020].

Armstrong, T. (2015) The myth of the normal brain: Embracing neurodiversity. *AMA Journal of Ethics*, 17(4), 348–352.

British Dyslexia Association (n.d.) *Dyslexia*. Available at: www.bdadyslexia.org.uk/dyslexia [Accessed 9 April 2020].

British Dyslexia Association (2010) *What is Dyslexia?* Available at: www.bdadyslexia.org.uk/dyslexia/about-dyslexia/what-is-dyslexia [Accessed 7 April 2020].

British Dyslexia Association (2020) *About Dyslexia*. Available at: www.bdadyslexia.org.uk/dyslexia/about-dyslexia [Accessed 7 April 2020].

Cambridge Dictionary (n.d.) *Intellectual*. Available at: https://dictionary.cambridge.org/dictionary/english/intellectual [Accessed 8 April 2020].

Davis, R.D. & Braun, E.M. (2011) *The Gift of Dyslexia: Why Some of the Brightest People Can't Read and How They Can Learn*. London: Souvenir Press.

Department for Education (2019) *Key Stage 4 Performance 2019 (Revised)*. Available at: www.gov.uk/government/statistics/key-stage-4-performance-2019-revised [Accessed 16 April 2020].

Education Endowment Fund (2017) *Attainment Gap 2017*. Available at: https://educationendowmentfoundation.org.uk/public/files/Annual_Reports/EEF_Attainment_Gap_Report_2018.pdf gap [Accessed 8 December 2022].

Flanagan, B. (2003) Who wnats to be a millioniare? *The Guardian*, 5 October. Available at: www.theguardian.com/uk/2003/oct/05/benflanagan.theobserver [Accessed 16 August 2020].

Gilchrist, J., Holden, C. & Warren, J. (2018) *Specific Learning Difficulties (SpLDs) and Visual Difficulties: A Guide for Assessors and SpLD Practitioners*. Available at: www.sasc.org.uk/SASCDocuments/Visual_Difficulties_guidance_for_SpLD_practitioners_Final_June2018.pdf [Accessed 9 April 2020].

Glutting, J., Adams, W. & Sheslow, D. (2000) *Wide Range Intelligence Test: WRIT*. Wilmington, DE: Wide Range.

Kaplan, B.J., Wilson, B.N., Dewey, D. & Crawford, S.G. (1998) DCD may not be a discrete disorder. *Human Movement Science*, 17(4–5), 471–490.

Kirk, J. & Reid, G. (2001) An examination of the relationship between dyslexia and offending in young people and the implications for the training system. *Dyslexia*, 7(2), 77–84.

Klein, C. (1998) *Dyslexia and Offending*. London: Dyspel.

Nicolson, R.I. & Fawcett, A.J. (2007) Procedural learning difficulties: Reuniting the developmental disorders? *Trends in Neuroscience*, 30(4), 135–141. https://doi:10.1016/j.tins.2007.02.003.

Office for National Statistics (ONS) (2019) *Overview of UK Population: August 2019.* Available at: www.ons.gov.uk/peoplepopulationandcommunity/populationandmigration/populationestimates/articles/overviewoftheukpopulation/august2019 [Accessed 14 April 2020].

Rose, S.J. (2009) *Identifying and Teaching Children and Young People with Dyslexia and Literacy Difficulties: An Independent Report from Sir Jim Rose to the Secretary of State for Children, Schools and Families*. London: Department for Children, Schools and Families.

Sinclair, J. (2012) Don't mourn for us. *Autonomy, the Critical Journal of Interdisciplinary Autism Studies*, 1(1), 1–5.

United Nations (2019) *2019 Revision of World Population Prospects*. Available at: https://population.un.org/wpp [Accessed 14 April 2020].

Chapter 2

Theories of Dyslexia

LYNN LOVELL

A brief history of dyslexia

The previous chapter outlined definitions of dyslexia and explained what they mean. It also suggested some key points to bear in mind while reading this book. In this chapter, we will explore the possible causes of dyslexia, bearing in mind that there is no overall consensus in this area.

Dyslexia was first identified and reported by a German professor of medicine, Adolf Kussmaul, who named it '*wortblindheit*', meaning 'word blindness' (Kirby, 2018). In doing so, he recognized that some individuals, though they had good vision and general ability, appeared unable to read or recognize words. This first report of dyslexia therefore considered it from a medical point of view. Kussmaul did not consider vision to be a factor in the difficulties he observed in his patients.

Rudolf Berlin was the first person to use the term 'dyslexia' to describe individuals who had difficulty with words. Berlin was a German ophthalmologist who agreed that the difficulties seen were not caused by problems with vision. He also went further and put forward the idea that dyslexia may be due to a physical difference in the brain (Kirby, 2018).

Research into dyslexia was also occurring in the UK, and in 1896, William Pringle Morgan, who was a general practitioner, published an article outlining the case of a boy recognized as having normal intelligence and eyesight who was unable to recognize or retain words. Morgan felt that the difficulties were present from birth and also agreed that these were caused by a difference in the brain, specifically the left angular gyrus (Morgan, 1896). The view that dyslexia was congenital and originated in the brain was supported by British practitioners in other professions, such as the ophthalmologist James Hinshelwood (1900).

Samuel Orton, an American neurologist, was the first practitioner to systematically study a large number of individuals with dyslexic-type difficulties. Focusing on language disabilities, Orton rejected the idea that the difficulty observed originated in the left angular gyrus. Instead, Orton proposed that children with these problems were unable to 'turn off' the right, visual side of their brain to enable effective engagement of the left side of the brain, responsible for word reading (Orton, 1937). Orton stated that the impact of this was that letters appeared twisted to the individual, a difficulty he termed 'strephosymbolia', meaning 'twisted symbols' (Gaurdiola, 2001). Orton therefore was the first researcher to link a brain impairment to a visual difficulty as the cause of dyslexia.

These early works identified dyslexia as originating in the brain but having an impact on the appearance of text, and this underpins theories that remain today. As you will see, dyslexia is still felt to be caused by an impairment in the brain, but the exact nature of this is still under discussion. The impact of this impairment is also debated, and it is believed to affect not just vision but other areas as well, including auditory pathways, motor coordination and memory.

Until Orton's work was published, dyslexia had been studied by ophthalmologists and neurologists, but following Orton's more thorough research, the subject began to appeal more widely to different professional fields (Gaurdiola, 2001). In 1959, Hermann shared the view of neurologists that dyslexia was hereditary; meanwhile, psychologists, sociologists and those working in education highlighted the impact of environmental factors on dyslexia. In doing so, they began to show that dyslexia could be influenced by a range of factors. More importantly the idea that the environment could negatively impact on dyslexia also suggested that it could have a positive effect and thus paved the way for specialist teaching methods to be developed, as outlined later in this book.

The three-level framework

The interacting factors identified by different researchers, both past and present, are effectively encapsulated by Morton and Frith's three-level framework (1995), reproduced here:

<table>
<tr><td rowspan="3">Environment</td><td>Biological</td></tr>
<tr><td>Cognitive</td></tr>
<tr><td>Behavioural</td></tr>
</table>

This framework captures the following key points:

1. Dyslexia is likely to be biological in origin, originating in the brain and influenced by our genetic make-up.
2. These biological differences impact the mental processes involved in completing literacy activities (cognitive ability).
3. Due to this, we see an impact on reading, writing and spelling, as well as some other areas, such as motor coordination and organization (behavioural) (Rose, 2009).
4. Each area outlined can be impacted by environmental factors. As an example, having a home environment where a diverse range of languages is used can help individuals develop vocabulary skills, which can positively impact on their ability to recognize a greater range of words when reading. The converse may also be true: limited access to diverse spoken vocabulary can limit the number of words an individual knows and is able to apply to their reading. It should be noted that this latter point does not suggest that a core biological difference is not present in dyslexia, only that environmental factors will have an influence on the impact of this, positively or negatively.

This framework will be used throughout the following discussion to reconcile what can appear to be conflicting views on the causes of dyslexia. To take the work of Orton as an initial example, he felt that the inability to turn off parts of the brain (at the biological level) interfered with the ability to see words correctly (a cognitive process) and thus impacted on reading (behavioural).

From the 1970s onwards, research into dyslexia started to increase, and from this research came seminal works that remain popular and respected to the current day. The theories resulting from these seminal works are outlined below. As you will see, they seek to highlight Frith's view that: 'Dyslexia can be defined as a neuro-developmental disorder with a biological origin and behavioural signs which extend far beyond problems with written language' (Frith, 1999: 192).

Phonological deficit theory

The first theory that will be discussed is the phonological deficit theory. This theory proposes that dyslexia is caused by a difficulty with identifying and utilizing phonemes, which are the individual speech sounds in words (Vellutino *et al.*, 2004). As an example, the word 'cat' has three phonemes: c, a and t (as sounds, not letter names). The theory states that individuals with dyslexia struggle to recognize these sounds and to blend and segment sounds in words. This affects their ability to identify syllables, onset and rime, alliteration, rhyming words and so on.

The origins of the phonological deficit theory can be traced back to the work of Liberman *et al.* (1974), which showed that difficulties with reading were linked to difficulties with identifying phonemes and syllables in speech. In 1983, Bradley and Bryant identified difficulties with rhyme and alliteration in those who struggled to read. Dyslexia was linked to difficulties with rhyming tasks by Rack *et al.* (1992) among others. This research continued, and the idea that difficulties with phonological awareness may be the cause of dyslexic-type difficulties has remained a popular theory. This is supported by a great number of studies, including longitudinal studies such as those by Wagner *et al.* (1994) and Muter *et al.* (2004).

Stanovich (1986) agreed that a phonological deficit was present in those with dyslexia and that this affected the ability to recognize words. This is because the inability to identify sounds results in difficulty linking sounds to their written representation, that is, knowing that a phoneme (sound) is linked to a grapheme (letter/s) (Rack *et al.*, 1992). This could be compounded by poor orthographic awareness, where individuals may find it hard to recognize how letters in words are organized (Vellutino *et al.*, 2004).

Perhaps the most well-known proponent of the phonological deficit theory is Professor Margaret Snowling, who has written numerous articles and books on it and other related topics over the past 40 years. Professor Snowling was awarded a CBE for her contribution to the field of dyslexia in 2016 (Snowling, n.d. [online]) and continues to advocate that a core cause of reading difficulties is difficulty with phonological skills, which impacts on the ability to decode words for reading (Snowling *et al.*, 2019).

The Rose Report (2009) also advocates the view that dyslexia is a difficulty with phonological awareness and states that effective intervention to address reading difficulties will involve specific methods to improve children's phonological knowledge. As you will see later in this book, specialist teaching does indeed include the explicit teaching of phonological skills to aid reading and spelling. This approach has been shown to be successful in a number of studies (Vellutino *et al.*, 2004).

The phonological deficit theory is based at the cognitive level, as good phonological awareness is a mental process that allows us to read more effectively. A difficulty with reading, therefore, is the behavioural outcome of a phonological difficulty. However, the origins of this deficit are felt to stem from differences in brain structure (Ramus, 2003), though the nature of such differences is unclear.

Double deficit theory

Alongside the phonological deficit theory, a deficit in rapid naming was also proposed as a cause of reading difficulties (Li *et al.*, 2009). This latter theory stated that those who struggle to read may have difficulty either with retrieving information from memory at a good speed or with articulating information quickly in order to name items rapidly (Hulme *et al.*, 1995; Hulme *et al.*, 1999). This was measured through tasks that asked study groups to name familiar items at speed. Deficits in this area then led to reading difficulties, with individuals unable to retrieve words from memory in order to read fluently.

These two theories – phonological deficit and rapid naming – were initially felt to be independent of one another: a phonological impairment impacting on reading accuracy and comprehension, and a rapid naming impairment impacting on speed of work, reading fluency and comprehension. However, in 1999, Wolf and Bowers proposed that the two difficulties may occur together in some learners. This 'double deficit' was felt to cause more significant reading difficulties than either of the two causes by itself. This was an important point as interventions that seek to address just one of these areas may not fully support the individual's needs.

In 2009, Rose proposed that difficulties with phonological awareness and verbal processing speed (measured through rapid naming tasks) were both key characteristic features of dyslexia, alongside difficulties with verbal memory. All of these areas need to be addressed if we are to successfully support individuals with dyslexia.

Cerebellar theory

In contrast to the phonological deficit theory, the cerebellar theory focuses on brain differences as the cause of dyslexia. The cerebellum is a part of the brain that is felt to impact on a range of activities, including phonological tasks and processing speed, that are related to reading (Fulbright *et al.*, 1999). This theory therefore accounts for difficulties in both phonological awareness and rapid naming. In addition, the cerebellum, if impaired, is felt to cause difficulties in the language area of the brain (known as Broca's area), as well as impacting on the automatization of skills and motor ability (Nicolson *et al.*, 2001). This theory then has the benefit of also accounting for the language and motor difficulties that Rose (2009) states may co-occur with dyslexia.

The cerebellar theory was established by investigating not only literacy difficulties but also a range of other areas, such as motor ability and balance, speed of processing information and memory (Nicolson *et al.*, 2001). In relation to motor ability and balance, research showed that individuals with dyslexia struggled when asked to perform a balance task while completing a secondary task such as counting backwards, and determined that this may be because balance takes considerable effort for those with dyslexia (Nicolson & Fawcett, 1990). This may help to explain why those with dyslexia sometimes report struggling to complete two tasks at a time (Augur, 1985).

With regard to cognitive ability, research has shown that individuals with dyslexia struggle with a range of phonological tasks, such as segmenting words and rhyming (Nicolson & Fawcett, 1994). As such, proponents of cerebellar theory acknowledge that individuals with dyslexia do show a phonological deficit as well, one that persists throughout their childhood (Nicolson & Fawcett, 1990). This has again been linked to abnormalities in the cerebellum. Research in this area has also shown that memory and processing speed can be weaker in younger individuals with dyslexia (Nicolson & Fawcett, 1994).

Such research as described above is indirect in that it looks at the behavioural difficulties caused by poor cerebellar function, but the cerebellar theory has also been supported by direct methodology. PET (positron-emission tomography) has identified reduced cerebellar function in those with dyslexia when performing a sequencing task (Nicolson *et al.*, 2001), and there is also evidence to suggest that a metabolic imbalance in the cerebellum is evident in some individuals with dyslexia (Rae *et al.*, 1998). The implication is that these differences could cause the range of difficulties seen in those with dyslexia.

It would seem that the cerebellar theory provides an explanation for a wide range of the behavioural signs seen in those with dyslexia. To summarize, it is believed that the core difficulty related to the cerebellum is in the automatization of skills, that is, the ability to complete a task subconsciously, without deliberate thought (Nicolson & Fawcett, 1990). This then impacts on the speed and efficiency with which individuals can perform a range of tasks.

Cerebellar theory therefore advocates a biological cause of dyslexia, one that impacts at the cognitive level on language, processing and phonological skills. This then causes behavioural difficulties in literacy, language and motor skills. Nicolson and Fawcett (1990) suggest that this explains the range of difficulties shown in those with dyslexia and thus is a comprehensive explanation as to the cause of this specific learning difficulty or difference.

Magnocellular theory

The magnocellular theory mirrors the early work on dyslexia, which suggested that it is a brain-based difficulty that impacts on vision. In 1990, Lovegrove showed that a visual deficit impacted on an individual's reading ability. In the study, those who found it hard to read were not as sensitive to image changes ('flicker') as others and thus could not respond to changes quickly. Therefore, they found it hard to process incoming visual information at the same speed as others.

This theory was further developed by Stein and Walsh (1997), who agreed that an inability of the brain to move smoothly from one image to the next could impact on reading. That is, if the individual could not move between incoming visual information quickly enough, this would impact on how they saw words on a page. They attributed this to magnocells within the brain, which are responsible for the detection of movement and forms of objects (Pam, 2013). This was believed to explain why individuals with dyslexia report blurring or movement of text when reading. It was later determined, however, that magnocells are not responsible for visual persistence (Stein, 2000).

Despite this, theories around the role of the magnocellular system and its impact on literacy skills endure, supported by physical evidence from post-mortem studies. These studies have shown that the magnocellular region of the brain is smaller in individuals with dyslexia than in others (Livingstone *et al.*, 1991). Stein continues to argue that magnocells have an impact on visual ability and can affect the stability of incoming images and the ability to determine visual depth (Stein, 2001). This, then, could still account for the visual difficulties that some individuals with dyslexia report experiencing and also explain why they struggle to access written materials.

In addition, comparative difficulties in auditory processing pathways have been linked to the difficulties with phonological awareness experienced by those with dyslexia. This was felt to be due to an inability to discriminate between high and low frequencies in sounds, which then makes it hard to discriminate between similar sounds (Stein & Walsh, 1997). Tallal *et al.* (1993) suggest that individuals with reading difficulties find it hard to process incoming sound efficiently and thus find it harder to identify sounds presented close together, as they are in words. This then impacts on the ability to hear the sounds in words and to apply this knowledge to sound out words when reading and spelling.

The overall theme of this research is that there are inefficiencies in auditory and visual processing in those with dyslexia that explain both visual and phonological difficulties. It is therefore argued that such delays could also impact on other areas, such as balance and motor skills (Stein & Walsh, 1997). Very much like the cerebellar theory, magnocellular theory seeks not to replace previous research but to explain a range of the difficulties seen as having a cause based in the brain. This then impacts on the ability to see and hear words and sounds, which is necessary for reading and writing.

Temporal sampling theory

This early research on auditory processing paved the way for more recent exploration into auditory difficulties as a cause of dyslexia, which we will now explore in more detail.

There are a number of terms that need to be explained here if we are to understand the impact of auditory difficulties on phonological skills and, in turn, reading:

- Rhythmic timing: This is the rhythm of speech and the timing with which words are spoken. Some sounds are spoken together, such as 'ch', others separately. It is these intonations that people with dyslexia may struggle with, according to research into auditory difficulties (Goswami *et al.*, 2013).
- Prosody: The stress placed on syllables and the pattern of these within speech. As an example, in the name 'Harry Potter' the stress is put on the first and third syllables: 'HAR-ry POT-ter'. Being able to hear these changes allows us to separate speech sounds, and thus a deficit may make it hard to recognize sounds in order to sound words out.
- Amplitude modulations: Defined as 'speech energy' or 'signal intensity', this is the energy created by our jaws, tongue and so on when we speak. Understanding this energy as it is used in speech is felt to be necessary for understanding.
- Rise time: How quickly speech energy reaches its peak. A deficit in detecting this is felt to be a notable area of difficulty for those with dyslexia (Goswami, *et al.* 2013).

A mismatch in the timing with which these areas of speech are detected is felt to be the cause of difficulties with phonological awareness, which then lead to difficulties with reading. In simpler terms, the nuances of speech are not detected at the same time to provide a coherent interpretation of language. This has been named temporal sampling theory (Goswami *et al.*, 2013).

Like magnocellular theory, temporal sampling aims to define dyslexia as a difficulty with the processing of auditory information in the brain (the biological level), which impacts on the cognitive processes of sound recognition. This, in turn, has a negative impact on literacy skills.

Working memory

According to Rose (2009), deficits in working memory are a key characteristic of dyslexia, alongside phonological awareness and processing speed. We have already looked at research around the latter two areas, so it is appropriate to now turn our attention to theories around memory. One of the most widely known and well respected of these theories is the working memory model (Baddeley & Hitch, 1974). This model proposes that our storage of short-term information in memory is dependent on whether it is language or visual-spatial information, both of which are controlled by a central system. As such, these are the components of working memory:

- The phonological loop: This stores both written and verbal language information. It is aided by verbal rehearsal, where our 'inner voice' repeats information in order to support retention of the information.
- The visual-spatial sketchpad: This is where visual and spatial information is stored, such as memory of an image or directions. This system is also felt to aid spatial awareness, that is, where we are with regard to ourselves and others.
- The central executive: This is a key aspect of the working memory model. It is believed to 'coordinate' information from the phonological loop and visual-spatial sketchpad. Not only this, but the central executive is thought to have the additional role of filtering information, allowing us to decide what information requires our attention and what does not (Baddeley, 1986).

  It is important to note that, over time, the proponents of this theory came to feel that it had limitations, notably in that it did not link short-term and long-term memory. To address this, Baddeley added an additional component to the working memory model in 2000: the episodic buffer.
- The episodic buffer: This 'buffer' was felt to communicate with all components of the original model but to be primarily responsible for linking information in short-term memory to long-term memory. Although information within this buffer is also felt to be temporary, it is suggested that it links visual and language-based information to enable the learning of phonological information (Baddeley, 2000).

  As the episodic buffer has a role in the learning of phonological information, this suggests that a difficulty in the working memory system could prevent the efficient storage of phonological information in memory. This theory, then, is biological in origin, which, like many other theories, suggests that an impairment in the necessary systems of the brain impacts on phonological skills. This would impact on the ability to retain and recall sound information, making the learning of new words and the ability to sound these out difficult. It would also impact on our ability to recall words from a bank of words that can be recognized by sight (the lexicon).

Genetics and hereditary factors

From theories of dyslexia, we move on to widely accepted facts. There is a high probability that dyslexia is hereditary. Thus, if you have a family member or members with dyslexia, the likelihood that you will have dyslexia is higher. This risk increases if both parents and/or a sibling have dyslexia, and this has been shown to be independent of environmental factors, such as family socio-economic status (Scerri and Schulte-Körne, 2010). This gives rise to the theory that dyslexia is genetic in origin, passed on from parents to children in their genes.

It is important to note here that humans have somewhere in the region of 20,000–30,000 genes, which are contained within our 23 pairs of chromosomes. These contain genetic information that we inherit from our parents (National Human Genome Research Institute, n.d.). Because there are so many genes, they have names composed of letters and numbers. To complicate matters further, research into the genetic basis of dyslexia has identified loci on genes that may be responsible for this specific difficulty; that is, specific parts of the gene that may be responsible for the difficulties seen in those with dyslexia. These have been identified within chromosomes 1, 2, 3, 6, 11 and 15 (Scerri & Schulte-Körne, 2010).

The large majority of loci that have been linked to dyslexia are believed to cause certain cells, known as neurons and axons, to not develop or migrate as they should do in the early developmental stages of the individual (Scerri & Schulte-Körne, 2010). This affects the left side of the brain, a theory in keeping with the early work of Morgan in 1896 and subsequent research. One recent review of this area states that 'the emerging picture is that risk genes for dyslexia alter brain development differentially in the left hemisphere, thereby altering speech and language development so as to make the acquisition of written language more difficult' (Peterson & Pennington, 2015).

Genetic theory is solidly grounded in a biological reason for dyslexia and does not compete with any of the previous theories outlined. Genetic markers on genes can be said to be responsible for changes in the brain that lead to the cognitive difficulties seen in those with dyslexia, along with the literacy and other difficulties that follow. However, genetic research in relation to dyslexia is complicated (Fisher & DeFries, 2002), and any such research will need to navigate the complex interacting factors that can contribute to literacy and related difficulties. For this reason, we are unlikely to see any advances such as genetic screening for dyslexia and early identification based on genetic information for some time, if ever.

The multiple deficit model

Morton and Frith's three-level framework (1995) has been shown throughout this chapter to unify the varying theories on the causes of dyslexia and the difficulties displayed. However, it could be viewed as a somewhat simplistic view that does not account for a range of interacting factors. In 2006, Pennington proposed a multiple deficit model (MDM) that aimed to unite not only theories of dyslexia but also other co-occurring conditions and environmental factors.

In the MDM, Pennington proposes four levels, each of which has an impact on the factors within that level and on subsequent levels. The top level is etiologic, which means it is the cause of difficulties. This level consists of both genetic and environmental influences that can be both risk factors, causing negative outcomes, or protective factors, which may promote positive outcomes or limit the extent of difficulties. As an example, if you have a sibling with dyslexia, your genetic risk is higher than that of someone without a family history of dyslexia. However, if you are genetically predisposed to have a strong memory capacity, this may reduce the impact of any resulting dyslexic-type difficulties.

These varying factors at the etiologic level could result in a range of differences at the neural level, according to Pennington (2006). The neural level would be equivalent to Morton and Frith's biological level (1995). However, Pennington expands on this, suggesting that differences at this level can be seen to be interacting and responsible for the range of co-occurring specific deficits that are often seen, such as dyspraxia and dyscalculia (see Chapter 3). Even if only some neural pathways are affected by genetic and environmental factors, this can change other neural systems, leading to a wider range of difficulties stemming from differences in the brain.

At the remaining levels, Pennington again adheres to Morton and Frith's three-level framework (1995) in suggesting that the higher levels affect cognitive processes such as phonological awareness, which then result in behavioural outcomes (i.e. difficulty with reading, motor skills and so on). The difference in the MDM is that these difficulties are supposed to result from risk and protective factors at the genetic and environmental levels. These, the theory proposes, all interact to produce various behaviours, not just those identified as common to dyslexia but also to other SpLDs. This then accounts for not only the very varied signs of dyslexia identified by different researchers but also the overlap of these signs with other conditions such as dyspraxia and dyscalculia (see Chapter 3).

What does this mean for teachers and specialist assessors?

For educators, knowledge of the various theories of dyslexia helps to paint a picture of the possible causes of SpLDs. This knowledge, while often complex, can be utilized when we plan support for learners with dyslexia and other specific difficulties. We cannot change the underlying aetiology of dyslexia or the cognitive difficulties that this may cause, but we can respond to the various resulting behaviours, which will present differently in each learner.

While we recognize that every learner will be different, we can see that there are commonalities as to the causes of these difficulties, and this leads us to be able to create programmes that can address a great many of the challenges that those with dyslexia face while recognizing that such approaches should be individualized. In the classroom, this is the key to shared aims, high expectations and effective differentiation.

References

Augur, J. (1985) Guidelines for Teachers, Parents and Learners. In M. Snowling (ed.), *Children's Written Language Difficulties*, pp.147–171. Windsor: NFER Nelson.

Baddeley, A.D. (1986) *Working Memory*. Oxford: Oxford University Press.

Baddeley, A.D. (2000) The episodic buffer: A new component of working memory? *Trends in Cognitive Sciences*, 4(11), 417–423.

Baddeley, A.D. & Hitch, G. (1974) Working Memory. In G.H. Bower (ed.), *Psychology of Learning and Motivation*, 8, pp.47–89. New York, NY: Elsevier.

Bradley, L. & Bryant, P.E. (1983) Categorizing sounds and learning to read – a causal connection. *Nature*, 301(5899), 419–421.

Fisher, S.E. & DeFries, J.C. (2002) Developmental dyslexia: Genetic dissection of a complex cognitive trait. *Nature Reviews Neuroscience*, 3(10), 767–780.

Frith, U. (1999) Paradoxes in the definition of dyslexia. *Dyslexia*, 5(4), 192–214.

Fulbright, R.K., Jenner, A.R., Mencl, W.E., Pugh, K.R. *et al.* (1999) The cerebellum's role in reading: A functional MR imaging study. *American Journal of Neuroradiology*, 20, 1925–1930.

Goswami, U., Gerson, D., Astruc, L., Huss, M. & Mead, N. (2013) Dyslexia – in tune but out of time. *Trends in Cognitive Sciences*, 15, 3–10.

Guardiola, J.G. (2001) The evolution of research on dyslexia. *Anuario de Psicologia*, 32(1), 3–30.

Hermann, K. (1959) *Reading Disability: A Medical Study of Word Blindness and Related Handicaps.* Springfield, IL: Charles C. Thomas.

Hinshelwood, J. (1900) Congenital word blindness. *The Lancet*, 155(4004), 1506–1508.

Hulme, C., Roodenrys, S., Brown, G.D.A. & Mercer, R. (1995) The role of long term memory mechanisms in memory span. *British Journal of Psychology*, 86, 527–536.

Hulme, C., Newton, P., Cowan, N., Stuart, G. & Brown, G. (1999) Think before you speak: Pauses, memory search, and trace reintegration processes in verbal memory span. *Journal of Experimental Psychology: Learning, Memory, and Cognition,* 25, 447–463.

Kirby, P. (2018) A brief history of dyslexia. *Psychologist*, 31(3), 56–59.

Li, J.J., Cutting, L.E., Ryan, M., Zilioli, M., Denckla, M.B. & Mahone, E.M. (2009) Response variability in rapid automatized naming predicts reading comprehension. *Journal of Clinical and Experimental Neuropsychology*, 31(7), 877–888.

Liberman, I.Y., Shankweiler, D., Fischer, F.W. & Carter, B. (1974) Explicit syllable and phoneme segmentation in the young child. *Journal of Experimental Child Psychology*, 18(2), 201–212.

Livingstone, M.S., Rosen, G.D., Drislane, F.W. & Galaburda, A.M. (1991) Physiological and anatomical evidence for a magnocellular defect in developmental dyslexia. *Proceedings of the National Academy of Sciences*, 88(18), 7943–7947.

Lovegrove, W.J., Garzia, R.P. & Nicholson, S.B. (1990) Experimental evidence of a transient system deficit in specific reading disability. *Journal of the American Optometric Association*, 61, 137–146.

Morgan, W.P. (1896) A case of congenital word blindness. *British Medical Journal*, 2(1871), 1378.

Morton, J. & Frith, U. (1995) Causal Modelling: A Structural Approach to Developmental Psychopathology. In D. Cicchetti & D.J. Cohen (eds), Wiley series on personality processes. *Developmental Psychopathology, Vol. 1. Theory and Methods* (pp.357–390). New York, NY: John Wiley & Sons.

Muter, V., Hulme, C., Snowling, M.J. & Stevenson, J. (2004) Phonemes, rimes, vocabulary, and grammatical skills as foundations of early reading development: Evidence from a longitudinal study. *Developmental Psychology*, 40(5), 665–681.

National Human Genome Research Institute (n.d.) *Human Genome Project FAQ.* Available at: www.genome.gov/human-genome-project/Completion-FAQ [Accessed 26 May 2022].

Nicolson, R.I. & Fawcett, A.J. (1990) Automaticity: A new framework for dyslexia research? *Cognition*, 35(2), 159–182.

Nicolson, R.I. & Fawcett, A.J. (1994) Comparison of deficits in cognitive and motor skills among children with dyslexia. *Annals of Dyslexia*, 44(1), 147–164.

Nicolson, R.I., Fawcett, A.J. & Dean, P. (2001) Developmental dyslexia: The cerebellar deficit hypothesis. *Trends in Neurosciences*, 24(9), 508–511.

Orton, S.T. (1937) *Reading, Writing and Speech Problems in Children*. New York, NY: W.W. Norton & Co.

Pam, N. (2013) *Magnocellular System.* Available at: https://psychologydictionary.org/magnocellular-system [Accessed 1 May 2020].

Pennington, B.F. (2006) From single to multiple deficit models of developmental disorders. *Cognition*, 101(2), 385–413.

Peterson, R.L. & Pennington, B.F. (2015) Developmental dyslexia. *Annual Review of Clinical Psychology*, 11, 283–307.

Rack, J.P., Snowling, M.J. & Olson, R.K. (1992) The nonword reading deficit in developmental dyslexia: A review. *Reading Research Quarterly*, 27(1), 28–53.

Rae, C., Lee, M.A., Dixon, R.M., Blamire, A.M. *et al.* (1998) Metabolic abnormalities in developmental dyslexia detected by 1H magnetic resonance spectroscopy. *The Lancet*, 351(9119), 1849–1852.

Ramus, F. (2003) Developmental dyslexia: Specific phonological deficit or general sensorimotor dysfunction? *Current Opinion in Neurobiology*, 13(2), 212–218.

Rose, J. (2009) *Identifying and Teaching Children and Young People with Dyslexia and Literacy Difficulties: An Independent Report from Sir Jim Rose to the Secretary of State for Children, Schools and Families*. London: Department for Children, Schools and Families.

Scerri, T.S. & Schulte-Körne, G. (2010) Genetics of developmental dyslexia. *European Child & Adolescent Psychiatry*, 19(3), 179–197.

Snowling, M. (n.d.) *St. Johns College – Biography*. Available at: www.sjc.ox.ac.uk/discover/people/professor-maggie-snowling [Accessed 29 April 2020].

Snowling, M.J., Hayiou-Thomas, M.E., Nash, H.M. & Hulme, C. (2019) Dyslexia and Developmental Language Disorder: Comorbid disorders with distinct effects on reading comprehension. *Journal of Child Psychology and Psychiatry*, 61(6), 672–680.

Stanovich, K.E. (1986) Matthew effects in reading: Some consequences of individual differences in the acquisition of literacy. *Reading Research Quarterly*, 21(4), 360–407.

Stein, J. (2000) The neurobiology of reading difficulties. *Prostaglandins Leukotrienes and Essential Fatty Acids*, 63(1–2), 109–116.

Stein, J. (2001) The magnocellular theory of developmental dyslexia. *Dyslexia*, 7(1), 12–36.

Stein, J. & Walsh, V. (1997) To see but not to read: The magnocellular theory of dyslexia. *Trends in Neuroscience*, 20, 147–152.

Tallal, P., Miller, S. & Fitch, R.H. (1993) Neurological basis of speech: A case of the preeminence of temporal processing. *Annals of the New York Academy of Sciences*, 682, 27–47.

Vellutino, F.R., Fletcher, J.M., Snowling, M.J. & Scanlon, D.M. (2004) Specific reading disability (dyslexia): What have we learned in the past four decades? *Journal of Child Psychology and Psychiatry*, 45(1), 2–40.

Wagner, R.K., Torgesen, J.K. & Rashotte, C.A. (1994) Development of reading-related phonological processing abilities: Evidence of bi-directional causality from a latent variable longitudinal study. *Developmental Psychology*, 30, 73–87.

Wolf, M. & Bowers, P.G. (1999) The double-deficit hypothesis for the developmental dyslexias. *Journal of Educational Psychology*, 91(3), 415.

Chapter 3

Other Specific Learning Difficulties Explained

Implications for Specialist Interventions and Classroom Practice

RACHEL BURN AND KAYLEIGH CHANG

Chapters 1 and 2 have set out the complex nature of dyslexia and the continuing investigation and discussion of its causes. We accept dyslexia as a neurodevelopmental disorder of biological origin that presents along a spectrum, with no cut-off points (Rose, 2009), and that is evident in an individual's cognitive abilities and processing of information, especially in learning and in the acquisition and mastery of literacy skills. Individuals across the entire range of intelligence experience dyslexia, and it has many associated strengths. Every individual with dyslexia has a personal profile of strengths and challenges, and their behaviour, skills and level of attainment will be influenced by their environment, life experiences and exposure to learning opportunities. There is much evidence that dyslexia has a familial link, related to a range of inherited genes and a range of risk factors that influence its presentation and severity (Muter, 2020).

The Rose Report (2009) made clear that while dyslexia has difficulties with literacy at its core, other difficulties are also common, for example coordination, mental calculation, organization and concentration. However, difficulties in these areas are not, by themselves, indicators of dyslexia.

It is essential, as educators, that we acknowledge the individual at the centre of any diagnosis and understand that those who experience 'pure' dyslexia are the exception rather than the rule (Muter, 2020; Willcutt & Pennington, 2000).

Co-occurring developmental disorders have been recorded in pre-school children (Gooch *et al.*, 2014). Most youngsters identified as poor readers also experience attention, maths, language or visual-motor difficulties as well, and sometimes a combination of these. Research continues to indicate the many overlaps of specific learning difficulties (SpLDs), and it is unlikely that any specific learning difficulty exists in isolation (Hulme & Snowling, 2008). Indeed, Kaplan *et al.* (2001) found that 25% of those with either developmental coordination disorder (DCD), dyslexia or attention deficit hyperactivity disorder (ADHD) had all three.

The prominent view is that genes do not cause learning disorders; rather, genes and cognitive risks are shared across learning disorders (Pennington, 2006). Genes create risks for a child's development; some of these are shared risks, and the cumulative effect of multiple genes builds risk. Curran (2021) identifies the commonalities, biologically, between the neurodiverse conditions of ADHD, autism spectrum disorder (ASD) and obsessive compulsive disorder (OCD) and emphasizes the need to consider each individual as a unique human with varying capabilities. Risks can be modified by protective factors such as environment or effective teaching (Muter, 2020). For example, poor phonological processing can be supported by phonological awareness training.

There has been a shift from the single deficit model of dyslexia (Muter, 2020), according to which one set of genes is common to dyslexia while another predisposes a person to another learning difficulty. It is now believed that genes are shared. It is the brain's ability to connect its different regions, not just the strengths or weaknesses of a particular region, that determines cognitive function. The wide range of variation in the behavioural representation of a learning difference can be explained not by the existence of a single deficit but by the cumulative effect of multiple risk and protective factors. This supports the understanding of dyslexia as being on a continuum (mild through to severe) and as part of an overlapping and complex recipe for neurodiversity.

'Neurodiversity' is a term that has entered the language of learning difficulties more recently and has quickly gained favour owing to its acknowledgement of the unique person and the individual strengths and challenges at the centre of any single diagnosis. The concept of neurodiversity helps the idea that neurological differences are recognized and respected as part of human diversity – celebrating people's differences and nurturing the message of the potential in all, including those with a learning difference.

The BDA (2022a) sets out a number of conditions that are commonly co-occurring neurotypes with dyslexia:

- Anxiety and mental health

- ADHD (including attention deficit disorder [ADD])
- ASD
- Developmental language disorder (DLD)
- Dyscalculia and maths difficulties
- Dyspraxia/development coordination disorder (DCD)
- Visual difficulties.

Anxiety and mental health

Anxiety and mental health are included within this group as they are commonly associated with SpLDs. Studies have established that young people with learning differences are more likely to experience feelings of anxiety, depression and low self-esteem (British Dyslexia Association, 2022a). Within the school environment, a young person's reluctance to engage in particular tasks – for instance, writing – particular lessons or school as such may be the first indicator that they are experiencing difficulties with learning that may be the result of a neurological developmental disorder.

Slower cognitive processing is common within the range of SpLDs; feeling unable to keep up with teachers/peers, coupled with apprehension of failing to finish or to offer responses quickly, can feed the development of anxiety. In addition, young people may be labelled as unmotivated or even lazy; they may fail to attain the levels expected of them across the curriculum. Children quickly form views of themselves as learners and compare themselves to others; on recognizing that they are falling behind, their confidence is bound to be negatively impacted, and anxiety builds.

Negative feelings around the ability to learn and being labelled 'slow', 'behind' or 'needing to try harder' swiftly grow and damage mental health. Young people may develop strategies, such as work avoidance, joking, excessive talking or withdrawing, to hide below the teacher's radar. They may act out at home and/or school by behaving inappropriately, and physical symptoms, such as nausea or breathing difficulties, may develop.

It is vital that behaviours or symptoms that suggest anxiety, depression and emotional difficulties are addressed swiftly, and it is important that learning difficulties are carefully considered as playing a part in young people's poor mental health. Schools and parents must work closely to put in place suitable support. This may include outside support services, such as targeted mental health services (TAMHS) or child and adolescent mental health services (CAMHS).

Attention deficit hyperactivity disorder (ADHD)

ADHD is a neurobiological condition that is considered to be one of the most common childhood disorders present through adolescent into adulthood (ADHD Foundation, 2022). The condition involves impulsivity, hyperactivity and inattention; symptoms include challenges in remaining focused, maintaining attention and managing behaviour and hyperactivity.

There are three subtypes recognized:

- Type 1 – Inattention
- Type 2 – Hyperactivity and impulsivity
- Type 3 – All of the above.

ADD is classified as a subtype of ADHD (Type 1) in that it involves inattention but not hyperactivity or impulsivity.

Pennington identifies the core difficulty in ADHD as that of inhibition, which is itself an executive skill and which could be viewed as comparable to the core weakness with phonology in those with dyslexia (Pennington and Bishop, 2009). Barkley (2005) purports that deficits in executive function result in the inability to link the part of the brain that holds knowledge to the part that controls behaviour. That is, those with ADHD may have knowledge and experience but are not able to explain this further. They may present as demanding of attention and praise in the classroom and often find it difficult to work on one task for extended periods of time, particularly if movement and choice are restricted. It is widely accepted that differences in the dopamine receptors in the frontal lobe of the brain play a role in ADHD. The ADHD neurotype was first recognized in those boys in class who were unable to stay in one place and concentrate, but it is important to emphasize that ADHD is diagnosed in both boys and girls and is not caused by poor parenting or lack of education; nonetheless, the risk factors, as with other SpLDs, can be modified by compensatory factors, such as the learning environment or teaching approaches.

In school children, ADHD is diagnosed by a medical clinician, for example a paediatrician or child psychiatrist. The pathway to diagnosis can be complex and may take months or years. There are two main routes for diagnosis: parents may seek a referral via their GP, or the young person's school can make a referral to a community paediatrician or service such as CAMHS. Increasingly, ADHD is being diagnosed later in life.

Commonly, ADHD is regarded and recorded in school as a 'behavioural problem', and it is the case that an individual with ADHD is more likely to underachieve in the education system. Youngsters with ADHD are often labelled as disruptive, attention seeking and lacking in motivation and are often chastised and underestimated owing to a lack of attention to detail and inability to finish one task before being drawn to another. Half the children with ADHD in a clinical sample had reading difficulties (Stevenson *et al.*, 2005), and this combination of difficulties can create a perfect storm of underachievement, with a high proportion of those young people avoiding education or being excluded from it. In addition, adults with ADHD are more likely to be engaged in antisocial and risky behaviour (Barkley, 2005). Yet, ADHD, as with other SpLDs, is diagnosed in individuals across the spectrum of intelligence. Indeed, those with ADHD can become high achievers.

The ADHD Foundation (2022) identifies the positive aspects of ADHD. It is often said of youngsters with ADHD, 'But he/she can concentrate when he/she wants to', and indeed this is the case. Those with ADHD can become hyper-focused and highly driven to succeed; they tend to be goal- and achievement-driven and to have high levels of energy. Many individuals with ADHD talk about how their mind 'races', working very quickly, and how they are the drivers of teams and tasks. They take risks and avoid details and processes; they focus on the 'goal' and look for the quickest way of getting to it.

The combination of these traits – being easily distracted and being driven by success and new challenges – with the literacy difficulties associated with dyslexia and the common weaknesses of poor working memory and auditory processing difficulties can be very challenging within the classroom. It is therefore important that schools, teachers and parents carefully consider ways to promote and use the strengths of those with ADHD and dyslexia to combat and compensate for the difficulties.

Here are some ideas for such adaptations and support strategies:

- Keeping tasks fun and engaging; using multisensory active learning.
- Chunking tasks and providing mini goals and clear achievement outcomes.
- Supporting organization and memory by providing visual prompts.
- Reducing repetitive tasks and unnecessary time fillers.
- Limiting demands of listening and increasing the opportunities for doing.
- Ignoring 'fiddling' and 'jigging', instead viewing these as strategies to support concentration; therefore, promoting inobtrusive methods/tools, for example silent fiddle toys/adapted chairs to allow movement.
- Using humour to de-escalate negative interactions and events.

- Encouraging metacognition and the model 'think before I do'.
- Using positive re-enforcement to acknowledge and reward often.
- Ignoring negative behaviour and providing time and space for reflection.
- Providing extra support in examinations – extra time is less likely to be an effective arrangement for those with ADHD than rest breaks and cues to return to task.

Youngsters with SpLDs, but particularly those with dyslexia and co-occurring ADHD, can be viewed as litmus paper pupils – that is, they provide the teacher with immediate feedback on the quality of the teaching and learning taking place. If the child with ADHD/dyslexia is losing focus, it will be clearly evident, while others in the class may present as engaged.

It is important to remember when teaching those with ADHD that impulsivity often leads to regret. Children, adolescents and adults with ADHD may be more likely to speak before thinking and therefore to unintentionally cause offence or annoy others by calling out or moving around the room.

Autism spectrum disorder (ASD)

Autism is a lifelong developmental disability. One out of one hundred individuals are said to be on the autism spectrum, and there are approximately 700,000 autistic young people and adults in the UK (National Autistic Society, 2022). Autism is also regarded as a specific learning difficulty (British Dyslexia Association, 2022a) and can be co-occurring with dyslexia.

Autism affects individuals in unique ways, but there are commonalities in their difficulties, and many individuals have significant strengths in a wide range of areas.

An autistic condition has to be diagnosed by a medical professional or a professional with specialist qualifications, and they must present with difficulties in three key areas.

All those with an autistic condition have difficulties with social communication and social interaction; interpreting verbal and non-verbal language is highly challenging. They may need longer to process information and may find decoding social communication, such as facial expressions, very demanding. They tend to process language literally and can often misunderstand the subtleties of verbal and physical communication. Some may be unable or extremely reluctant to speak, while others have highly developed vocabularies and writing skills, but they struggle to comprehend tone of voice or sarcasm and use repetition of vocabulary or phrases without fully understanding the meaning; in some cases, this is experienced as 'echolalia'.

Those with autism find recognizing or understanding the feelings and intentions of others challenging. They find it difficult to express their own feelings and so find it hard to form and maintain relationships with others, particularly those they do not know. Socializing in larger groups can be extremely stress-inducing for those on the autism spectrum, and they may come across to those who do not know them or understand the condition as insensitive or socially inappropriate, for example making rude comments that would normally go unsaid, like the child who tells the headteacher his breath smells of coffee.

Autistic individuals may prefer to be alone, either because this is less stressful or because they do not seek comfort from others; nonetheless, many recognize their difficulties with socializing and long to share the company of others. Youngsters on the autism spectrum may communicate and socialize more readily with those older or younger than themselves, and they may not be interested in 'fads' or 'fashions'. They may tend to direct conversations around their personal interests, failing to show interest in the views or conversations of others.

Another key area of difficulty within the definition of autism is repetitive and restrictive behaviour, whether it be a special interest, a need to repeat behaviours over and over or a tendency to maintain routines to deal with feelings of anxiety. This can be explained by a difficulty in being able to imagine or predict events or the reactions of others. Extreme anxiety presents psychologically or physically, and reactions and attempts to lessen these feelings can come across to others as unexplained or extreme. Those on the autism spectrum are often described as rigid in their thinking and find it difficult to come off task. This can be viewed as having a keen hobby or an 'obsession', but often this becomes a strength or indeed a specialism, and the ability to be hyper-focused and driven to perfection is regarded by many employers as an asset. Such keen interests can lead to high achievement and innovation. There are numerous international innovators or activists who are autistic.

Sensory overload is commonly experienced as autistic individuals may be hyper-sensitive to sound, visual stimulus and sensations of touch, smell and taste. They may alternatively be under-sensitive. For example, they may find changes in temperature intolerable or find certain background noises unbearable; they cannot 'filter', ignore or block out such sensations, often creating extreme anxiety or sensory discomfort, and the individual may 'shut down' or 'melt down'. For this reason, many environments are highly challenging for an individual with autism, for example public transport, busy schools and areas with loud children or barking dogs. Reactions to such stimuli can be seen by others as extreme or irrational, but to the individual with autism, it is overwhelming and distressing. It is for this reason that schools often develop safe spaces or specialist units to provide the most appropriate environment for some or part of the school experience. Workplaces can be very challenging, too, but with careful consideration and often simple changes, places and situations can become autism friendly.

Owing to the wide range of strengths and difficulties presenting for the individual with autism, programmes of support must be personalized and monitored closely. In general, there are some key principles for quality-first teaching and individual support for those with autism in the mainstream school:

- Establishment of routines and systems of pre-warning of change.
- Visual cues for learning, including for organization and daily routine.
- Carefully considered and adapted learning environments and provision of strategies and tools to allow the individual with autism to manage sensory overload, for example provision of headphones or limiting bright lighting.
- Direct teaching of social skills, including non-verbal and verbal communication – for example, provision of scripts to assist in given situations.
- Direct teaching of how to adapt to new situations.

Autism can often go undiagnosed, particularly in girls, and this can mean that youngsters are misdiagnosed or labelled as difficult. This may continue into adulthood, and many individuals on the autism spectrum are not diagnosed until much later in life. It is therefore clear that educators should be alert to the strengths and difficulties associated with autistic conditions and be ready to support and seek understanding of the individual's needs, whether through referral and diagnosis or by adapting their own teaching and learning strategies, resources and environment.

Developmental language disorder (DLD)

The delayed acquisition of speech and language skills is not uncommon in early childhood. This can be related to a delay in using speech sounds to communicate, difficulties pronouncing speech sounds, speech impediments or problems understanding verbal communication from others. Such difficulties may be recognized by parents, by health professionals (such as health visitors and GPs) or in pre-school settings such as playgroups or nurseries. Sometimes, the difficulties will not be recognized until the child begins school. Often, with help, including being referred to a speech and language therapist, they make progress and 'catch up', but in some children, substantial difficulties with language persist.

DLD is a type of speech, language and communication need (SLCN) (British Dyslexia Association, 2022a), previously known as specific language impairment (SLI). Recent research indicates that, on average, in a class of 30, two children will experience DLD to such an extent that their academic progress will be negatively affected (RADLD, 2022).

DLD is a specific, persistent and significant difficulty with oral communication – speaking and understanding language. Children with DLD are otherwise healthy and have developed in other areas within expected ranges. They have otherwise 'normal' underlying abilities, and the difficulty is 'hidden'. The difficulties with talking and understanding language cannot be explained by other conditions or illnesses, for example hearing impairment, head injury, cerebral palsy or autism. It is thought that it may run in families (RADLD, 2022).

In most cases, a diagnosis of DLD comes from a medical professional when a child is aged five or over and has already received speech and language therapy, but difficulties have not been resolved.

The diagnosis of DLD includes language difficulties that:

- persist into adulthood
- are unlikely to be overcome without support
- impact academic progress and everyday life.

Children and adults with DLD may experience:

- misdiagnosis – their difficulties may be overlooked, misdiagnosed or misinterpreted, sometimes as poor behaviour, lack of motivation or poor attention/listening
- social isolation or difficulties forming and maintaining relationships with peers and others – they may find it hard to follow and join in with conversations, particularly if lots of people are talking at once
- difficulties making academic progress and accessing learning, as learning is mostly facilitated via language
- difficulties mastering reading or writing
- behavioural problems and/or frustration and disengagement from learning

- anxiety and/or mental health problems
- social and economic disadvantage.

The ability to understand and utilize language to communicate and learn cannot be underestimated, and those with DLD experience considerable difficulty accessing the curriculum and demonstrating their knowledge and understanding without effective support. Many difficulties faced are shared with those common to dyslexia – for instance, youngsters with DLD may take longer to process verbal instructions, they may struggle to understand complex directions and they may find it difficult to organize their thoughts into sentences. Thus, their difficulties may be particularly evident when they are required to read and comprehend language or to express themselves in writing. In this way, difficulties in the classroom can present similarly as difficulties associated with dyslexia, but children with DLD may not have specific difficulties with decoding single words or with spelling. DLD may co-occur with other learning difficulties – for example, dyslexia and DLD may go unrecognized and undiagnosed but nevertheless impact an individual's academic progress and ability to communicate verbally with others.

There are a wide range of resources that may be used to support the development of language, for instance Talk Boost KS1 and KS2 Intervention Packs (ICAN, 2022). As with all children and young people, involving them in designing and monitoring the progress of programmes and interventions to support their progress is very impactful.

Educators are able to support youngsters with DLD via appropriate support within quality-first teaching and individual support, including:

- simplifying language (verbal and written)
- providing opportunities to pre-learn and overlearn, including re-enforcement via supporting adults in the classroom
- using visual cues to support new language and instructions
- using direct teaching of language skills, using specialized resources (e.g. Talking Tins)
- providing opportunities to understand personal strengths, and strategies to compensate for difficulties
- using assistive software and information and communications technology (ICT) to provide opportunities to support all ages
- offering exam access arrangements, including modified papers.

Individuals with DLD are sociable and often have strengths and talents in a variety of other areas. Support from professionals, including speech and language therapists and specialist educators, has the potential to make a positive impact on outcomes and experiences for those with DLD.

Dyscalculia and maths difficulties

The origins of mathematical difficulties in children and adults can be diverse and complex. As with difficulties with mastering literacy, the effect of underdeveloped mathematical skills upon the individual is significant, not only in their academic life but in many aspects of daily living, work and recreation. Difficulties with maths can be overwhelming for each person; a lack of confidence and security with maths can be evident in difficulties telling and dealing with time, using and managing money and coping with everyday tasks such as following recipes or playing games with family or friends.

Mathematical difficulties should be considered as a continuum, not as a distinct category, with a range of causal factors (Jarrett, 2020). The acquisition and mastery of maths skills is easily impacted by a school absence or periods of poor mental health, such as anxiety, and 'falling behind' or developing a 'maths phobia' can prevent a person from making progress with maths or from even seeking support. Teachers observe that a significant number of children withdraw from learning maths as early as seven years old (Chinn, 2022). It is therefore essential to appreciate that difficulties with maths can be related to environmental factors and therefore may not be related to SpLDs. They may be part of the range of learning difficulties associated with dyslexia, or they may constitute a specific learning difficulty solely related to the acquisition and mastery of mathematics – this would be regarded as dyscalculia.

Dyscalculia is a specific and persistent difficulty in understanding numbers that leads to a diverse range of difficulties with mathematics that are not expected given the individual's age and level of education. It is experienced across all ages and abilities. Jarrett (2020) chaired the BDA committee to establish a definition of dyscalculia, distinguishing it from other maths difficulties and placing it at one end of the spectrum of maths learning difficulties. In dyscalculia, the learner's persistent and specific difficulties with maths must include those with number sense, including subitizing, comparing symbolic and non-symbolic magnitudes and ordering. This can be seen in the most basic aspects of number and arithmetic. The individual who experiences dyscalculia has no concept of numerical magnitude; they find it very challenging to see patterns of relationships between numbers, even when these are demonstrated to them. A learner may often remain in the 'counting trap' (Bird, 2022). The prevalence and causes of development dyscalculia (DD) are not as widely researched; nevertheless, it is generally agreed that dyscalculia is congenital and neurological in origin, like dyslexia, and although it is hard to be precise regarding prevalence owing to definitions and diagnosis still being in the early stages, it is estimated that 6% of the population has dyscalculia (British Dyslexia Association, 2022b).

Cognitive processing difficulties associated with dyslexia may impact an individual's development of mathematical skills. Poor verbal working memory, phonological processing deficits (such as slower processing speeds) and weak processing of number-related information are common challenges that can negatively impact an individual's ability to recall number facts, sequences of numbers and the steps required to solve mathematical problems and to comprehend written maths questions. Dyslexic learners often also experience issues with mastering numeracy skills; however, mathematics is not necessarily a 'weakness' for those who experience dyslexia, and indeed for some learners who experience dyslexia, maths is an area of strength.

Many mathematical problems, whether in the classroom or in real life, are embedded within words, either written or verbal. The language of maths and word-related maths tasks can be made difficult by an individual's challenges in reading, whether it be decoding new words or comprehending longer pieces of text. Memory difficulties, like those commonly associated with dyslexia, cause barriers to achievement in maths. Issues with verbal working memory make mental arithmetic very challenging, and it is difficult to sequence and retain numbers while carrying out longer mathematical problems. Slow processing speeds can make classroom maths particularly hard; learners who require more time to process information and/or organize their responses can find the system of questioning in the classroom highly challenging, and this exacerbates anxiety issues. The ability to quickly retrieve words or concepts from the memory is something maths tasks rely heavily on, and so those with rapid naming difficulties are placed at a disadvantage. When learners have visual processing difficulties, the way maths is laid out visually can create difficulties, and the individual may miss or misinterpret what is written or find it hard to visually represent their ideas in the expected way. Difficulties with fine motor skills, particularly when these are demonstrated in poor handwriting and an inability to set out work neatly on a page, also create considerable issues for learners when they are writing out maths work. These issues commonly facing learners with SpLDs mean that maths can be a particularly hard subject to master, and this in turn negatively influences self-esteem and the confidence to pursue interests and talents in other subjects, for instance physics or engineering, or even to be able to progress in their careers, for example in nursing.

It is therefore clear that whatever the cause of an individual's lack of attainment, progress or confidence in mathematics, it is essential that educators take early opportunities to offer effective support. For those at the far end of the maths difficulties spectrum – those with dyscalculia – the level of support will need to be higher, more personalized, delivered on an individual basis and over an extended period of time. Suitable strategies for supporting those with difficulties in maths through quality-first teaching and individual support should include the following:

- Clear understanding of gaps in knowledge and understanding through sound assessment.
- A calm approach, giving time and opportunities for overlearning and questioning.
- A structure programme of support that is cumulative.
- Multisensory methods and resources for teaching and learning.
- Breaking concepts and tasks down into manageable chunks.
- Direct teaching of the language of maths, and provision of materials for prompts (e.g. cue cards).
- Visual cues and re-enforcement in resources and learning environment.
- Small group or individual support.
- Awareness and consideration of how anxiety and self-esteem may influence teaching and learning.
- Use of concrete materials, such as Numicon, Cuisenaire rods and counters.
- Provision of extra time for thinking and developing/using visual methods for working out problems.

Difficulties with mathematics can be overcome, and progress can be made, but it is essential that adequate support is put in place early. Each individual must be encouraged to develop an understanding of their own strengths and difficulties and given 'tools' and strategies to apply and adapt their learning of maths in everyday life.

Dyspraxia and/or development coordination disorder (DCD)

Dyspraxia and DCD are interchangeable terms for the specific learning difficulty associated with motor control and planning. Dyspraxia is a subtype of DCD (British Dyslexia Association, 2022a). It is known as a common, lifelong disorder affecting fine and/or gross motor coordination. DCD is distinct from motor difficulties caused by other motor disorders, such as cerebral palsy, or those impacted by illness or disease, such as stroke or brain injury.

DCD is a common condition, affecting about 3% of adults (Kirby & Gibbon, 2018). It presents as unique strengths and difficulties for every individual, but persistent, long-standing difficulties in at least one aspect of motor control have to be evident for a diagnosis. In young children, the most common path to diagnosis is via an occupational therapist (OT). Referrals can be made via a GP or community paediatrician or directly to the local OT service. As with other SpLDs, behaviour and difficulties change over time, and early diagnosis, intervention and appropriate support have positive impact upon motor development for each individual.

The condition is found across intellectual abilities. As with other SpLDs, most individuals with dyspraxia also have another neurological developmental disorder. For example, 70% of children with DCD also show evidence of dyslexia and phonological problems (O'Hare & Khalid, 2002). Slow processing is a shared difficulty with other SpLDs, such as dyslexia (Pennington, 2006). Another commonly shared risk factor with dyslexia is weakness in verbal memory. Common difficulties are challenges in following instructions, attention, sense of direction and sequencing, copying from the board, the concept of time and processing information.

Coordination difficulties affect an individual's functioning and participation in learning, life skills and employment. The main impact for those with DCD is on physical skills, such as movement; however, DCD may affect communication (including speech), handwriting and drawing skills, planning and study skills, and play. Children often show difficulties mastering self-care skills, such as dressing and feeding; they regularly are slower in meeting physical developmental milestones, such as learning to walk or to ride a bike; they show delay in physical play, such as balancing and using play equipment; on entry to school, children with dyspraxia show difficulty with self-care, pen control and handwriting, and PE.

Support and interventions for those with DCD are often recommended and sometimes delivered by an OT or physiotherapist; nonetheless, there are many ways children and young people can be supported:

- Gross motor programmes.
- Fine motor programmes.
- Concrete, visual reminders of daily routines.
- Extra time for dressing and organizing equipment.
- Adaptive resources, such as sloping writing boards, specialist pens (e.g. triangular/soft grip), larger keypads for computer.
- Handwriting books – wider lines.
- Handwriting programmes.
- Copies of notes, handouts to avoid note-taking.

- Alternatives to written recording, e.g. dictaphone, voice recognition software or supportive writing software (Crick, Claro, etc.).
- Exam access arrangements – extra time, scribe, use of laptop with assistive software.

As children with DCD develop, they may acquire many motor/coordination skills, for instance neat handwriting; nevertheless, tasks requiring dexterity or gross motor skills and organization and planning continue to be a challenge and take longer to master and perform.

References

ADHD Foundation (2022) *Home – ADHD Foundation*. Available at: www.adhdfoundation.org.uk [Accessed 17 May 2022].

Barkley, R. (2005) *ADHD and the Nature of Self-Control*. New York, NY: Guilford Press.

Bird, R. (2022) *Specialist in Dyscalculia and Arithmetic Difficulties*. Available at: www.ronitbird.com [Accessed 15 May 2022].

British Dyslexia Association (2022a) *Neurodiversity and Co-occurring Difficulties*. Available at: www.bdadyslexia.org.uk/dyslexia/neurodiversity-and-co-occurring-differences [Accessed 15 May 2022].

British Dyslexia Association (2022b) *Dyscalculia and Maths Difficulties*. Available at: www.bdadyslexia.org.uk/dyslexia/neurodiversity-and-co-occurring-differences/dyscalculia-and-maths-difficulties [Accessed 15 May 2022].

Chinn, S. (2022) *Home page*. Available at: www.stevechinn.co.uk [Accessed 15 May 2022].

Curran, A. (2021) *The Neurobiology of ADHD*. Available at: https://vimeo.com/544986241 [Accessed 15 May 2022].

Gooch, D., Hulme, C., Nash, H. & Snowling, M. (2014) Comorbidities in preschool children at family risk of dyslexia. *Journal of Child Psychology and Psychiatry*, 55(3), 237–246.

Hulme, C. & Snowling, M. (2008) *Developmental Disorders of Language Learning and Cognition*. Chichester: Wiley.

ICAN (2022) *ICAN, the Children's Communication Charity*. Available at: https://ican.org.uk [Accessed 15 May 2022].

Jarrett, P. (2020) Webinar: Understanding, identifying and supporting learners with dyscalculia and maths learning difficulties. British Dyslexia Association. Available at: www.bdadyslexia.org.uk/events/a-brief-overview-to-understanding-identifying-and-supporting-learners-with-dyscalculia-and-maths-learning-difficulties [Accessed 15 May 2022].

Kaplan, B., Dewey, D., Crawford, S. & Wilson, B. (2001) The term comorbidity is of questionable value in reference to developmental disorders. *Journal of Learning Disabilities*, 34(6), 555–565.

Kirby, A. & Gibbon, H. (2018). Dyslexia and employment. *Perspectives on Language and Literacy*, 44(1), 27–31.

Muter, V. (2020) *On Demand: Literacy Disorders: 'Tricky' profiles – how to assess, interpret and intervene SASC authorised*. Available at: www.patoss-dyslexia.org/online-courses/on-demand-literacy-disorders-tricky-profiles-how-to-assess-interpret-and-intervene-sasc-authorised/10315?OccId=14788 [Accessed 15 May 2022].

National Autistic Society (2022) *What is Autism*? Available at: www.autism.org.uk/advice-and-guidance/what-is-autism [Accessed 15 May 2022].

O'Hare, A. & Khalid, S. (2002) The association of abnormal cerebellar function in children with developmental coordination disorder and reading difficulties. *Dyslexia*, 8(4), 234–248.

Pennington, B. (2006) From single to multiple deficit models of developmental disorders. *Cognition*, 101(2), 385–413.

Pennington, B.F. & Bishop, D.V. (2009). Relations among speech, language, and reading disorders. *Annual review of psychology, 60*, pp.283-306.

RADLD (Raising Awareness of Developmental Language Disorder) (2022) *Developmental Language Disorder*. Available at: www.radld.org/about/dld [Accessed 15 May 2022].

Rose, J. (2009) *Identifying and Teaching Children and Young People with Dyslexia and Literacy Difficulties*. Available at: www.thedyslexia-spldtrust.org.uk/media/downloads/inline/the-rose-report.1294933674.pdf#:~:text=Identifying%20and%20Teaching%20Children%20and%20Young%20People%20with,most%20severe%20difficulties%20invariably%20require%20more%20specialist%20support [Accessed 15 May 2022].

Stevenson, J., Langley, K., Pay, H., Payton, A. *et al.* (2005) Attention deficit hyperactivity disorder with reading difficulties: Preliminary genetic findings on the involvement of the ADRA2A gene. *Journal of Child Psychology Psychiatrist*, 46(10), 1081–1088. https://Doi:10.1111/j.1469-7610.2005.01533.x.

Willcutt, E.G. & Pennington, B.F. (2000) Comorbidity of reading disability and attention-deficit/hyperactivity disorder: Differences by gender and subtype. *Journal of Learning Disabilities*, 33(2), 179–191.

Chapter 4

Reading and Spelling

Part 1: Reading

BRENDA FERRIE

The purpose of this part is to look at models of reading. These models have been used to help us understand the complexities of reading and how children learn to read.

What is reading? Reading is the complex cognitive process of decoding symbols to derive meaning. It is a form of language processing. Success in this process is ultimately measured by our ability to understand what we have read, although there are a number of skills to master on the way. Reading is a means for language acquisition, communication and sharing information and ideas. It involves a number of elements, such as visual and auditory processing, memory, vocabulary knowledge and one's own schemata and experience.

In his book *Teaching the Brain to Read* (2005), Dr Duncan Milne tells us that while spoken language is about 25,000–150,000 years old and the brain therefore has defined circuits for speech, written language and reading are much newer, only 4000 years old. The brain therefore does not have a specifically defined region for reading and has to recruit services from different areas, creating a complex network of neural connections between them. No two brains have identical neural circuits for reading. It is a complex process of recognizing symbols in the visual system and translating them into pronunciations in the speech areas that are then related to the meanings of words.

To understand the reading process, we need to start with the symbols or alphabet because without knowing what the symbols mean, we cannot make sense of them. All written languages are an expression of a spoken language and evolved when we needed to record what had been said. Unlike the Chinese alphabet, which is logographic (i.e.

based on picture symbols), the alphabet we use to write English is based on sounds. It has its early origins in hieroglyphics. Over time, these were refined by the Greeks, the Romans, the Christians and then printing presses to become the letters we use now. However, because England has been invaded by so many different peoples over time, all bringing their own languages with them, the English written system is very much a hybrid of different spellings and pronunciations. It is therefore considered to be an opaque written system, with 44 sounds represented by only 26 letters, unlike languages like Spanish, which have a much more regular one-to-one sound-to-symbol mapping. In English, there is more than one way to spell a particular sound. For example, the 'long e' sound can be spelt 'ee' (as in 'tree'), 'ea' (as in 'dream'), 'ie' (as in 'chief') or 'ei' (as in 'receive') to name a few. And to make things even more complicated, certain graphemes, like 'ea', can make more than one sound, for example (ē) in cream, (ĕ) in bread and (ā) in steak. The way our alphabet system works is known as the alphabetic principle, and understanding how this works is crucial to being able to 'crack the code'.

Dr Milne (2005) writes that in a simple model of word reading, there are two circuits: the upper or phonological route, which decodes the symbols into individual sounds and blends them into words, and the lower or orthographic circuit, which recognizes groups of letters or whole words and pronounces them without the need to recompose them by blending the sounds. When we learn a new word, we normally go through the upper circuit to identify sounds and then blend them together, but after seeing the word or group of letters many times, the brain makes an image or lexicon of it and thereafter is able to retrieve it as a whole word using the faster and more efficient lower circuit. This automatic process enhances reading fluency and speed.

Beginner readers need to be taught to read using both upper and lower circuits because English words are both phonically regular and irregular. This is why it is important to teach both letter names and sounds from the outset. Otherwise you may have a child trying to decode the word 'said' using letter sounds. They need to know that these irregular words are not phonically decodable and must be recognized as 'sight words' and read as whole words using the lower circuit. When I make flashcards for high-frequency or tricky words, I draw eyes or ears around the word so that the learner can instantly know how to read it. Some people use a green colour for phonically regular words and red for phonically irregular words. This helps children to instantly recognize what strategy they can use.

However, this model of reading only takes into account word reading, which is only part of the process. Rose introduced the simple view of reading model to replace the searchlights model in 2009 when he published his report *Identifying and Teaching Children and Young People with Dyslexia and Literacy Difficulties*, which followed his 2006 report *Independent Review of the Teaching of Early Reading*. This model was originally articulated by Gough and Tunmer (1986), who proposed that successful reading comprehension was the product of two components: decoding and linguist or language comprehension (R = D × L). The model therefore has two axes – decoding and language comprehension – dividing the model into four quadrants. It can therefore be used for informal assessment by determining where a learner sits within the quadrants. Good language comprehension and good decoding would equate to typically developing children; good language comprehension and poor decoding are indicative of dyslexia; good decoding and poor language comprehension may indicate a learner with development language disorder; and poor decoding and poor comprehension may indicate a child with delayed development across the spectrum of learning.

Scarborough's (2001) rope model of reading clearly illustrates the components that constitute language comprehension and decoding. Language comprehension, she says, consists of background knowledge (facts and concepts), vocabulary, language structures (syntax, punctuation), verbal reasoning (inference, predicting) and literacy knowledge (genres, print formats). Decoding focuses on word reading and decoding and includes phonological awareness (awareness of sounds and blending), word decoding (letter/sound mapping, word derivatives, spelling rules and conventions) and sight recognition of irregular words. Fluent readers are able to execute and coordinate the components of word recognition and text comprehension simultaneously.

The argument between the phonics and the whole language approaches to teaching reading, sometimes referred to as the 'reading wars', has been ongoing for a long time, and the methods in teaching reading tend to see-saw in popularity from the whole-word or language approach to decoding and phonics. The phonics approach is often considered a 'bottom-up' approach. Its advantage is that once students master the basics of the alphabetic principle, especially those with good vocabularies, they can start to read quite a large range of children's literature. Conversely, because the English language is such an opaque language, with a considerable number of irregular conventions, letter/sound mapping can be quite difficult for some learners to master. Sir Jim Rose, however, is adamant that phonics is fundamental to learning to read.

The 'top-down' whole language approach was advocated by Ken Goodman in his paper 'Reading: A psycholinguistic guessing game' (1967), in which he argues that reading is not a precise process of learnt conventions but rather that children could use available language cues – syntactic, semantic and graphic – to make decisions about what to accept, reject or refine in terms of acquiring information from these cues. He says that efficient reading is based on the ability to select the fewest, most productive cues necessary to produce guesses rather than the precise perception and identification of letters, morphology, rules and other elements involved in the reading process. This model has been refuted by scientific research in favour of the belief that good readers do not rely on guessing but on precise and detailed attention to letters and words and that, if anything, it is poor readers who compensate for inadequate decoding ability by guessing using semantic cues and context.

The early models of reading involved three integrated processors: the orthographic processor, the meaning processor and the context processor (Bielby, 1994). The orthographic processor received visual information from the printed text by identifying letters and by recognizing the sequential organization of the word. This was then sent to the meaning processor, which identified the word. The meaning processor also received information from the context processor, which helped to select the correct response when homonyms were involved. For example, if we read 'a table mountain', we would not think of a table where we would eat dinner. But this early model did not take into account the phonological processor.

Seidenberg and McClelland's connectionist model (1989) included the phonological processor because if printed language is going to have a meaning, we have to learn it in the first instance through the phonological processes of spoken language (Bielby, 1994). The complete model therefore includes two-way interactive processes between the context processor, the meaning processor, the phonological processor and the orthographic processor.

We can therefore access the meaning of text through two possible routes: the direct route from the orthographic processor to the meaning processor and the indirect route through the phonological processor, which synthesizes the sounds of the words. An example in *Making Sense of Reading* (Bielby, 1994) illustrates how children would interpret the sentence 'Tell me wear he went'. An older child would say that the sentence did not make sense as they would employ the faster, direct route, whereas a younger child would be more dependent on the indirect route, decoding the word so that the pronunciation gives the correct word.

The dual route is further explored by Coltheart's dual cascaded model (*et al.* 2001). This model refers to the lexical route and the non-lexical route. The lexical route involves recognizing and decoding known words and requires access to an extensive database of knowledge, such as the spelling of the word stored in the orthographic lexicon, the pronunciation of the word stored in the phonological lexicon and the word meaning stored in the semantic system. There are in fact two lexical routes. The first accesses the word, its meaning and its correct pronunciation without having to go through the semantic processor. But if the word was then mispronounced, the reader may recruit the semantic processor. In a later paragraph, I use the example of a reader saying 'a row of chairs' but mispronouncing the word 'row' so that it rhymes with 'cow' and then self-correcting. The non-lexical route is independent of the lexical route and deals with words through previously learnt grapheme–phoneme correspondence (GPC) and rules.

Stuart and Stainthorp (2016) refer to the two routes as lexical-semantic and phonological. In their explanation of how children learn to read, they say that children already have a store of word meanings and pronunciations acquired through use in daily life. Therefore, developing lexical-semantic processes requires storing knowledge of the letter sequence of the written word (its orthography) and linking the letter sequence to its meaning.

However, children will encounter words that are not familiar to them, and therefore the lexical-semantic process involves storing knowledge of the letter sequence, inferring its meaning from the context, working out the correct pronunciation from the letter sequence and linking the sequence to the word's meaning and pronunciation.

Then, on subsequent encounters with the word, the learner can recall the correct meaning and pronunciation of the word in a rapid, automatic process that does not require conscious awareness on the part of the reader.

This process can be used by skilled readers to access 'exception' words like 'yacht' and 'meringue' that do not conform to GPC rules and thus are not regular words. Because both word meanings and pronunciations are stored, learners can distinguish between homophones like 'sail' and 'sale'.

The phonological processor in reading depends on previously stored knowledge of GPC rules, which is used to decode phonically regular words and non-words. If used to read 'exception' or irregular words, this would lead to mispronunciations. To develop phonological processing, the learner needs to develop an understanding of the alphabetic principle, explicit awareness of GPC, sequences of phonemes and correspondences through phonics teaching and how to blend. The correct pronunciation is vital to give the word its correct meaning.

An example of this may be if a learner were asked to read the sentence 'please line up the chairs in a row' and mispronounced 'row' as rhyming with 'cow' rather than with 'grow', the sentence would not make sense, and the learner may correct themselves if the correct word was stored in the meaning processor and vocabulary knowledge. Similarly, they may read the word 'treacherous' with the long e (as in 'teacher') if they have not previously encountered the word 'treacherous' and do not know its meaning. Mispronunciations of words will impact on comprehension.

Word reading also progresses through various phases (Ehri, 1997), which can be classified as:

- Pre-alphabetic: environmental and visual cues without knowing what the letters represent – for example, a young child may be able to read 'Sainsbury' because they can associate the sign with the spoken word.
- Partial alphabetic: some connection between sounds and some letters in phonically regular words.
- Full alphabetic: more established GPC and awareness of exception words and irregular words.
- Consolidated alphabetic stage: confident GPC, recognition of exception and irregular words and developing knowledge of morphology.

Morphonology is an understanding of how words are made up – their derivations, roots, suffixes and prefixes. It is an important tool that contributes to fluent and accurate reading.

So far, we have talked about the different mechanisms that learners use to access single-word reading. But this is only half the story. If we refer to the simple view of reading, we see that the second axis is language comprehension. This should not be confused with reading comprehension. Language comprehension is a learner's awareness of sentence structure, punctuation and the way that written language represents spoken language in terms of intonation and genre.

There has also been a great deal of research by Maggie Snowling (2019) into the benefits of enriched language in terms of reading acquisition. Therefore, vocabulary knowledge, general knowledge and speaking and listening skills play significant parts in the process of learning to read.

And this is still not the whole story of learning to read. While it is so easy to become overly focused on word reading and decoding, which are of course very important in the reading process, we must not forget the principal reasons for learning to read, which include conveying instructions, acquiring new knowledge, and enjoyment. Although, during a child's development, the balance shifts over time from 'learning to read' to 'reading to learn', we must also remember to focus on reading to learn and reading for enjoyment even in the very early stages.

Children with dyslexia will often have a much higher interest level and knowledge compared with their ability to access text. There is always a danger that they will be discouraged from enjoyment of reading because of their difficulty in accessing text and because they will consequently be reading at a level well beneath their interest and intellect. Reading helps children acquire knowledge and learn the meaning of words; knowledge and learning the meaning of words develops reading. There is a synergetic effect.

The opposite is also true: the less you read, the less knowledge you acquire. Keith Stanovich (1986) coined this as the Matthew effect in reading.

We therefore need to teach word reading separately from text reading. In reading, we need to teach:

- phonological awareness so that the child becomes phonemically aware of the sounds in the words. This is an ability that develops both innately and through teaching. It is hierarchical and involves counting syllables, counting sounds, manipulating sounds, rhyming and blending
- one-to-one correspondence of letter names and sounds for phonically regular words, which is best achieved using alphabet letters and constructing words
- the alphabetic principle and awareness of the alternative spellings for different sounds
- word-reading strategies for phonically regular words, such as practising reading phonetically regular non-words, using resources such as Toe by Toe by Keda Cowling or the game Chunks by Smart Kids
- word-reading strategies for phonically irregular words, including flashcards, neurolinguistic programming, shapes, colours and words within words
- morphology and knowledge of spelling rules and syllable division
- language comprehension skills, such as punctuation, syntax and recognizing the genre through layout
- vocabulary development and storytelling
- guided reading to support reading for pleasure and knowledge. Paired and shared reading techniques can be used to support continued fluency. There is nothing more frustrating than being stopped in the middle of a sentence to 'sound a word out'. It interrupts fluency and can be highly demotivating. In paired and shared reading activities, it really does not matter how many of the words the child reads

independently as long as they are supported, enjoy the experience, are engaged, interact with the text and answer questions.

Independent reading does, however, require that the learner can access a high percentage of words independently. Care should be taken that texts have a high interest level even if they have a lower reading level. Assistive technologies are an important resource. Reading pens help learners access the words that they may not be able to read. They also act as readers for GCSE texts, along with Read Write and other technologies. Children who find reading difficult should be encouraged to access audiobooks so they do not succumb to the Matthew effect.

But before helping learners with their reading, we must check their visual processing. Visual difficulties affect many reading skills, from tracking and being able to follow print to unstable and moving letters. The SpLD Assessment Standards Committee website has a useful questionnaire, and learners who may have visual processing difficulties should be referred to an optometrist. Despite the controversies around colour glasses and overlays, many learners say that they have helped their reading.

In assessment for reading at Level 5, we need to do a single-word reading text and a prose reading text. The single-word reading text will help us determine how well a learner can recognize the graphemes and know their sounds, decompose a word into its constituent sounds and recompose it using the correct pronunciations through blending. It will inform us about their knowledge of exception and irregular sight words.

We also do a prose reading exercise to determine reading behaviour. This is often called a miscue analysis. See the appendix for more on what miscues are and what they tell us.

There are many reasons why learners with dyslexia find reading difficult. In the first instance, they may have difficulties with phonological awareness, which is one of the key underlying deficits of developmental dyslexia and a vital ability underpinning literacy development. If they cannot identify the sounds, they will be unable to match the letters to those sounds and 'crack the code'. Poor and unstable GPC is one of the main characteristics of dyslexia. Another contributory factor may be visual processing issues. If the letters are unstable, the learner will find it hard to make lexicons and therefore continue to be reliant on decoding rather than developing rapid and orthographic recognition of words.

In summary, therefore, reading is a highly complex task that involves many different skills and involves a number of different parts of the brain. Our opaque written English

Holds the book too close

Reads without expression – word by word

Ignores punctuation

Re-reads to make sense

Can use context clues well

Can retell the story

Does not recall what they have read

Is stressed by reading

Is reluctant and gives up

Reads too fast to conceal mistakes

Reads too slowly

Has sore eyes or headaches

Complains about letters moving

Uses a colour acetate or wears glasses

Any other comment:

References

Bielby, N. (1994) *Making Sense of Reading*. Southam, Warwickshire: Scholastic.

Coltheart, M., Rastle, K., Perry, C., Langdon, R. & Ziegler, J. (2001) DRC: A Dual Route Cascaded model of visual word recognition and reading aloud. *Psychological Review*, 108, 204–256.

Ehri, L.C. (1997) Learning to Read and Learning to Spell are One and the Same, Almost. In C.A. Perfetti, L. Rieben & M. Fayol (eds), *Learning to Spell: Research, Theory, and Practice Across Languages* (pp.237–269). Mahwah, NJ: Lawrence Erlbaum Associates.

Goodman, K. (1967) Reading: A psycholinguistic guessing game. *Journal of the Reading Specialist*, 6(4), 126–135.

Gough, P.B. & Tunmer, W.E. (1986) Decoding, reading, and reading disability. *Remedial and Special Education*, 7, 6–10.

Milne, D. (2005) *Teaching the Brain to Read.* Hungerford: Smart Kids Publishing.

Rose, J. (2006) *Independent Review of the Teaching of Early Reading*. London: Department for Education and Skills.

Rose, J. (2009) *Identifying and Teaching Children and Young People with Dyslexia and Literacy Difficulties: An Independent Report from Sir Jim Rose to the Secretary of State for Children, Schools and Families*. London: Department for Children, Schools and Families.

Scarborough, H. (2001) Connecting Early Language and Literacy to Later Reading (Dis)abilities: Evidence, Theory, and Practice. In S.B. Neuman & D.K. Dickinson (eds), *Handbook of Early Literacy*, pp.97–110. New York, NY: Guilford Press.

Seidenberg, M.S. & McClelland, J.L. (1989) A distributed developmental model of word recognition and naming. *The American Psychologist: Psychological Review*, 96(4), 523–568.

Snowling, M.J. (2019) *Dyslexia: A Very Short Introduction*. Oxford: OUP.

Stanovich, K.E. (1986) Matthew effects in reading: Some consequences of individual differences in the acquisition of literacy. *Reading Research Quarterly*, 21(4), 360–407.

Stuart, M. & Stainthorp, R. (2016) *Reading Development and Teaching*. London: Sage.

Part 2: Spelling

SUZY SHEPPARD

Glossary

- Etymology: word origins and their link to meaning
- Grapheme: letter (group of letters)
- Grapheme–phoneme correspondence (GPC): the relationship between sounds and the letters that represent those sounds (also known as phonics)
- Morpheme: the smallest meaningful element of speech
- Morphemic awareness: the ability to use morphemes as a basis of building words
- Orthography: the study of a writing system's spelling patterns
- Orthographic awareness: being aware of common letter patterns or rules
- Phoneme: speech sounds
- Phonological awareness: the ability to discriminate sounds and manipulate individual phonemes

Introduction

As well as learning to read, a vital part of becoming literate is being able to spell. The idea that symbols can represent spoken language and that a message can be made by making marks is the first stage in this seemingly complex process.

Spelling skills develop in a predictable way (Rowe, 2015). First, children recognize that letters make sounds. They can then correctly recall these letter/sound correspondences in reading and later reproduce them in their writing. Nevertheless, as with reading, spelling is not a natural skill and needs to be explicitly taught.

This section will focus on these questions:

- What is spelling and how do children become proficient spellers?
- How can we teach spelling more successfully?
- What difficulties can occur along the way, and how can we, as practitioners, help children overcome these?

What is spelling?

In the simplest terms, spelling is the representation of speech sounds (phonemes) with their corresponding letters or group of letters (graphemes) to form written words. In the English language, there are 44 phonemes represented by 26 letters; 24 of the phonemes are consonant sounds, while 20 are vowel sounds. As there are more phonemes than graphemes, in English we need to combine several letters to make all our phonemes. This correspondence of graphemes to phonemes (GPC) is more commonly known as phonics.

20 vowel phonemes/graphemes			
Phoneme	**Example**	**Grapheme**	
Short vowels			
/ă/	apple	a	
/ĕ/	egg, bread	e	ea
/ĭ/	igloo, gym	i	y
/ŏ/	orange, swap	o	a
/ŭ/	umbrella, son	u	o
Long vowel sounds			
/ā/	train, play, made, acorn	ai, ay, a-e, a	
/ē/	tree, me, treat, chief, pony, donkey	ee, e, ea, ie, y, ey	
/ī/	night, ride, cry, island, lie	igh, i-e, y, i, ie	
/ō/	boat, snow, oboe, alone	oa, ow, o, o-e	
/ū/	blue, dew, unicorn, tube	ue, ew, u, u-e	
/ōō/	spoon, tissue, route, blew, use	oo, ue, ou, ew, u-e	
Other vowels			
/oo/	book, would, put	oo, ou, u	
/oi/	boil, toy	oi, oy	
/ou/	mouse, cow, bough	ou, ow, ough	
R controlled vowels			
/ar/	star, grass	ar, a	
/or/	fork, awe, autumn, call, snore, board, door, fought, daughter	or, aw, au, a, ore, oar, oor, ough, augh	
/er/	herb, blurt, girl, pearl, worm	er, ur, ir, ear, or	
/air/	stairs, bears, snare	air, ear, are	
/ear/	fear, peer, sphere	ear, eer, ere	
schwa	picture, banana	unstressed vowel	

24 consonant phonemes/graphemes			
Phoneme	**Example**	**Graphemes**	
/b/	bat, wobble	b	bb
/c/	cat, king, lick, chemist, quilt	c	k, ck, ch, q
/d/	dog, paddle	d	dd
/f/	fish, waffle, phone, graph	f	ff, ph, gh
/g/	good, giggle	g	gg
/h/	help	h	
/j/	June, angel, edge, forge	j	g, dge, ge
/l/	lamb, llama, apple	l	ll, le
/m/	man, mummy, comb	m	mm, mb
/n/	necklace, sunny, knot	n	nn, kn
/p/	poster, flapper	p	pp
/r/	rose, horror, wrestle	r	rr, wr
/s/	sandal, ice, house, cement, scene	s	ce, se, c, sc
/t/	table, rattle	t	tt
/v/	van, stove	v	ve
/w/	window, whistle, queen	w	wh, u
/x/	fox	x	
/y/	yellow	y	
/z/	zip, breeze, pins, rose	z	ze, s, se
/sh/	ship, brochure, television, dictation	sh, ch, si, ti	
/ch/	child, watch	ch, tch	
/th/	other	th	
/th/	thong	th	
/ng/	swing, ankle	ng, n	

However, spelling is more than the simple process of encoding speech sounds with their corresponding grapheme(s), and as you can see from the tables above, some phonemes are represented by more than one grapheme, especially long vowel phonemes, for instance the long /a/ can be spelt multiple ways ('play', 'train', 'cake', 'alien'). Moreover, a single grapheme can represent more than one phoneme: for instance, the grapheme 'ough' can be pronounced 'bough', 'bought', 'through' or 'dough'.

The continuous influx of people from our neighbouring countries over the course of the last several thousand years has resulted in English being a 'rich and luxurious language' (Walker, 1999: 101). Moreover, it has also resulted in 'layers of spellings' from the Celts, Romans, Vikings and French (Henry, 2003) and presented our children with some unusual spelling patterns and rules, at times appearing 'illogical and inconsistent' (Walker, 1999: 101).

Despite the English language containing an array of linguistic patterns and rules, most of these spellings are consistent and therefore can be learnt and their exceptions noted (orthography). An understanding of where words originate (etymology) can also help with understanding word construction, especially with the addition of affixes (morphology).

About 3% of all English words are spelt irregularly (Crystal, 2003) – that is, they do not follow any rules – and therefore an internal spelling lexicon can also be created for these. See the previous chapter for a discussion on Milne's dual route to reading.

Learning to spell

It would be sensible to suppose that the development of reading and the development of spelling skills are inextricably linked: reading is the process of decoding graphemes to phonemes, whereas spelling deals with encoding phonemes to graphemes. Milne's reading model refers to the upper and lower routes. In spelling, children also need to use both of these routes, but using the opposite process of phoneme to grapheme, the upper/phonological circuit is used for phonically regular words, and the lower/orthographic circuit is used for phonically irregular words, where we need to teach a number of other strategies (Milne, 2005).

However, the relationship between reading and spelling is more complex (Ehri, 1987) and indeed not a simple one-way relationship. The 'exposure to written language is not enough to ensure proficient spelling skills' (Snowling, 2000: 76), and children do not learn to spell by simply reversing the skills developed from the process of learning to read. What is known is that children do apply patterns and rules learnt from spelling to help with their reading (Davis & Bryant, 2006) and, conversely, they learn about rules in reading and apply these to spelling (Frith, 1985).

A good phonological awareness is essential for successful spelling development. If a child cannot distinguish the sounds within spoken words, they will have difficulty recognizing and learning the necessary GPC. A child's phonological awareness at four years old is a strong predictor of spelling ability at age eight (Bradley & Bryant, 1991).

Alphabetic knowledge is also essential, knowing that written letters represent sounds. Once children understand that written letters represent speech sounds and have knowledge of letter names (from singing the alphabet), they use this to help them to spell (Bourassa & Treiman, 2010). Their first attempts at spelling words often involve using these names to represent the sounds that they hear in words, such as the letter 'r' to write 'are' or 'gnys' to write the word 'genius' (Bissex, 1980).

Good phonic skills are also necessary for effective spellings. If a child has good phonic skills, they become good spellers (Chall & Pop, 1996). However, these skills alone are not sufficient to develop competent spelling skills (Fletcher & Caplan, 2014): children also need explicit teaching (Nicolson, 2014; Stone, 2014).

Ordinarily, children's phonological skills develop throughout pre-school and Reception year, and they begin to learn phonics in readiness for reading (as discussed above) and spelling. This starts with simple CVC (consonant/vowel/consonant) words and quickly moves on to consonant digraphs (sh, ch) and blends (sm, nt) to produce four-letter (CCVC and CVCC) words. At this stage, proficient decoding skills (reading) produce more accurate encoding skills (spelling). The early learning goal for children in Reception is to be able to spell words by identifying sounds in them and representing the sounds with a letter or letters and also be able to write simple phrases and sentences that can be read by others (Department for Education, 2021).

Although spelling develops initially through a phonological route, where children use their awareness of sounds and letter names to experiment with writing and spelling, as their phonological awareness builds, they increase spelling accuracy by applying spelling rules for regular words. However, not all words follow rules, and therefore an internal lexicon is created for irregular words (Snowling, 1987).

Once children have learnt that there is more than one way of spelling a specific phoneme, their choice of grapheme will depend on their knowledge of alternative graphemes learnt through reading, and indeed children as young as Reception use both their phonics and their orthographic knowledge to help them spell (Reece & Treiman, 2001). They move from a phonetic understanding of spellings to a more rule-based orthographic understanding, or 'mapping' (Ehri, 2014), one where spelling patterns and rules are understood and learnt.

It is thought, however, that children also begin to learn about spelling rules from an early age, even before they are taught, and this is thought to be extrapolated from reading

(Cassar & Treiman, 1997). They are sensitive to both vowel and consonant rules, for instance never using 'ck' at the beginning of a word (Hayes *et al.*, 2006).

Studies seem to suggest that morphemic awareness is also a predictor of spelling ability (Green *et al.*, 2003). Most words in the English language contain more than one morpheme, and, as such, morphology is important in the development of spelling. Morphemes are either free (usually root words) or bound (affixes), and their use is governed by rules.

Consequently, knowledge of morphemes is important in the development of spelling skills. It is well documented that improving children's awareness of morphology has a positive effect on their spelling of words. This is essential when there is more than one way to represent a sound. For instance, the end sounds of 'socks' and 'fox' are the same, but spelling differs for morphological reasons (the suffix plural -s has been added to sock as it represents more than one sock, whereas the word 'fox' ends with that phoneme). The use of morphemic structures also helps children with spelling. For instance, in one study, the word 'turning' was spelt correctly, but the same children had difficulties spelling the word 'turnip' (Deacon & Bryant, 2006).

Knowledge of affixes also helps our developing spellers as they tend to be spelt the same way in different words, regardless of variation in speech. Take, for instance, the affix -ed used for past regular verbs ('wanted', 'kissed', 'killed'). These sound very different but are all governed by the same add -ed rule. And it is this consistency that is important in spelling development.

It has been found that children spell more correctly if teaching of spelling incorporates morphology (Bourassa *et al.*, 2006; Bowers *et al.*, 2010). Information from brain imaging confirms that all three areas – phonological, orthographical and morphological – are activated during spelling (triple word form theory) (Richards *et al.*, 2006).

Stages of spelling development

Over the years, several stage models have emerged. They all agree that children learn:

- a large number of letter combinations
- orthographic rules
- morphological rules
- to map phonemes to graphemes.

Frith's (1985) model is composed of three stages of spelling and reading development: the logographic stage, where the learner recognizes the word as a visual unit but does not know about letters in the word; the alphabetic stage, where the learner starts to use GPC; and the orthographic stage, where learners have a good knowledge of letter/ sound relationship. Ehri (2003) also suggests that children go through semi-phonetic, phonetic and morphemic spelling stages. Regular words are spelt using the phonological approach, encoding as the word to be written is spoken. Synthetic phonics facilitates learning the reversible process of both decoding for reading and encoding for spelling using the upper circuit (Milne, 2005). When children spell in the Early Years Foundation Stage (EYFS), often only one or two sounds of a word are represented, whereas in Year 1, GPC becomes secure, and regular words are spelt more conventionally. Irregular words are best spelt using the orthographic (lexical) circuit, which recognizes similar spelling patterns and morphemes (Milne, 2005; Treiman, 2017). Both morphemic and phonetic spelling patterns are used by Year 2 (Ehri, 1987).

Gentry (1982) proposes five stages of spelling development. The pre-communicative stage is when children use arbitrary shapes, squiggles or words learnt by heart. The second stage (semi-phonetic) is when the relationship between letters and sounds is realized. Letters are used to represent sounds in words but are often missing vowels. The third stage (phonetic) is when children produce spellings that closely represent the sounds in words. The fourth stage is the transitional stage, during which children start to use their knowledge of spelling rules. They often rely on their visual memory or knowledge of grapheme–phoneme rules. The last stage is referred to as the correct stage, when spelling is generally correct, including irregular words (see table below for further details).

Stage models have been criticized for presuming that all children pass through the stages in the same order. However, they can be useful; some research (Bourassa & Treiman, 2014; Bourassa et al., 2006) has shown that children with dyslexia tend to make the same mistakes that younger, typically developing children make. Stage models of spelling development can therefore be useful for teachers to map development of their pupils. Spelling errors of learners who find spelling difficult are similar to those made by younger children at an earlier stage. Therefore, it is easier for a teacher to track back to that stage to ascertain what skills need to be retaught or revisited.

Stage	Gentry (1982) Progress through the stages is gradual. Strategies from more than one stage may coexist.	Frith (1985) Building on earlier stage models.	Ehri (2002)
Stage 1	**Pre-communicative (3–5)** Children start to recognize that writing represents speech. An intended message is 'written'. At this stage, children have no knowledge of GPC, and random letter strings are used. The message cannot be read by the reader. Writing consists of mostly upper-case letters.	**Logographic** Children begin to recognize a small number of whole words by sight. Few words are spelt. The errors that are made are non-phonetic.	**Semi-phonetic** Children begin to try out 'writing' by making marks on the page and giving them meaning. They then move on to copying print, and although letters are used, they have no understanding of GPC. However, the names of letters are quickly learnt and used for semi-phonetic spellings. The first and/or last sound(s) of a word are represented with the names of letters.
Stage 2	**Semi-phonic (4–6)** Children begin to understand GPC; however, spelling is still largely 'invented'. Children begin to put letters together to represent words, and words may be one to three letters in length, with the salient sound in the word being represented, for instance 'r' for 'are'. More consonants than vowels are used, and children tend to write the initial and final letters of the word.	**Alphabetic** Children may use onsets and rimes to find patterns within words and match GPCs. Spelling is mainly phonetic. Some errors may be semi-phonetic.	**Phonetic** Children's knowledge of GPC increases, and spellings become more phonetically plausible.

Stage 3	**Phonetic (5–7)** Children are now able to represent all sounds with letters, and regularly spelt words are mostly spelt correctly. Children use common spelling patterns. However, orthographic rules are still missing, but words can be read.	**Orthographic** Children may use spelling patterns and units of words that are common to written English. They have an awareness of orthographic rules.	**Morphemic** Children begin to learn spelling rules and patterns. Morphemic rules are also learnt, and spelling becomes more consistent.
Stage 4	**Transitional (6–11)** Children start to apply their knowledge of orthographic and morphological rules and have a basic understanding of the conventions of spelling. Therefore, they can spell more words correctly. Most common words are spelt correctly. Vowels now present in each syllable.	n/a	n/a
Stage 5	**Correct spelling (11+)** Children now have a concrete understanding of spelling. They now know the English orthographic system and its basic rules. They understand word structure.	n/a	n/a

The National Curriculum in the UK

In line with children's cognitive development and with knowledge about how children learn to spell, the UK government has provided comprehensive guidelines for teaching spelling in the updated National Curriculum for English (Department for Education, 2014). It includes a broad overview of what should be taught/learnt at each year group as well as a more detailed list of each phonic, orthographic and morphemic element.

Children should be able to spell words quickly and accurately through knowing the relationship between sounds and letters (phonics) and understanding the morphology (word structure) and orthography (spelling structure) of words. This advice to teachers corresponds to the evidence of how children learn to spell (Department for Education, 2014).

By the end of Year 1, children should understand GPCs. They should be able to spell words containing the 44 phonemes along with common exception words – words that are phonetically irregular. They may make phonically plausible attempts to spell words that they have not yet learnt. They should also be able to name the letters of the alphabet (in order) and use this knowledge to help them differentiate the alternative spelling of the same phoneme. Orthographic rules are taught, and morphemic rules are also beginning to be examined, with the additions of simple affixes.

At the end of Year 2, children continue to be able to make phonically plausible attempts to spell words they have not yet learnt. They have learnt new ways of spelling phonemes, including common homophones. More affixes are added, and they are encouraged to use their ever-increasing morphemic knowledge to spell longer words. Children start to look at the etymology of words, which helps with their understanding of why some words are not spelt as they are pronounced, for instance 'table'.

Phonic knowledge should continue to support spelling into Key Stage 2, but increasingly, children understand the role of orthography, morphology and etymology. In lower Key Stage 2, children should be able to spell words accurately using their phonic and morphemic knowledge and their increasing awareness of etymology. Further prefixes and suffixes are understood and used, increasing spelling knowledge.

In upper Key Stage 2, they should now be able to spell words that they have not yet been taught by analogy, using what they have learnt about how spelling works in English.

Difficulties learning to spell

This final section will look at some of the difficulties that children can have with spelling development and in particular those with dyslexia. It will also offer some tried and tested strategies to support spelling development.

By looking at spelling errors from free writing tasks, it is possible to ascertain that poor spelling affects both the quality of the writing in terms of the language used, with often a discrepancy between written and oral language, and the quantity of writing produced. Looking at the relationship between spelling, handwriting and compositional skills showed that children with dyslexia displayed no difference in the speed of their handwriting in a routine task, but during free writing, they wrote significantly fewer words a minute, revealing that spelling can affect both the quality and quantity of writing (Sumner *et al.*, 2013).

Spelling errors from free writing can be analysed to look for any patterns in misspelled words – these gaps in spelling knowledge can then be addressed. Using spelling error analysis, misspelled words can be grouped by either phonological, morphological or orthographical error (integrated POM approach) (Devonshire *et al.*, 2013; Kelly & Phillips, 2016). This information can then be used to track back along the stages and explicitly teach what is missing (McMurray & McVeigh, 2016), not rote teaching a weekly spelling list but rather emphasizing the importance of word patterns and spelling rules (Goswami, 1992).

Phonological awareness difficulties

To be able to spell proficiently, children must be able to segment words into sounds. The phonological awareness deficits of dyslexia mean that dyslexic children are not aware of the individual sounds in words and will need to be explicitly taught how to analyse speech and separate sounds. Phonological awareness relies on both auditory and sequential discrimination. The ability to segment sounds, blend sounds into words, segment words into sounds and manipulate phonemes is normally achieved by the age of six (Lundberg, 2009; Schuele & Boudreau, 2008). However, phonological awareness and memory deficits make it difficult to process sounds in a word, remember them, recall corresponding graphemes and write them in the correct order. Deficits impact on the ability to hear letter clusters and syllables, leading to spelling difficulties (Schreiber, 2008). Furthermore, rapid naming difficulties may impede automaticity, the fluent retrieval of phonemes/graphemes without subconscious effort. A child with dyslexia may experience:

- difficulties in distinguishing sounds in oral language
- auditory processing difficulties in which rapid auditory changes may interfere with the ability to differentiate similar sounds or difficulty identifying sounds presented in quick succession
- phonological memory deficits, leading to challenges in holding phonological information
- rapid naming deficit, leading to a lack of automaticity and fluency in letter or word retrieval. More time is needed to recognize and process verbal information, and

the child may have difficulty remembering and following instructions and trying to find the right words to say or letters to write.

In order to support children in the classroom, teaching and learning should be multisensory. In addition, the following would also be beneficial:

- Provide quiet learning areas.
- Sit facing children, slow down speech, and model correct syntax and pronunciation.
- Allow for longer thinking and talking time.
- Limit instructions given at one time – the same applies to giving information.
- Use lots of visual aids.
- Continuously check for understanding.
- Repeat instructions often.
- Ask children to explain what they are going to do/are doing/have done.
- Share nursery rhymes, rhymes with movement, songs, poems and riddles.
- Read rhyming and alliterative books.
- Arrange to go on class/group listening walks and sound hunts.
- Play stamping and clapping games or sorting of syllables.
- Use alliteration games/silly sentences.
- Use mirrors to see how the mouth forms when speaking to aid articulation and sound discrimination.

Difficulties learning phonics

Systematically taught synthetic phonics is common in the EYFS and Year 1 to support the understanding of the letter/sound relationship by learning phonemes and their graphemic representations, blending them to read and also learning that the process is reversible for writing. Children with normal visual memory and processing recognize letters (their shapes and patterns) and track text from left to right without issue. Normal auditory memory and discrimination allows children to:

- recognize individual letter sounds and sounds of letter groups and patterns
- correspond and sequence sounds to visual representations
- discriminate sounds, including those within words

(Reid, 2003)

Dyslexic individuals find GPC, recall and manipulation challenging, with visual memory and processing difficulties in:

- recognizing letter patterns, shapes and orientations
- recalling letters seen and corresponding sounds
- recognizing that more than one letter can represent a sound or that a variety of letter patterns can represent a single sound
- text movement due to visual stress; identifying letters and keeping track of place in text
- mapping visual representations of sounds.

Moreover, auditory memory and discrimination difficulties – such as sound recognition and discrimination, sound retention and/or sequencing, sound discrimination within words and corresponding sounds to visual representations – lead to poor fluency in reading and spelling (Reid, 2003).

There are some strategies that can be used along with a daily structured phonics programme (Jolly Phonics or Letters and Sounds) (Department for Education and Skills, 2007; Jolly Learning Ltd., 2018):

- Monitoring student progress and providing follow-up support.
- Multisensory teaching, for example songs, letter/sound hunts, games.
- Creating class letter/sound books and e-books.
- Cue cards and visuals for confusing letters (b/d).
- Alphabet strips, phoneme mats, working walls.
- Overlearning.
- Coloured overlays/paper.

Frequent repetition for dyslexic learners is key. Sound-to-symbol linkage must become automatic, so one-to-one teaching strategies may include:

- A multisensory, structured intervention programme, for example Conquering Literacy (Kelly & Phillips, 2016), to reinforce phonics acquisition.
- Supervised multisensory sound–symbol linkage practice with Nessy Reading and Spelling, AcceleRead AcceleWrite or Wordshark (Brooks, 2016; Nessy Learning Ltd., n.d.; Wordshark, 2019).
- Teaching/re-teaching blending and decoding skills as well as segmenting and encoding skills to embed the reversible process.
- Personalized letter/sound cue cards.
- Securing sound/symbol linkage before introducing new ones.
- Different coloured pens for upper-/lower-case letters, vowels, letter groups and patterns.

- Games to reinforce learning.
- Wooden letters, sand/glitter trays, Roll 'n' Write alphabet.

How does this impact on spelling development?

As previously stated, regular words are spelt using the phonological approach, encoding as the word to be written is spoken. Synthetic phonics facilitates learning the reversible process of both decoding for reading and encoding for spelling using the upper circuit (Milne, 2005). During the early years (EYFS), often only one or two sounds of a word are represented, whereas in Year 1, as GPC becomes secure, regular words are spelt more conventionally. Irregular words are best spelt using the orthographic (lexical) circuit, which recognizes similar spelling patterns and morphemes (Milne, 2005; Treiman, 2017). Both morphemic and phonetic spelling patterns are used by Year 2 (Ehri, 1987).

However, the phonological approach relies on auditory and sequential discrimination, which can be challenging for dyslexic children. Phonological awareness and memory deficits make it difficult to process sounds in a word, remember them, recall corresponding graphemes and write them in the correct order. Deficits impact on the ability to hear letter clusters and syllables, leading to spelling difficulties (Schreiber, 2008). Dyslexic individuals may not recognize high-frequency words and letter patterns in text due to visual processing and memory difficulties, in turn impacting on the lexical route to spelling. The dyslexic brain stores information differently from non-dyslexic brains, so sound or similar element analogies are not used instinctively and must be explicitly taught.

Strategies to help learn spelling rules within the classroom:

- Sound buttons.
- Teaching morphology of words and usage.
- Explicitly teaching spelling rules – this is essential for all learners but even more so for learners who are having difficulties remembering how to spell.
- Mnemonics to remember tricky/irregular words.
- Word walls and working walls with key spelling patterns, rules and vocabulary.
- Multisensory practice, including technology.
- One-to-one support.
- Magnetic letters to practise spelling (remove pressure of writing).
- Sand/glitter trays, collage, rainbow writing, Plasticine.
- Syllabification (hand under chin/mirror/clap) to break words down.
- Writing syllables in different colours to aid recall.
- Personalized pictures with spelling patterns.

- A structured intervention programme, for instance Conquering Literacy (Kelly & Phillips, 2016).
- Repetition and overlearning of spelling patterns.
- Supervised practice with Nessy Reading and Spelling, AcceleRead AcceleWrite or Wordshark (Brooks, 2016; Nessy Learning Ltd., n.d.; Wordshark, 2019).
- Personalized spelling lists linked to class topics. Group words together to give meaning and context.
- Recording spellings on a device.

This part has looked at how children develop their skills as spellers. The first step is becoming aware of the individual sounds made by spoken language and mapping these onto letter(s) through GPC. Due to the complexity of the English language, children begin to realize that not all sounds can be mapped one to one, and so spelling patterns and rules need to be learnt. Rules, spelling patterns, affixes and learning about the origins of words all help children to develop a command of English spelling conventions and to accept that there are some spelling 'exceptions' that must be learnt by rote (although not as many as most people believe).

However, some children with dyslexia may find many of these typical routes difficult and will need extra help to navigate their way through. This may start with an inability to distinguish the smallest sounds in spoken language (phonemes) and map them onto individual letters (graphemes). Phonological memory deficits of dyslexia may impede the process of encoding all the sounds of a particular word and holding them in memory for long enough for it to be written down. Sequencing difficulties, both auditory and visual, may also cause difficulties writing the correct sounds in the correct place in order to spell a word correctly.

Some strategies have been listed that will help children who are finding spelling difficult, especially those with dyslexia. However, there are no hard and fast rules, and the rule here is to use what works for your child.

References

Bissex, G.L. (1980) Patterns of development in writing: A case study. *Theory into Practice*, 19(3), 197–201.

Bourassa, D. & Treiman, R. (2010) Linguistic Foundations of Spelling Development. In D. Wyse, R. Andrews & J. Hoffman (eds), *The Routledge International Handbook of English Language and Literacy Teaching*, pp.182–192. Abingdon: Routledge.

Bourassa, D.C. & Treiman, R. (2014) Spelling Development and Disability in English. In C.A. Stone, E.R. Silliman, B.R. Ehren & G.P. Wallach (eds), *Handbook of Language and Literacy: Developmental Disorders*, second edition, pp.569–583. New York, NY: Guilford Press.

Bourassa, D.C., Treiman, R. & Kessler, B. (2006) Use of morphology in spelling by children with dyslexia and typically developing children. *Memory & Cognition*, 34, 703–714.

Bowers, P.N., Kirby, J.R. & Deacon, S.H. (2010) The effects of morphological instruction on literacy skills: A systematic review of the literature. *Review of Educational Research*, 80, 144–179.

Bradley, L. & Bryant, P. (1991) Phonological Skills Before and After Learning to Read. In S.A. Brady & P.D. Shankweiler (eds), *Phonological Processes in Literacy*, pp.65–74. London: Erlbaum.

Brooks, G. (2016) *What Works for Children and Young People with Literacy Difficulties?* Available at: www.interventionsforliteracy.org.uk/wp-content/uploads/2017/11/What-Works-5th-edition-Rev-Oct-2016.pdf [Accessed 7 December 2022].

Cassar, M. & Treiman, R. (1997) The beginnings of orthographic knowledge: Children's knowledge of double letters in words. *Journal of Educational Psychology*, 89(4), 631–644.

Chall, J.S. & Pop, H.M. (1996) *Teaching and Assessing Phonics: Why, What, When, How: A Guide for Teachers*. Cambridge, MA: Educators.

Crystal, D. (2003) *English as a Global Language*, second edition. Cambridge: Cambridge University Press.

Davis, C. & Bryant, P. (2006) Causal connections in the acquisitions of an orthographic rule: A test of Uta Frith's developmental hypothesis. *Journal of Child Psychology and Psychiatry*, 47(8), 849–856.

Deacon, S. & Bryant, P. (2006) Getting to the root: Young writers' sensitivity to the role of root morphemes in spelling of inflected and derived words. *Journal of Child Language*, 33(2), 401–417.

Department for Education (2007) *Letters and Sounds: Principles and Practice of High Quality Phonics, Primary National Strategy*. Available at: https://assets.publishing.service.gov.uk/government/uploads/system/uploads/attachment_data/file/190537/Letters_and_Sounds_-_Phase_One.pdf [Accessed 19 August 2020].

Department for Education (2014) *The National Curriculum in England: Complete Framework for Key Stages 1 to 4*. Available at: www.gov.uk/government/publications/national-curriculum-in-england-framework-for-key-stages-1-to-4 [Accessed 10 July 2020].

Department for Education (2021) Statutory framework for the early years foundation stage. Available at: https://www.gov.uk/government/publications/early-years-foundation-stage-framework--2 [Accessed: 13.3.23].

Devonshire, V., Morris, P. & Pluck, M. (2013) Spelling and reading development: The effect of teaching children multiple levels of representation in their orthography. *Learning & Instruction*, 25, 85–94.

Ehri, L.C. (1987) Learning to read and spell words. *Journal of Literacy Research*, 19(1), 5–31.

Ehri, L.C. (2002) Phases of acquisition in learning to read words and implications for teaching. *British Journal of Educational Psychology: Monograph Series*, 1, 7–28.

Ehri, L.C. (2003) Systematic Phonics Instruction: Findings of the National Reading Panel.

Ehri, L.C. (2014) Orthographic mapping in the acquisition of sight word reading, spelling memory, and vocabulary learning. *Scientific Studies of Reading*, 18, 5–21.

Fletcher, H. & Caplan, M. (2014) *Anyone Can Spell It: A Guide for Teachers and Parents*. Farnham: Helen Arkell Dyslexia Centre.

Frith, U. (1985) Beneath the Surface of Developmental Dyslexia. In J.C. Marshall, K.E. Patterson & M. Coltheart (eds), *Surface Dyslexia in Adults and Children*, pp.301–330. London: Routledge.

Gentry, J.R. (1982) An analysis of developmental spelling in GNYS AT WRK. *The Reading Teacher*, 36, 192–200.

Goswami, U. (1992) Phonological factors in spelling development. *Journal of Child Psychology and Psychiatry*, 33, 967–975.

Green, L., McCutchen, D., Schwiebert, C., Quinlan, T., Eva-Wood, A. & Juelis, J. (2003) Morphological development in children's writing. *Journal of Educational Psychology*, 95, 752–761.

Hayes, H., Treiman, R. & Kessler, B. (2006) Children use vowels to help them spell consonants. *Journal of Experimental Child Psychology*, 94, 27–42.

Henry, M. (2003) *Unlocking Literacy: Effective Decoding and Spelling Instruction*. Baltimore: MD Brooks.

Jolly Learning Ltd. (2018) *Jolly Phonics*. Available at: www.jollylearning.co.uk [Accessed 12 August 2020].

Kelly, K. & Phillips, S. (2016) *Teaching Literacy to Learners with Dyslexia*, second edition. London: Sage Publications.

Lundberg, I. (2009) Early precursors and enabling skills of reading acquisition. *Scandinavian Journal of Psychology*, 61(4), 611–616.

McMurray, S. & McVeigh, C. (2016) The case for frequency sensitivity in orthographic learning. *Journal of Research in Special Educational Needs*, 16(4), 243–253.

Milne, D. (2005) *Teaching the Brain to Read*. Hungerford: Smart Kids Publishing.

Nessy Learning Ltd. (n.d.). Available at: www.nessy.com/en-gb [Accessed 5 December 2022].

Nicolson, T. (2014) Dyslexia: Reading and Spelling: Some Teaching Suggestions. In I. McLean & J. Clements (eds), *The Australian Dyslexia Learning Difference Handbook*. Erina, NSW: Learning Difference Convention.

Reece, C. & Treiman, R. (2001) Children's spelling of syllabic /r/ and letter-name vowels: Broadening the study of spelling development. *Applied Psycholinguistics*, 22, 139–165.

Reid, G. (2003) *Dyslexia: A Practitioner's Handbook*, third edition. Chichester: John Wiley and Sons.

Richards, T.L., Aylward, E.H., Field, K.M., Grimme, A.C. *et al.* (2006) Converging evidence for triple word form theory in children with dyslexia. *Developmental Neuropsychology*, 30(1), 547–589.

Rowe, D.W. (2015) The development of a descriptive measure of early childhood writing: Results from the Write Start! writing assessment. *Journal of Literacy Research*, 47, 245–292.

Schreiber, L. (2008) *Development of Phonological Awareness Skill*. Available at: www.speechpathology.com/articles/article_detail.asp?article_id=342 [Accessed 19 August 2020].

Schuele, C.M. & Boudreau, D. (2008) Phonological awareness intervention: Beyond the basics. *Language, Speech, and Hearing Services in Schools*, 39(1), 3–20.

Snowling, M. (1987) *Dyslexia: A Cognitive Developmental Perspective*. Oxford and Cambridge: Blackwell Publishing.

Snowling, M. (2000) *Dyslexia,* second edition. Chichester: Wiley Blackwell.

Stone, L. (2014) *Spelling for Life: Uncovering the Simplicity and Science of Spelling*. London: Routledge.

Sumner, E., Connelly, V. & Barnett, A.L. (2013) Children with dyslexia are slow writers because they pause more often and not because they are slow at handwriting execution. *Reading and Writing*, 26(6), 991–1008.

Treiman, R. (2017) Learning to spell: Phonology and beyond. *Cognitive Neuropsychology*, 34(3–4), 83–93.

Walker, J. (1999) Teaching Basic Reading and Spelling. In J. Townsend & M. Turner (eds), *Dyslexia in Practice: A Guide for Teachers*, pp.93–129. New York, NY: Kluwer Academic/Plenum Publishers.

Wordshark (2019) *Wordshark*. Available at: www.wordshark.co.uk/wordshark/schools [Accessed 10 July 2020].

Chapter 5

How to Support Learners with Dyslexia in the Classroom and During Intervention

General Strategies/Principles

SARA WATTS AND KAREN BARTLETT

As has been discussed in previous chapters, learners who are diagnosed with dyslexia will have difficulties with reading accurately, easily and at an appropriate speed (Rose, 2009). Being able to correctly recognize words, assign meaning to them and then also remember them in order to gain overall meaning of the text may be a challenging task. When reading is effortful, when it requires conscious thought, it becomes a significantly more challenging task to not only remember but also to make sense of what has been read. Difficulties may arise because too many words are unfamiliar and therefore are not decoded automatically; a visually similar word may be read incorrectly, and the more familiar word may not make sense, causing confusion; words may also sound the same when read out loud but have different spellings and different meanings, again causing misunderstanding. The reader then must decide which is the correct meaning that fits the sentence.

These processes require thinking time; the reader needs to be able to process the information before being able to decide exactly what the word is, what it means and whether it makes sense. While this additional processing is taking place, the learner may well be missing out on additional information as well as falling further behind in the activity.

Difficulties with fluent reading are only part of the story; older learners may have developed coping strategies to ameliorate weak reading skills, and so difficulties with well-sequenced, fluent and cohesive writing may now be the main issue. The learner also needs to record their thoughts and ideas; they need to be able to demonstrate their knowledge and understanding. The teacher needs to be able to see that they are acquiring new skills and knowledge. If the learner does not complete classwork, homework, lecture notes, essays, examinations or assignments to the required standard, how can the teacher be sure that the learner is listening, learning and working to their potential? The dyslexic learner's possible strengths in oral language or problem solving or with creative skills may not offer much assistance when the task requires quick reading and writing. The aim of quality-first teaching and classroom adjustments is therefore to minimize these barriers to learning and to enable the learner to access the curriculum, showing how their thoughts and ideas are progressing.

Take a few minutes to consider one of your learners who is dyslexic. What difficulties do they show on a day-to-day basis? How do their support needs vary in different subjects or for different tasks? Does the learner show varying levels of confidence, resilience and motivation across the curriculum and for different tasks? Put yourself in their position; consider the difficulties they experience lesson by lesson, day by day; consider how much energy and resilience are required, and compare this to a learner who is not dyslexic.

There are several adjustments that can be made to support the dyslexic learner, from the learning environment and teaching and learning strategies (quality-first teaching) to the use of access arrangements and assistive technology, as well as targeted intervention. The dyslexic learner is likely to find automatic reading, spelling and writing hard as a result of underlying difficulties with:

- phonological awareness (recognizing, isolating and manipulating the sounds in words)
- short-term sequential memory (remembering sounds or information in the correct sequence)
- processing speed (being able to quickly retrieve information from long-term memory)
- working memory (being able to hold and use information)
- concentration and attention (remaining focused and on task) – as the result of either co-occurring difficulties such as ADHD or tiredness
- visual and auditory processing difficulties (being able to accurately process visual or auditory information)

- motor coordination – gross and fine motor control difficulties may co-occur with dyslexia.

(Alloway & Alloway, 2015; Kelly & Phillips, 2016; Nicolson & Fawcett, 1999; Ramus, n.d.; Rose, 2009; Snowling, 2008; Stein, 2018)

As the dyslexic learner develops greater understanding of their difficulties and recognizes the increasing gap between themselves and their peers, associated difficulties with confidence, self-esteem, motivation and resilience can occur. Anxiety and the fear of failure can be very debilitating, making it extremely hard to focus and to learn. The impact of anxiety and low self-esteem should not be underestimated. For a struggling learner, knowing that your needs and difficulties are understood, that your strengths and efforts may not always be seen but are recognized and that you are valued as a learner is extremely powerful. A positive and secure relationship between the learner and the teacher is the foundation on which other adjustments are built.

The British Dyslexia Association (BDA) has produced the *Dyslexia Friendly Schools Good Practice Guide* (2018). This is a celebration and collection of good practice from local education authorities, regional children's services and schools across the UK. The result is a hugely valuable resource of tried and tested practical teaching tips and methods within a whole-school approach. Along with contributions from eminent specialists, this book will enable specialist teachers, classroom teachers and teaching assistants to see the best strategies and ideas for working with dyslexic children. It will also enable policy makers, advisers and senior leadership teams in schools to adopt and embed dyslexia-friendly good practice.

There are chapters on the process of becoming a dyslexia-friendly school, as well as help identifying children with dyslexia and providing support for reading, spelling, writing, maths and teaching of foreign languages. There is a dyslexia-friendly classroom observation checklist, which is extremely useful, as well as a very helpful dyscalculia lesson checklist.

When considering the range of adjustments and strategies that may be implemented to support a dyslexic learner, it is sensible to start with the learning environment. An ideal learning environment for those with dyslexia may include the following:

- A room free from distractions, quiet, without flickering lights and not a walkthrough classroom.

- The learner seated towards the front so they can see and hear the teacher clearly.
- A well-lit room.
- A coloured or pastel background on the interactive whiteboard, which reduces contrast and glare.
- Information written on the interactive whiteboard that is clear and easy to read. Cluttered and 'busy' information could be confusing and cause overload.
- Equipment available on the table or workstation, for example pens, highlighters, pen grips, writing slope, sticky notes, a mini whiteboard, voice recorder/Talking Tins, overlays, coloured paper, a dyslexia-friendly dictionary and keyword maps.
- Table and chairs at the appropriate height.

Classroom adjustments (quality-first teaching)

Quality-first teaching is a set of guidelines laid out by the Department for Education to ensure the best possible learning outcomes for all children (Department for Children, Schools and Families, 2008). The premise incorporates interactive, kinaesthetic teaching, allowing individuals to learn in different ways, ideal for the dyslexic learner. Five basic principles are considered necessary for successful teaching with dyslexic learners: it must be structured, multisensory, cumulative, phonics based and with opportunities for developing automaticity, including overlearning (Kelly & Phillips, 2016). The Special Educational Needs and Disabilities (SEND) Code of Practice (Department for Education, 2014) states that high-quality teaching that differentiates for individuals is the first step in responding to learners with SEN and will meet the needs of most children. Some learners may need additional or different support, which must be provided by the school or college.

When considering which classroom adjustments are appropriate, there will be considerable overlap between different age groups; the needs of the individual learner are paramount, and so strategies may be used in primary and secondary settings and may also be adapted for use in further or higher education. A range of the following strategies may be appropriate depending on the needs of the individual learner, and should take place in conjunction with appropriate differentiation. The dyslexic learner may also have creative, musical or practical skills as well as hobbies and areas of particular interest, which could be incorporated. It is recommended that learners who are presenting with visual and/or auditory difficulties in the classroom have a full vision and hearing test to rule out any underlying causes.

Here are some practical ideas that can be incorporated into quality-first teaching to improve outcomes for learners with dyslexia.

Oral language

- Create a rich oral language learning environment.
- Explicitly teach new keywords or subject-specific words.
- Have vocabulary mats available for keywords or subject-specific words.
- Link new vocabulary to prior knowledge.
- Use drama or music activities when introducing new topics and vocabulary, for example role play and singing activities.
- Remember that group work and group discussions can reduce the pressure on the individual learner.
- Do fun activities such as games, especially those with a competitive element, for example barrier games.
- Set up class or group listening walks and sound hunts.
- Revise or revisit new vocabulary regularly.
- Use vocabulary webs to break new words into the constituent sounds, syllables, meaning and linked words.

Instructions

- Give succinct, short instructions and chunk these into small steps.
- Give instructions in the order they need to be completed.
- Try to avoid adding new steps at the end of the list of instructions.
- Provide memory aids with oral instructions, including visual aids such as numbered lists on the whiteboard, activity planners or 'first, next and last' lists.
- Pause when giving information, to allow time to process.
- Check understanding – ask other learners to explain what they are going to do or what they have done.
- Allow learners to ask questions.
- Repeat instructions using the same vocabulary and in the correct order, giving thinking time again.
- When giving instructions, face the learners, slow down speech and model correct syntax and pronunciation.
- Use open questions and develop shared thinking approaches. Allow planning and rehearsal time before giving answers.
- Allow thinking and talking time to encourage collaborative thinking; this reduces the pressure on the learner to give the correct answer independently.

- Use classroom routines and repetition to encourage automaticity.
- Do fun activities and games involving repetition, sequencing and recall; for example, 'I went to the shops and bought ...'

Reading

ACCURATE READING

- Use paired reading or reading buddies for reading activities in topic work.
- Have a reader or reading pen or reading software to complete activities requiring accurate reading skills.
- Use coloured overlays and reading rulers, and adjust screens if appropriate.
- Consider the layout of any handouts, reduce clutter or busyness, enable keywords and important information to be quickly identified.
- Explore reading on iPads or e-readers where it is possible to change the font size, background colour, etc.

COMPREHENSION

- Give extra time to complete reading activities.
- Listen to audiobooks to develop an enjoyment of stories.
- Use hi-lo (higher chronological age and lower reading age) books or large-print books on non-glossy paper.
- Do not expect learners to read aloud in class unless they want to.
- Use reading comprehension and guided reading activities advocating reading for meaning.
- Use picture books and images to develop comprehension skills without the need to decode.
- Read to the class or provide audiobook versions and then discuss the story.
- Model and explicitly teach comprehension strategies.
- Explore the story by retelling or sequencing through movement, role play, pictures and story maps (see resources such as Pie Corbett).
- Develop skimming and scanning skills.
- Develop study skills, for example highlighting text in different colours, to identify new or unfamiliar vocabulary or information relating to a particular character; develop note-taking skills.

Spelling

- Explicitly teach new topic words.

- Have word lists or vocabulary mats available.
- Use spelling dictionaries, for example the *ACE Spelling Dictionary* (Moseley, 2011) or the *School Spelling Dictionary* (Maxwell & Rowlandson, 2012).
- Teach multisensory strategies to practise and overlearn new spellings, for example 'look, cover, write, check', rainbow writing or using finger paints or sand trays.
- Develop a whole-school spelling policy; use one colour to mark the quality of the written work and a different colour to identify a specific number of spellings, for example three or four, in any piece of work.
- Differentiate homework spelling lists, take a mastery approach and give spellings appropriate to the learner.
- Personalize spelling lists linked to class topics. Group words together to give meaning and context.
- Allow use of a personal, electronic spellchecker.

Writing

RECORDING INFORMATION

- Minimize copying where possible and provide handouts.
- Allow older learners to take photos of information on interactive whiteboards, for example mind maps developed from class discussions.
- Supply notes of core lesson content for further annotation by the learner.
- Teach note-taking skills.

EXTENDED WRITING

- Allow learners who write slowly or need longer to formulate their responses extra time to complete written activities.
- Use a variety of approaches, for example cartoon strips, labelled pictures, songs or raps, flow charts, mind maps, storyboards or diagrams, leaflets and PowerPoint presentations.
- For learners who write slowly, allow additional time and ensure that this normal way of working is considered in tests and exams.

LEGIBILITY ISSUES

- For learners who find legible writing difficult, consider the use of a scribe or assistive technology or alternative strategies, for example cartoon strips and PowerPoint presentations.
- If appropriate, have pen grips, writing slopes and coloured paper easily available.

- Teach planning skills, encouraging the learner to develop an individualized approach.

Developing phonological skills

- Develop rhyme with movement, songs, poems, riddles and tapping or clapping games.
- Read rhyming and alliterative books.
- Play with words to explore beats, rhyming and syllables.
- Use songs, letter and sound hunt games.
- Use alliteration games and silly sentences to reinforce sound recognition.
- Have a Sound of the Week and share this with parents for homework.
- Use phonic phones, mirrors or Talking Tins to improve awareness of mouth movement with the sound made and the spoken letter.
- Use alphabet arcs with wooden or magnetic letters to develop and reinforce alphabet skills.
- Follow a daily structured phonics programme, for example Jolly Phonics (Jolly Learning Ltd., 2018) or Letters and Sounds (Department for Education Skills, 2007).
- Use multisensory teaching, including musical and creative activities as well as cue cards and visuals for confusing letters, for example 'b'/'d' confusion.

Focus and concentration

- Remember that dyslexia can occur with other specific difficulties, for example ADHD or dyspraxia, which may result in difficulties with concentration or focus.
- Bear in mind that some learners with dyslexia may not have additional co-occurring difficulties but due to tiredness, stress and anxiety may struggle to maintain focus and concentration throughout the day.
- Say the learner's name first and pause until you have their attention before giving instructions or new information.
- Develop strategies not only to keep learners on task but also to recapture their attention if they do become unfocused.
- Teach the learner ways of remembering instructions and new information – personalize it to the individual learner.
- Provide learning and movement breaks; consider adjusting the length of sessions to the learner's individual attention span.
- Use timers to help extend a learner's attention span.
- Link the learning topic to areas of personal interest or the real world.
- Minimize distractions from the learning environment, for example flickering lights

and noisy ventilators. Headphones and screens can be useful in busy classrooms if learners are easily distracted by others.

- Use games, competition, reward systems and other incentives to create motivation and encourage and maintain attention.
- Use a multisensory approach, with a mix of activities, for example words, images and diagrams, to keep activities interesting and maintain focus.
- Allow for tiredness or off days.

Memory

- Allow pupils to use a Talking Tin (Talking Products, 2020), a dictaphone, a whiteboard or sticky notes to record words, sentences or instructions.
- Support writing with writing frames, and explicitly teach note-taking and planning strategies. There is a range of planning strategies, from mind maps and visual approaches to more structured lists and flow charts. Different learners will prefer different approaches and may need the opportunity as well as the time to explore their preferred way of working.
- Multitasking is very difficult, so don't give instructions or new information while the learner is doing something else, for example reading, writing or copying from the board.
- Provide labels with the learning objective or homework already on them, which can be stuck into books.
- Allow older learners to photograph board work or provide them with a printout of the work.
- Provide visual supports, for example visual timetables, task planners, mind maps, working walls and table mats with keywords and vocabulary facts on them to reduce the load on memory.
- Make learning multisensory so pupils can make as many connections to the learning as possible by firing up all the senses. Connections in the brain are improved, and a stronger memory is formed.
- Allow learning or movement breaks.
- Minimize the stress that can occur from forgetting – for example, give praise for asking or for good listening.
- Use study buddies for learners who may need help with remembering what to do next.
- Ensure that learning is built on the previous knowledge and information is presented in smaller chunks. If possible, develop links across the curriculum, particularly with skills or information that will be used in other subjects.

Organization

- Make sure deadlines are recorded accurately in homework diaries.
- Ensure that resources are easily accessible and labelled clearly.
- For older learners, plan how to meet the deadlines of longer writing assignments; include time to complete research as well as the planning, writing and proofreading elements of the assignment.
- Encourage life skills such as problem solving, stress management, communication and decision making.
- Encourage topic/subject notes to be kept in colour-coded folders.
- Teach learners how to create and organize subject folders and topic folders on the computer.
- Monitor progress, and give the learner regular, constructive feedback.
- Trial assistive technologies such as online calendars and reminder apps to help meet deadlines and schedule seminars and meetings.
- Try using study mentors as a useful point of contact, not only to teach organizational and study skills but also to be available at high-pressure times, for example during exams, to provide additional support that is targeted towards learners with SpLDs.

Regardless of the age of the learner, the benefits of metacognition cannot be underestimated. Enabling a learner to have good understanding of how they learn best and how they can use their strengths to ameliorate areas of difficulty is extremely powerful. Taking the time to reflect on how they have tackled the task or completed a piece of work, considering which strategies worked well and so could be used again, will result in improved learning outcomes and progress, as well as have a positive impact on confidence and self-esteem.

One-to-one targeted intervention

Dyslexic learners will often require targeted one-to-one intervention if they are to acquire automatic reading and spelling skills as well as being able to produce written work to the required standard. Weak literacy skills may often mask underlying visual or problem-solving skills, and so the true potential of the dyslexic learner may not be recognized, resulting in underachievement and possible frustration, stress and anxiety.

Targeted intervention needs to be structured, cumulative, sequential and multisensory, with opportunities for overlearning (Rose, 2009). Multisensory teaching involves several different senses being used simultaneously, resulting in a stronger memory being formed, as the memory is embedded along a variety of neural pathways. Therefore, activities that combine visual, auditory, tactile and kinaesthetic actions are multisensory and will lead to more successful learning (Kelly & Phillips, 2016).

It is key to start from where the learner is at and to master the required learning outcome before moving on. It is important to consider their individual circumstances and to consider what would be useful for that learner. For example, a primary-aged learner is likely to need to focus on acquiring robust phonological awareness skills to support the development of their literacy skills, whereas an adult learner may need to acquire skills relating to their employment, as well as strengthening literacy and organizational skills.

A typical intervention programme should cover the following areas:

- Alphabet skills
- Phonological awareness skills
- Phonics
- Word reading and spelling for both regular and irregular words
- Reading comprehension skills
- Writing skills
- Study and/or organizational skills.

Alphabet skills

Being able to recite the alphabet correctly, knowing the letter names of both upper- and lower-case letters and having an idea of where a letter comes in the alphabet are very useful. Hickey (1977), Briggs (1992) and Combley (2001) describe a way of dividing the alphabet into groups to make this process easier. It is important that all learners can give the letter names and sounds for all upper- and lower-case letters; if a learner does not have this knowledge, they will struggle to develop their reading and spelling skills (see Adams, 1990 for a review of research in this area).

There is a range of fun, multisensory activities for developing familiarity with the alphabet. An alphabet arc and wooden or plastic letters (letter cards do not give tactile feedback) are easy to acquire and can be used to complete a variety of activities; finger painting, playdough letters, making letters out of different materials and textures and shaving foam can all add fun and colour. For a range of suggestions, see Chapter 9, 'The Alphabet', in *Overcoming Dyslexia: A Practical Handbook for the Classroom* (Broomfield & Combley, 2003).

Phonological awareness skills

Phonological awareness is recognizing, isolating and manipulating the sounds in words. It is not the same as phonics. Phonics is GPC, that is, linking sounds and letters. Bruck and Treiman (1992) and Goswami (1994) suggest that intervention should not focus solely on phonemes as phonics programmes often have but should also consider the level of phonological awareness a learner has. It is key to ensure that the learner has a sense of rhythm, can recognize beginning, medial and end sounds and syllables in words and can blend and segment sounds, along with other sound recognition and manipulation skills. There are several phonological awareness programmes available, for example *Sound Linkage* (Hatcher *et al.*, 2014).

Phonics programmes

The age of the learner and their skill level will obviously influence the starting point for the teaching programme as well as the type of teaching programme used. There are a number of programmes available, some of which are included here.

- Use a multisensory structured intervention programme, for example Conquering Literacy (Kelly & Phillips, 2016), Alpha to Omega (Hornsby *et al.*, 1999), Units of Sound (Units of Sound, 2018) and Toe by Toe (Cowling & Cowling, 1993).
- For supervised multisensory sound/symbol linkage practice, try, for example, Nessy Reading and Spelling (Nessy Learning Ltd., 2017), AcceleRead AcceleWrite (Clifford & Miles, n.d.) or Wordshark (Wordshark, 2019).
- Teach and re-teach blending and decoding, segmenting and coding skills to embed the reversible process. Create personalized letter/sound cue cards to secure the sound/symbol linkage before introducing new ones.
- Strengthen and embed alphabet, upper- and lower-case letter, vowel and consonant recognition, for example by using different coloured pens or different coloured letters for upper- and lower-case letters, for vowels and for letter groups.
- Play games such as Trugs (Read Successfully, n.d.), bingo pairs for matching and rhyming or Go Fish.
- Explicitly teach spelling rules, one rule at a time, ensuring the rule is mastered before moving on.
- Develop a morphological approach to the teaching of words, for example 'heal', 'healthy' and 'healthier', to encourage learners to see the links between related words.

Reading comprehension

- Use guided reading activities, teaching segmenting and blending, spelling patterns.

- Explicitly teach model reading comprehension strategies, including literal comprehension, analysis, evaluation and inference, for example Rising Stars (2019), Think 2 Read (2016) and Brilliant Reading Comprehension (2020).
- Use reading comprehension support programmes, for example One Minute Reader (2020), Read Theory (2020) or Read Naturally Incorporated (2022).
- Discuss text in groups or with a partner to develop deeper understanding.
- Use computer-based software such as Lexia (Lexia Learning, 2020) or Engaging Eyes (Dyslexia Gold, n.d.) to help improve eye tracking.

Writing skills

- There are a range of programmes available to assist learners with developing transcription skills. Cursive writing supports spelling development and consolidation; however, older learners may find it more useful and more appropriate to develop robust keyboard skills.
- Developing effective planning skills is key, and it is important that learners utilize approaches that suit them and their preferred learning style. Approaches may include mind maps, flow charts, lists, task planners, cartoon strips, using sticky notes or oral recordings. Colour can also be a very powerful tool, with words/ideas/phrases being colour coded. Spending time reflecting on how tasks have been tackled and which approaches were useful and successful is a key component for any learner wishing to improve their writing skills.

Study skills

- Effective study skills are vital as learners progress through key stages and sit external exams and professional qualifications. Being able to organize and plan effectively to meet the demands of deadlines can be very challenging and may often require targeted input.

Teaching methodology

- Use a variety of games to reinforce the learning and to encourage a fun, relaxed approach to the development of these skills.
- Develop an understanding of preferred learning styles and use them when learning tricky spellings, for example mnemonics or funny pictures to remember challenging spellings.
- Ensure that support also incorporates direct teaching and opportunities to revisit and consolidate previous work.

- Overlearn skills so that the learner can transfer these skills to other tasks and so that task can be completed with greater automaticity, thereby embedding information in long-term memory.
- Use visual imagery and visualizations to support verbal cues and to help the learner remember information.
- Ensure that any normal way of working in the classroom becomes part of the learner's exam access arrangements if appropriate. For example, learners who are routinely given extra time to complete written activities or to process information or learners who routinely use a laptop or a scribe to complete written tasks should have the same access arrangement available in tests and exams.

References

Adams, M.J. (1990) *Beginning to Read: Thinking and Learning About Print*. Cambridge, MA: MIT Press.

Alloway, T.P. & Alloway, R.G. (2015) *Understanding Working Memory*, second edition. Los Angeles, CA: Sage.

Briggs, S. (ed.) (1992) *The Hickey Multisensory Language Course*. London: Whurr.

Brilliant Reading Comprehension (2020) Available at: https://brilliantpublications.co.uk [Accessed 5 November 2020].

British Dyslexia Association (2018) *Dyslexia Friendly Schools Good Practice Guide*, second edition. Dartford: Diamond Colour Print.

Broomfield, H. & Combley, M. (2003) *Overcoming Dyslexia: A Practical Handbook for the Classroom*. London: Whurr.

Bruck, M. & Treiman, R. (1992) Learning to pronounce words: The limitations of analogies. *Reading Research Quarterly*, 27(4), 375–388.

Clifford, V. & Miles, M. (n.d.) *AcceleRead AcceleWrite*. Available at: https://www.edtech.ie/product/acceleread-accelewrite/ [Accessed 7 December 2022].

Combley, M. (2001) *The Hickey Multisensory Language Course*, third edition. London: Whurr.

Cowling, K. & Cowling, H. (1993) *Toe by Toe*. Baildon, West Yorkshire: K & H Cowling.

Department for Children, Schools and Families (2008) *Personalised Learning: A Practical Guide*. Nottingham: DCSF Publications.

Department for Education (2014) *Special Educational Needs and Disability Code of Practice, 0–25 Years*. Available at: www.gov.uk/government/publications/send-code-of-practice-0-to-25 [Accessed 27 May 2022].

Department for Education and Skills (2007) *Letters and Sounds: Principles and Practice of High-Quality Phonics*. London: Department for Education and Skills.

Dyslexia Gold (n.d.) *Engaging Eyes*. Available at: www.DyslexiaGold.co.uk [Accessed 5 November 2020].

Goswami, U. (1994) Reading by Analogy. In C. Hulme & M. Snowling (eds), *Reading Development and Dyslexia*, pp.18–30. London: Whurr.

Hatcher, P., Duff, F. & Hulme, C. (2014) *Sound Linkage: An Integrated Programme for Overcoming Reading Difficulties*, third edition. Blackwell: Wiley.

Hickey, K. (1977) *Dyslexia: A Language Training Course for Teachers and Learners*. Staines, Surrey: Dyslexia Institute.

Hornsby, B., Shear, F. & Pool, J. (1999) *Alpha to Omega*, fifth edition. Oxford: Heinemann Educational Publishers.

Jolly Learning Ltd. (2018) *Jolly Phonics*. Available at: www.jollylearning.co.uk [Accessed 12 August 2020].

Kelly, K. & Phillips, S. (2016) *Teaching Literacy to Learners with Dyslexia: A Multisensory Approach*. London: Sage.

Lexia Learning (2020) *Lexia Core 5 Reading*. Available at: www.lexialearning.com [Accessed 15 May 2022].

Maxwell, C. & Rowlandson, J. (2012) *Barrington Stoke School Spelling Dictionary*, second edition. Edinburgh: Barrington Stoke.

Moseley, D. (2011) *ACE Spelling Dictionary*, fourth edition. Nottingham: LDA.

Nessy Learning Ltd. (2017) *Nessy*. Available at: www.nessy.com/uk/product/nessy-reading-spelling [Accessed 5 November 2020].

Nicolson, R.I. & Fawcett, A.J. (1999) Developmental dyslexia: The role of the cerebellum. *Dyslexia*, 5(3), 155–177.

One Minute Reader (2020) *One Minute Reader*. Available at: www.oneminutereader.com [Accessed 5 November 2020].

Ramus, F. (n.d.) Dyslexia, Phonological Processing. In H. Pashler (ed.), *Encyclopedia of the Mind*, pp.1–3. Thousand Oaks, CA: Sage.

Read Naturally (2022) *Read Naturally*. Available at: www.readnaturally.com [Accessed 7 December 2022].

Read Successfully (n.d.) *Trugs*. Available at: https://readsuccessfully.com [Accessed 5 November 2020].

Read Theory (2020) *Read Theory*. Available at: https://readtheory.org [Accessed 5 November 2020].

Rising Stars (2019) *Rising Stars*. Available at: www.risingstars-uk.com/subjects/english-language/cracking-comprehension [Accessed 5 November 2020].

Rose, J. (2009) *Identifying and Teaching Children and Young People with Dyslexia and Literacy Difficulties: An Independent Report from Sir Jim Rose to the Secretary of State for Children, Schools and Families*. London: Department for Children, Schools and Families.

Snowling, M. (2008) *Dyslexia: State of Science Review*. London: Government Office for Science.

Stein, J. (2018) The current status of the magnocellular theory of developmental dyslexia. *Neuropsychologia*, 130, 66–77. Available at: www.ncbi.nlm.nih.gov/pubmed/29588226 [Accessed 2 January 2019].

Talking Products (2020) *Talking Products Talking Tins*. Available at: www.talkingproducts.com/collections/talking-tins-learning-resources [Accessed 5 November 2020].

Think 2 Read (2016) *Think 2 Read*. Available at: www.think2read.co.uk [Accessed 5 November 2020].

Units of Sound (2018) *Units of Sound*. Dyslexia Action. Available at: www.unitsofsound.com [Accessed 5 November 2020].

Wordshark (2019) *Wordshark*. Available at: www.wordshark.co.uk/wordshark/schools [Accessed 5 November 2020].

Chapter 6

Identifying Strengths and Areas for Development for One-to-One/Small Group/Class Work

What to Assess/Screen For and How – Individual and Group Screening and Analysing Results

RACHEL BURN AND KAYLEIGH CHANG

This chapter aims to support the assessment phase of specialist teaching, which is an essential but complex process for all specialist teachers. It forms a key aspect of the Level 5 dyslexia qualification as it is essential that, as specialist teachers, we have established a clear background picture of a learner and clearly established their strengths and learning needs.

This chapter aims to show you:

- why screening and assessment are necessary
- how to set out the areas to assess
- how to screen classes, small groups and individuals to provide a baseline for teaching
- how to put together a comprehensive assessment plan to inform a programme of specialist dyslexia teaching
- how to identify strengths and areas for development for one-to-one/small group/class work
- how to analyse the results of screening assessments to determine appropriate teaching targets.

Key things to take away from this chapter:

- Knowing where your learner is now is essential in being able to take them forward.
- Screening is part of ongoing assessment for learning.
- Screening and assessment take a snapshot of a learner's skills and attainment.
- Some assessment should be left to specialist assessors.
- Assessment and screening produce quantitative and qualitative information.
- Your purpose for screening/assessment should be clear.
- Choosing the right assessment/screening tool is vital.
- Group screeners are helpful to identify those requiring further support and assessment.
- Individual assessment provides the foundations of individualized teaching programmes.
- It is important how you share the results of assessment with learners, parents and colleagues.

In screening and assessing a learner, as a specialist teacher, you will have the ability to collect, collate, analyse and present the data/information (quantitative and qualitative) to others and use it to make recommendations for classroom teaching and individual interventions. This is the sort of exercise you would be expected to be undertaking in a role as a specialist teacher for dyslexia.

The first stage of the process is to identify learners who may require additional input from a specialist teacher. This is often achieved by screening groups of learners.

What are we screening for?

As specialist teachers, we may be undertaking a wide range of roles either within a learning centre or while working independently. We may be advising other teachers and support staff on adaptations and interventions within their classroom via quality-first teaching, or we may be supporting the process of moving from general strategies to individually tailored programmes within the classroom and interventions. From the outset, we need to have clarity about what we are screening for as this will inform our choices on the range of screening tools we may utilize and the baselines we set. The criteria we are setting to screen for pupils requiring dyslexia-friendly teaching in the classroom may be very different from those we are setting for learners identified for small group guided reading with non-specialists to improve confidence or individualized specialist dyslexia teaching.

The first stage of screening is to be clear on what you are screening for. Within the Level 5 course you will be screening to identify learners who would benefit from an individualized phonics-focused literacy programme to develop a range of literacy skills.

What is the purpose of screening and assessment?

Screening identifies learners who require the intervention you are planning. Assessment is the underlying foundation of the learning you will be promoting and facilitating. Knowing your learner/s well allows for effective planning and teaching. It is crucial to understanding the learners' strengths as well as their challenges in order that we can utilize these strengths to support new learning. Knowing our learners' interests enables us to make good choices of activities and resources to engage them, to give them confidence and to allow new learning to build on existing knowledge.

Screening is the first stage of assessment. Its purpose for specialist teachers is to identify learners who may meet the criteria for intervention. To screen effectively, we have to understand precisely what we are trying to identify in our learners; for example, are we looking to identify learners who have difficulties with spelling, writing, reading comprehension, reading decoding or some/all of these? To devise or choose effective screening tools and methods, we need to understand what we are looking for. As specialist teachers of dyslexia, we are screening to identify learners who have difficulties with acquiring and mastering literacy skills, particularly reading, decoding and spelling, but for older learners we may explore further areas such as reading speed and fluency.

Screening whole classes

When screening a group of learners, we must be aware of the range of expected or 'normal' attainment and level of mastery of skills in order to be able to identify learners who are not meeting these expectations. For instance, this may be based on National Curriculum expectations or expected ranges for test results. It is therefore essential that you are clear on the baseline for your screening before undertaking it. The baseline may be set to identify the learner who is achieving lowest in the group or the learner who is most behind their personal expectations, or you may be looking for all the learners who come below a point in a test or who meet the essential criteria for the screening.

The baseline you set may be a raw score on one test, or it may be determined by a broader range of factors, such as length of time the learner has been experiencing difficulties or identified disparity between the learner's attainment in one or more areas and the expected attainment.

There are many ways in which we may choose to screen a group of learners to identify those who may require additional support, adaptations and interventions.

Effective screening should be relatively straightforward to administer to ensure that time is used efficiently. It can be constructed via a range of tools, including those that are qualitative and those that are quantitative; for instance:

- Liaison with education colleagues.
- Consultation with parents.
- Observation of learners.
- Reviewing learners' work undertaken with others.
- Administering and marking tasks.
- Reviewing the data collected by others.
- Administering, marking and analysing tests with groups or individual learners.
- Using commercial dyslexia screening tests.

Often, as specialist teachers, we may ask teaching colleagues, such as class teachers, special educational needs and disabilities coordinators (SENDCOs) or teaching assistants, for referrals for our interventions. This is beneficial to us in that teachers will already have extensive experience of assessing and teaching the learners and so will recognize those who may not be making progress in certain areas of the curriculum or learning skills. Teacher colleagues may have already gathered a wide range of qualitative information and quantitative data for us to review. We may be able to gather information about previous support strategies put in place and how the learner responded to them. There may also be information available from assessments or interactions with outside professionals that may give us information about the learners.

Although this information is extremely useful, we must be aware of some issues that affect our decisions based on it, such as how long ago other assessments or reports took place, as learners may well have made progress or developed since then. Does the teacher/support assistant understand what you are looking for? Are there judgements about expected attainment and progress in line with baselines you have established? For the purpose of screening, the identification of previous difficulties or provision of additional teaching interventions or adaptations to whole-class expectations may be another good indicator.

Parents, guardians and caregivers may refer a learner to a specialist teacher, either via a learning centre or on a private basis. When using information provided by parents as screening tools, it may be difficult to quantify and evaluate parents' opinions and judgements in comparison to those of others, but we should never underestimate how well parents know their children and are able to identify when the learner is experiencing some challenges that may require additional support to promote progress.

When recording or reporting for others on this screening process and how learners were directed to you, it is helpful to indicate who referred this learner and why. This provides a context and gives the reader a clear indication of core issues evident in the classroom or home setting. You should provide a clear account about the behaviour, progress and attitudes of the learner or of others that have caused concerns and provide a reason for the need for the input of a specialist dyslexia teacher.

For screening purposes, it is possible to analyse data on a group of learners and set a baseline for an individual or group of tests. This may relate to a cut-off point of scores or descriptor of a specific test used (e.g. 'below average' or standard score below 85). In these circumstances, it is imperative that you understand the test and the criteria for marking and can interpret the results available to you. Alternatively, you may be looking for a specific aspect, such as the learner with the lowest spelling score in the year group or learners identified as working below expected levels for reading.

It may be useful to review a learner's classwork to screen for those with difficulties, but this presents some issues. For example, you are not aware of how the learner was working on the day of the activity or how much support was given to aid the learner. As such, reviewing the learner's work during the screening process can be beneficial to support other assessment work but should not be used in isolation for either screening or assessment purposes.

There are of course 'dyslexia screening' tools available to purchase and administer within an educational setting. These are often computer based and generate reports or results that 'identify' how likely a learner is to be experiencing dyslexia. These screeners do not diagnose dyslexia, and their results need to be interpreted and shared with great caution to ensure they are not presented as accurate diagnostic judgements. Nonetheless, they can be useful screening tools to identify learners who may benefit from an additional specialist teaching intervention. We should be mindful that learners do not need to have a formal diagnosis of dyslexia provided by a suitably qualified professional to benefit from our specialist teaching; indeed, most learners we will teach will not have a diagnosis.

As specialist teachers, we therefore have a range of options to screen groups of pupils or individuals to identify candidates for our support, and in most cases we will have utilized several of these tools to make our judgement. The next stage, when a learner has been identified, is to undertake an assessment that goes into greater depth and provides all the information we require to be able to plan and implement an effective programme of teaching and learning.

Building a picture of the learner via assessment

As specialist teachers for dyslexia, our primary focus for an assessment to inform planning and teaching will be on the learner's literacy skills; however, in order to be able to identify the strengths of the learner, their needs and the strategies and resources that will best support them, our assessment has to be broader than attainment in literacy alone. Learners' attitudes to learning and their behaviours when learning in different environments and in response to different styles of teaching can provide essential information that helps us to make good choices.

The purposes of our assessment informing the design of a programme of study should include:

- Establishing where the learner is.
- Understanding what they need to know and understand next.
- Identifying the best ways we can teach the individual learner.
- Recognizing feelings and behaviours around learning that may impact progress.

Within the screening process you will very likely have collected some background information about the learner, but the first stage in the assessment process should be to conduct liaison with others to build a clear and detailed picture of the learner's background and experiences, including early developmental history, educational experience and progress and attitudes around learning and self-esteem. Having a secure picture of the learner before undertaking any face-to-face testing within your assessment ensures that you are able to place any results you obtain within a secure context as well as being able to plan and deliver the testing process itself in the most appropriate manner. For example, if you were to pick up in your liaison with colleagues that the learner finds concentrating very challenging, you would not set a test lasting a long time, or if you were to identify that a learner had very low self-esteem around reading, you would not begin the testing with a very challenging oral reading exercise.

To collect this background information, you will need to choose the most appropriate manner to consult with others, and you will need to work with teachers/support staff, parents/guardians and the learners themselves. Well-designed questionnaires that cover all relevant aspects and are straightforward for others to complete are often a good choice as they can then be filled in at a time that suits the consultee and can be reviewed in your own time. Designing questionnaires is more complicated than we often imagine prior to using them. They should be balanced in order to collate all the information necessary but should not be overly long or complicated. Tick boxes with 'yes' or 'no' are simple but often miss the detail or nuances required from full answers. We can use scales, such as 'strongly agree' to 'strongly disagree', and provide boxes for the consultee to complete if they wish to provide detail, but often these boxes are not completed, and so we are left with more questions than answers when we review questionnaires.

Discussion with the consultee may be more appropriate, particularly if you wish to establish a rapport and be able to question and unpick responses – to do this with questionnaires may mean going back to the individual completing it after you have reviewed it. When gathering the views and information from learners themselves, it would be best to speak with them directly as this is more likely to provide understanding of their feelings towards learning and to be able to draw out helpful details. For instance, the learner may say, 'I find reading hard', and then you would build this into a conversation to understand why, when, for how long, and so on.

Background information from teachers and support staff should include the following:

- Learner's strengths, academically, socially and outside the curriculum.
- Learner's difficulties and their degree – what is their greatest difficulty and what may be a lesser difficulty.
- Learner's attitude to learning and how this may change in different settings, subjects or types of tasks.
- Learner's attainment.
- Any previous assessment or involvement from outside professionals.
- Any current or previous adjustments provided or any interventions or support groups the learner has been involved with and how impactful these were.
- Recommendations for aspects of attainment to cover in a programme and targets to achieve in specific areas (e.g. reading or writing).

Background information from family/carers should include the following:

- Identification of early development from pre-natal and pregnancy through to schooling.
- Whether there have been any medical issues or concerns and whether the learner takes any medication.
- Whether the learner has had hearing checked and if there have been any previous or ongoing issues.
- Whether vision has been checked regularly and recently, and if it has not, whether there are any concerns, and whether eyesight tests should be recommended.
- How the learner met developmental milestones.
- Literacy experiences across the wider family. Are parents, siblings and other family members confident in their literacy skills? Do members of the family experience issues with literacy now or have they in the past?

When communicating with others, gathering information and then reporting on background information, there are key considerations that as professionals we must be mindful of, such as the fact that questions we ask may be emotive. It is essential that we are considerate of others' feelings while also asking personal questions at times. We should be prepared for unusual or challenging answers and be ready to remain non-judgemental; this is relevant for both families and educational professionals. Parents may feel embarrassed about their own literacy skills and/or the early experiences of the learner. The learner and/or their family may have experienced unsettling or upsetting circumstances and events. Teachers may feel uncomfortable that the learner's difficulties are being investigated, and they may not have identified or supported all of their needs in the past. The language and interactions we use when communicating and reporting on this background information are crucial – we should maintain a professional approach but also be open and accepting. We should enquire and then report only relevant facts and use sensitive language to do so, always considering the rights to privacy of others.

Pupil voice is an essential part of assessment as it informs those working with the learner about how the individual feels about learning and themselves as a learner. It also allows clear recommendations to be made, taking into consideration the need for personalized approaches to resources, activities and teaching and learning styles. This part of the assessment should be informative and sensitive to the audience, but it should also be a truthful reflection of the learner's positive and less positive views and feelings.

Classroom observation is a key aspect of the learner assessment. First, ensure that you choose when and where you observe and ensure that you are given permission. When planning and then reporting later, you should consider/explain if you were just observing or whether you became involved in the lesson/activity, as your interaction in the lesson may impact the learner's behaviour. For this reason, observation without interaction is most often chosen to be appropriate. Think carefully about what lesson is taking place and when in the day it is taking place as this might provide some insight into what is observed, and if you believe there is relevance in this to your observations – for example, the learner is lacking in focus because it is the last lesson of the day – then explain this within your analysis.

A full, detailed description of the support/intervention that has been in place previously for the learner is crucial for the assessment; therefore, ask about and make clear *who* has supported them in the past, *what* resources or strategies they have used and *when* it was – if it is ongoing, you should make it very clear that any future recommendations and input should involve close liaison and sharing of objectives and outcomes between professionals.

Assessment plans for assessing individual learners

The information gathered from interviews and/or questionnaires may provide us with vital information, but we will need to undertake testing with learners ahead of any planning for a teaching programme to ensure it is appropriate. We need to know where the learner is now and what they need to know/be able to do next. To do this effectively it is best to plan carefully, identifying the most appropriate testing materials for the learner as you understand them so far. This will include the test materials and also the timing of the testing. Consider the age and abilities of the learner before planning the testing. The testing may be planned over more than one session and separated by hours or days, but keep in mind the aim to complete the assessment efficiently and effectively.

The timeframe for testing should be planned and considered carefully. To be most effective we should test and then analyse the results as quickly after the test date as possible in order to then be able to plan and implement the programme soon after. Learners, particularly younger learners, may move forwards or backwards in their attainment and mastery of knowledge and skills in relatively short periods of time. For instance, over the summer holidays, learners may forget some of the spellings they learnt the previous academic year, or their writing may regress. If the learner is assessed at the beginning of a term and then teaching does not begin until just before the end of the term, the learner may have made progress in their phonics knowledge and ability to use this knowledge in reading and writing.

For Level 5 specialist teachers the recommendations are that formal, standardized tests should not be administered unless appropriate training in administering the tests and interpreting the data they provide has been undertaken.

When undertaking testing, the purpose of the test should be kept in mind and testing should cease when enough information has been gathered to provide the data required. It is unfair on the learner to continue testing, particularly when it is evident they are experiencing difficulties and even more so when they are aware that they are making errors and becoming frustrated or upset. Stop testing when you have identified enough errors, gaps or difficulties to cover in the teaching programme planned.

What should be assessed and why?

As with screening, when planning an assessment for a specialist teaching intervention, we must understand what we are looking for. For the purposes of a specialist dyslexia programme, there are key areas that should be assessed comprehensively:

- Phonics knowledge and mastery
- Reading: word reading, prose reading, accuracy, fluency and comprehension
- Writing: handwriting skills and free writing
- Spelling: regular and irregular
- Alphabet skills: knowledge and mastery
- Phonological awareness
- Oral language: receptive and expressive
- Self-esteem and attitude to learning.

For older learners, additional knowledge and skills may be assessed:

- Knowledge of subject words
- Academic reading
- Academic writing
- Speed of working
- Revision
- Organization.

Phonics

For a specialist dyslexia programme, phonics will be a core aspect of intervention, although not the only one. It is expected that teachers will use a structured, cumulative programme, and most often those commercially available are the most appropriate option. The BDA currently recommends the Conquering Literacy Programme (Kelly & Phillips, 2016). This programme, like most others, provides placement tests to allow teachers to test where on the programme the learner should commence and whether they need to complete all the programme or just parts of it. In the case of Conquering Literacy, the placement test forms the foundations of the phonics tests, but it is imperative that other tests should also inform the specialist teacher's understanding of how secure the learner is with phonics. Ultimately you will need to map the learner's needs for phonics intervention, and therefore you should use a variety of tests to identify which phonic units (or phonograms) the learner is not secure with. This means they may be able to read the phonics units but not be able to spell them. They may be able to read in a single-word test but make errors when reading in prose. The learner may be able to spell a phonic unit in a dictation but makes errors when free writing. Therefore, as well as relying on the placement test of the phonics programme, we should analyse all other tests to identify any gaps. The use of a mapping document while assessing for phonics is most helpful, and Kelly and Phillips' programme provides a downloadable version that can be adapted to the individual needs and preferences of the assessor.

Reading

The assessment of reading should be comprehensive and should cover the spectrum of reading skills. First, assessment plans should involve single-word tests, such as National Curriculum word lists and/or high-frequency, medium-frequency and common exception word lists. These tests will allow the teacher to identify whether the learner has automated sight word reading skills and to analyse errors to identify whether phonics or morphological strategies need to be taught.

Assessment of reading must include oral prose reading. The use of miscue analysis (covered in detail elsewhere in Chapter 4) allows the assessor to identify how the learner may deviate from the text when reading and whether there is a pattern to their errors, thus enabling an understanding of skills or strategies that need to be taught or secured. The miscue analysis will also provide evidence of the learner's fluency, reading behaviour and attitude to reading. A breadth of information can be gathered when closely observing a learner reading aloud. For example:

- Issues with tracking (e.g. using a pointer or skipping lines).
- Laboured reading (making no errors but reading slowly).
- Lacking intonation and expression.
- Missing punctuation.

The prose reading exercise can also be used to test comprehension. Informal questioning can identify whether the learner is able to recall facts and information from the text, as well as if they can use inference and deduction to interpret the meaning behind the words. This can be conducted with the learner able to refer back to the text so as to identify whether they can skim and scan to find information as well as asking some questions when they cannot refer back to identify if they have read the text effectively. For effective testing of reading fluency, reading behaviour and comprehension, the choice of text is extremely important. It may be helpful to use an age-appropriate or curriculum-appropriate text, but in some cases this level of text may be too challenging, and so too many errors are identified and the learner loses confidence. The text should be at a level that allows the learner to access and read the majority of the words – if this is a text that is lower than that expected for their age or key stage, then this should be discussed and used to add context to the analysis.

The testing of spelling should include word tests similar but not necessarily identical to those chosen to test word reading so that regular and irregular words are included among the words tested. This way, insecurity in using phonological and orthographic strategies can be identified. Then errors can be analysed to recognize patterns and instances of gaps in phonic, visual and morphological understanding of spelling.

To test spelling, the learner should also be asked to complete a piece of free writing. The spelling of words in free writing demands greater security and automaticity in the range of skills and knowledge required. As with the miscue analysis of reading, the errors identified within the free writing can be analysed to inform the planning of the programme. In some cases, the learner does not, or cannot, produce a piece of writing that provides enough evidence to inform planning, and so it is necessary to go back and review recent work completed outside the test, maybe looked at during the screening process, to identify other errors.

The free writing exercise also provides us with an opportunity to identify the learner's ability to express themselves in a written task. The learner's attitude towards the request may provide us with insight into their feelings about writing and can also provide an opportunity for discussion about this. The learner's understanding of their behaviour and study skills with respect to planning their writing can also be observed and questioned. This can be particularly useful for planning programmes for older learners. The amount of written text produced within the timeframe can inform us whether the learner is lacking in confidence in writing, but close observation of how the learner uses the time when writing is more enlightening. We should always watch closely, though not in an imposing or off-putting manner, to pick up on whether they hesitate frequently and whether these hesitations are because they cannot decide what to write next, whether they are thinking of a spelling or whether they are using self-editing skills to re-read their text as they go. Such qualitative information provides us with incredibly useful information to identify any issues that should be addressed via the programme.

After the writing exercise, the learner's text can be analysed to identify how confident they are in using punctuation, whether they use a rich vocabulary and how they construct their text in terms of grammar and use of literary devices to engage readers and structure their thoughts using paragraphs, and so on.

The free writing test provides us with information about the learner's handwriting. Although we may not have to include a structured handwriting programme within our planning (this would be an additional need), particularly for older learners, it is important that we consider the learner's posture, pen grasp, letter formation and writing style.

When planning an assessment for a specialist literacy programme, the testing of phonological awareness is a core element as it is expected that this will be an area in which the learner will require teaching, even for older learners. The informal testing should be formulated on the hierarchy of development within phonological awareness, and so a structured test is often the preferred choice for specialist teachers. The BDA provides an example of an informal test within the Level 5 dyslexia course materials.

An informal test of a learner's alphabet skills allows us to identify how automated their ability is to recite the alphabet and recognize the position and order of a letter or group of letters within the alphabet. A learner's ability to recite the alphabet is often not tested routinely in school after the early years, but learners may continue to lack confidence with this; and as they progress through education, they are expected to use the knowledge of the sequence of the alphabet as a tool and strategy to complete other tasks, such as using dictionaries, indexes or filing notes.

Oral language can be tested informally by listening to individuals during a pupil voice interview and during testing. We can also gain information from the background data. Questions to consider include the following:

- Does the learner understand my instructions?
- Does the learner ask for questions or comments to be repeated?
- Does the learner reply to questions fully?
- Does the learner hesitate significantly prior to offering a verbal response?
- Does the learner freely ask questions?
- What is the quality of the vocabulary used by the learner?

The assessment process provides many opportunities to investigate the self-esteem, attitudes, learning behaviours and metacognition of the learner from the screening stages through to the questionnaires, interviews and then the testing stage. This may be via the comments of others, the words or the behaviour of the learner themselves gathered and interpreted in the interview and testing session/s.

Identifying strengths and areas for development

The purpose of the assessment is to provide accurate, up-to-date and comprehensive information to identify strengths and areas for development via analysis and then target setting.

Identifying the learner's strengths and talents enables us to personalize the programme and make choices to best engage the learner and provide opportunities for learning to build on current knowledge, understanding and preferred learning styles.

The learner's strengths may include intrinsic and extrinsic factors – for example, resilience, support from family, proficient ICT skills, confident practical skills and broad vocabulary. These strengths allow us to design a programme that utilizes skills and interests, such as including songs for a learner who enjoys music and is able to remember songs well, emphasizing kinaesthetic strategies for a learner who is talented in sports, or using the theme of animals for the guided reading text and writing focus. Understanding that the learner may have a relative strength in their maths allows us to discuss and refer to this in the programme to continue to build self-esteem and a positive view of themselves as a learner.

When analysing and writing up reports of assessment, it is best practice to present positive comments ahead of difficulties and areas for development. Areas for development should be present as learning objectives – what the learner needs to be able to do, what the learner should know. When setting out recommendations for learning objectives, we should be brief and direct so that essential information is quickly accessible and not confused by unnecessary narrative or description.

All areas tested should produce information as to where the learner is now, where strengths are and what needs to be learnt next. This will support those teaching this learner to engage with them, design activities and resources that will be of interest and suit their style, as well as being a foundation for building self-esteem and rapport.

Areas for development should initially be set as longer-term aims giving an extended perspective for where the learner should be in around a half-term or longer, but they should still be specific and clear. These long-term aims should be set for each aspect the learner will be working on, for instance reading comprehension, phonics, sight word reading and free writing skills. Provide details here of long-term aims, which should cover individual literacy skills, National Curriculum attainment, independence, study skills, and so on. It is a good idea to think about the end of the teaching phase that the learner is in now and the phase they are about to enter. Take, for example, a Year 5 pupil: what will they achieve by the end of Key Stage 2, and how will they move into Key Stage 3? For older learners, this may be the end of their current course or courses.

Following analysis of assessment, recommendations for the learner's areas for development should be set and should ultimately be honed to SMART (specific, measurable, achievable, realistic, timely) targets (covered in Chapter 11). These SMART targets need to focus on the aims of the programme, and planned and formulated to be evaluated in a straightforward way. They should focus on what the learner will be able to do and what they will know after a set number of lessons or amount of time.

Within your recommendations, you will also set out how the learner should be taught, being clear about strategies such as multisensory techniques, structured programmes, resources, the time of day that you plan to teach (as different learners are better at focusing during different times of the day) and the length of lessons.

Reporting results

As part of the assessment process, we need to record and report a great deal of information. This information will ultimately be presented as a report and will inform the planning and teaching of an intervention.

When reporting on your assessment, for your own reflection and reference as well as for others who may access it, find time and space to explain how the assessment was set up and how the learner responded. Were they engaged? Did they indicate that they were challenged in any way? Try to identify what they were most comfortable with, and report any comments by the learner. Who was consulted as part of the assessment, and how was this conducted?

We understand, as professionals, that when we produce documents about a young person, their parents or guardians have the right to access them; therefore, at all times we should be professional in our tone and in the content we include.

In addition, in education, documents reporting on young people are filed in schools and are accessible to other members of staff (unless deemed confidential). On transfer between schools, such documents are also shared. In some circumstances, often without warning, outside agencies may request access to documents directly via the school or via requests of parents. These documents may be used for legal purposes, including in custody hearings or safeguarding matters. Therefore, although it is more than likely that only you will read this document, it must be written with an awareness that it may be shared and accessed by a wider audience. As such, a *formal* and *professional* tone must be maintained throughout, and the content must not only be accurate but also take into account the privacy of others. One key part of the document in which problems often arise is the 'Background' section, where it is necessary to give contextual information about the learner in terms of health, home circumstances and previous schooling. You should take care to protect the privacy of others, deciding on what information is relevant and wording it sensitively.

The Level 5 course requires the assessment process to ultimately result in a learner profile document. The primary purpose of this document is to present all the information you have collated in one document to set out clearly where the learner is now, whether there is a history of need and support and how this can inform future planning for effective teaching and learning.

You will be the main audience as on this occasion you will be planning a programme of intervention and so will need to know what the learner's strengths are and what and how they need to learn next. This document must give information to ensure that the teacher understands the individual's previous learning experience and is aware of what has gone well and what has not. The learner's current attainment levels must be established to know where to go next; this is important in establishing how individuals are performing in the curriculum and to see if it matches the information you found. The document may also be used by other teachers and support staff to inform their planning and teaching, and in the future it is expected that you will be doing this as the dyslexia specialist to share and promote best practice.

In summary, the screening and assessment process is a complex task that requires a depth of understanding of the causal theories of dyslexia, an appreciation of the strengths and difficulties often experienced by our learners and a confident familiarity with the impact on attainment and learning behaviours. This will enable us to ask all the necessary questions of the learner, and those close to them, to build a broad and detailed picture of their strengths and needs and to then make recommendations for learning targets with appropriate strategies and to construct effective interventions to meet them. Ultimately, this information needs to be organized and reported in a clear and professional manner so that both the assessor and others working with the learner understand where they are now and where they need to go in their learning next.

Chapter 7

Principles of Specialist Teaching

LUCY FLETCHER, JILL HUDSON AND SARAH YOUNG

Specialist teaching combines the fundamentals of good, quality-first teaching with the four main components of specialist pedagogy. These four essential elements, which serve as pillars of quality specialist teaching, are tuition that is multisensory, cumulative and structured and that also includes opportunities for overlearning. Employing these principles in small achievable chunks, using a 'little and often' approach, will aid progress and ensure improved outcomes for learners with dyslexia.

So what do these pillars mean, and how do they link with our knowledge of dyslexia? In order to answer this question, each 'pillar' will be explored.

Multisensory

People generally remember '10% of what they read, 20% of what they hear, 30% of what they see and 50% of what they see and hear' (Treichler, 1967, cited in Shams & Seitz, 2008: 5).

Multisensory techniques now feature prominently in most specialist programmes, as there is a wealth of experience and research acknowledging the effectiveness of this approach for all learners, but particularly for learners with dyslexia. Piaget (1969) originally recognized the need for 'concrete' materials and experiences to enhance learners' understanding, as highlighted by Mortimore (2008), in her research around dyslexia and learning styles. Most learners experience this themselves in their own learning journeys through remembering and understanding more effectively that which has been practised and discovered by themselves. This is an innate ability that young children demonstrate in the early years of their education, an ability that can be observed in any good early years setting. Research has shown that children as young as six can demonstrate greater performance when learning with multisensory cues than with unisensory information (Broadbent *et al.*, 2016).

A multisensory approach aims to incorporate as many of the learner's senses as possible, simultaneously, as outlined by Kelly and Phillips (2016), so it is more than just a kinaesthetic approach. It mainly focuses on visual, auditory, kinaesthetic and tactile channels working together at the same time. For example, painting a phoneme, while saying the name after hearing the teacher say it, employs kinaesthetic channels as well as visual and auditory ones.

Research into the causation of dyslexia reinforces the justification for a multisensory approach, as suggested by Gillingham and Stillman in 1956, involving the integration of sound, vision and touch (Thomson & Watkins, 2007). Each channel has a unique way of perceiving, interpreting and understanding symbolic information. The principles of multisensory teaching build on the learner's strong channels and develop the weaker ones. It involves making clear links between the visual, auditory, kinaesthetic and tactile senses. A link implies that at least two senses should be simultaneously engaged (Kelly & Phillips, 2016). This is crucial, as when senses are successfully linked, the transfer from short- to long-term memory is facilitated (ibid). Therefore, employing as many senses as possible *simultaneously* will improve both automaticity and speed of retrieval from memory (ibid).

What are the challenges of a multisensory approach?

In early years settings and Key Stage 1, the teaching and learning strategies employed are generally multisensory in nature. The difficulties for many learners, including those with dyslexia, are compounded by a number of factors once the learner has progressed through Key Stage 2 and beyond:

- The oral element of learning, for example oral repetition and discussion, is reduced.
- There is a greater expectation on reading and writing silently.
- The teacher dictates the time and purpose of oral contributions to learning.

This means a potential loss of essential learning channels for many learners. In relation to the causal theories of dyslexia, multisensory learning strategies address many of the deficits discussed by recent theorists in the field of research (Nicolson & Fawcett, 2008), such as:

- working and long-term memory

- naming, labelling and rapid naming
- phonological awareness
- verbal repetition
- visual processing: speed, attention and discrimination
- visuo/motor processing: speed and accuracy
- automaticity and multitasking.

Examples of multisensory strategies in the classroom are outlined in the table below.

Multisensory strategy	Example
Employ a **combination of visual/auditory/ kinaesthetic channels in any one task.**	Alongside talking through task instructions, use corresponding visual images. Use symbols/abbreviations/mind maps/ images as well as written words/sentences.
Use a WAGOLL (what a good one looks like) – modelling is a powerful tool.	Writing frames, sentence starters, worked examples, previous year's work, etc.
Teach learners to **visualize** (turns auditory input into visual memory).	'The Mind's Eye' is an effective strategy – closing your eyes and taking a photo in your head of words/facts/task.
Encourage learners to use their **own voice** (our own voice is the most memorable).	Discussion, recording and listening back, reading work aloud into iPads, etc.
Kinaesthetic strategies – muscle memory can be a very effective tool to strengthen memory.	Hand signals, dance, movement around the room (or the use of different areas/ rooms), use of playdough, glitter sand, water bottles.

One benefit of the multisensory approach is that it makes activities more engaging and fun for learners. Another, more specifically for learners with dyslexia, is that it has a significant impact on memory, increasing the chances of transferring knowledge from the short-term or working memory to the long-term memory.

Baddeley and Hitch's (1974) multicomponent 'working memory model' clearly helps us to explain why multisensory tuition aids memory.

Within this model, there is first the central executive, which acts like a triage nurse in A&E, quickly assessing patients, prioritizing them and directing them to the right place. The central executive is the decision maker of the model, determining the information that comes in and allocating it to the right place. The central executive is 'modality free', which means it can take in information from all of the senses. However, it also has a limited capacity and will ignore information if deemed irrelevant or once full capacity has been reached. When learners appear to be distant or disengaged in the classroom, this could be due to them reaching this sensory overload, as highlighted in the study by Bastien-Toniazzo *et al.* (2009, cited in Kelly & Phillips, 2016).

Second, the phonological loop stores and processes auditory information. Therefore, anything relating to sound will come into the brain via the central executive and be quickly redirected to the phonological loop. Similarly, the visuospatial sketchpad processes and stores any visual and spatial information.

Finally, in 2000, Baddeley extended the model by adding a fourth component, the episodic buffer, which interacts with both the phonological loop and the visuospatial sketchpad, binding all the information together. The episodic buffer also helps to store overlapping information into the long-term memory, integrating all the different sensory channels and therefore also aiding memory.

This model helps to explain that if information is received using just one sense, then it is processed by the brain in one way. However, if it is received via two different channels at the same time, then this increases the opportunities for the information to be processed more effectively, creating stronger connections between the various pathways of the brain and ultimately improving how information is both stored in and retrieved from the long-term memory. Multimodal processing also reduces the cognitive load because information from different modalities can be more easily chunked into the short-term memory and used to build long-term representations (Shams & Seitz, 2008).

Therefore, the multisensory approach is not just about levels of engagement but can also aid both memory and retrieval for learners with dyslexia.

Cumulative

The second pillar underpinning good specialist teaching is the idea that knowledge is cumulative, building on previous learning. The sequence must begin with the easiest and most basic concepts and progress methodically to more difficult concepts, with each element building on those concepts already known (Adams-Gordon, 2010).

The National Curriculum currently discusses knowledge in terms of components and composites (Rollett, 2019), the components being the building blocks of knowledge that lead to the composite, overall outcome. While the outcome or composite knowledge is often clearly defined within the National Curriculum, the components required to get there are not always as explicit. It is therefore the role of teachers within their quality-first teaching to break down the components into small steps, creating pathways to success. This can be achieved most successfully through the graduated approach, as outlined in the SEND Code of Practice (Department for Education, 2014), which uses assessment as a strategic tool for planning future teaching or interventions and then evaluating their success through the assess/plan/do/review cycle.

What are the challenges of the cumulative approach?

Current learning environments often rely heavily on memory, both in terms of tasks and testing, which can be particularly problematic for learners with dyslexia. For some learners, this can create gaps in their learning, which if left can accumulate, potentially preventing learners from acquiring complex skills and knowledge. When gaps in learning continue to emerge, it can weaken the foundations of knowledge and skill, like a precarious Jenga tower. Binder (1996) defines this as cumulative dysfluency, highlighting the importance of fluency in acquiring mastery over any skill.

Therefore, in order to fill these gaps, some learners require learning to be broken down into even smaller, achievable chunks, to ensure that none of the blocks have been missed and to create a solid foundation for knowledge and skills. This, combined with strategies to support memory, can aid learners and prevent the effects of cumulative dysfluency. Many interventions for supporting learners with dyslexia consequently include this cumulative approach, such as Precision Teaching, Toe by Toe (2021) and Nessy UK (2021), as a 'little and often' approach is frequently key in ensuring that small gaps of learning are filled, creating a secure footing on which learning can be built.

Other strategies for preventing gaps in learning are outlined in the table below.

Memory 'life' strategy	Example
Chunk information into bite-sized pieces.	'There are three things you need to know about this topic.'
Consider **readability of text.**	Consider font, font size, line spacing, background, paper colour; avoid block capitals, underlining and italics.
Revisit **multisensory strategies.**	Use mnemonics/images/colour coding as memory hooks. For example, SQ3R (survey, question, read, recite, review), 'Call the COPS' (capitals, order, punctuation and spelling) for proofreading, realia, YouTube clips, colour-coded subjects/topics/spelling patterns.

cont.

Memory 'life' strategy	Example
Be **inventive and 'wacky'.**	Use memory of loci, humour, for example PEEing (point, evidence, example), throughout your writing.
Limit distractions.	Remember that talking to a learner while they are writing will make them lose their train of thought.
Allow **'thinking time'.**	Use the five-second rule of 'thinking time' to allow students to process what you say and formulate a response.

Structured

The third essential pillar of quality specialist teaching is the importance of structure, whereby approaches are based on teaching knowledge in a specific order, such as teaching phonemes in a series of sequential steps. Rose (2009) advocates for structure to be included in specialist teaching throughout the Rose Review, based on evidence from Brooks (2007) as well as Singleton (2009).

Similarly, research has also shown that children benefit from explicit and systematic structured language instruction (Adams, 1990; Ehri, 2014; National Reading Panel, 2006, cited in Schlesinger & Gray, 2017). Effective trials of evidence-based interventions to develop oral language skills, a pre-requisite for learning to read (Snowling & Hulme, 2011), have also noted the success of programmes involving well-structured and multisensory teaching approaches.

Maintaining a clear structure throughout a programme of study works in a similar way to the cumulative effect, providing plentiful opportunities for filling the potential gaps in a learner's precarious brick towers and thereby creating a solid foundation on which future learning can be built. Introducing material gradually, in small, achievable chunks, can help to reduce the working memory load, as advocated by Gathercole and Packiam Alloway (2007). Reid (2009) also states that small steps of progress should be logical, making clear, explicit links and connections.

Tasks that are structured and directed towards an individual's preferred learning style, such as visual and kinaesthetic learning channels, are also likely to be more effective, as many learners with dyslexia often exhibit tendencies towards visuospatial learning styles, as outlined by Mortimore (2008).

Brooks (2007), in his advocacy of effective interventions, also highlights the importance of structure within individual lessons. A well-structured lesson, following a predictable pattern and routine, helps to create a safe space for learning, where learners feel secure enough in their learning to take risks and explore concepts outside their comfort zone. This corroborates Vygotsky's (1978) widely held theory on scaffolding learning, which describes the point at which learners are out of their comfort zone or, as Vygotsky defined it, their 'zone of proximity'. It is at this point that teachers can skilfully 'scaffold' or 'layer' new learning concepts, encouraging learners to develop new ideas comfortably, without feeling too overwhelmed or confused. MacKay also supports and summarizes this view, stating that 'secure, happy learners learn – stressed, anxious learners do not' (2012: 23).

Clear structure should not mean that teachers feel too restricted within a set programme, as most good structures allow for some level of flexibility within them. There is also the skill of the specialist teacher, who is able to adapt to and accommodate the needs of the learner while also maintaining the integral elements that the structure creates.

Overlearning

Another way of helping the transferral of information to the long-term memory, to aid recall and help automaticity of skill, is overlearning. This is essential because, as Ebbinghaus (1885, cited in Growth Engineering, 2020) described, retention of information decreases rapidly over a relatively short period of time unless you do something with the material.

Ebbinghaus (1885, cited in Growth Engineering, 2020) found memory retention to be 100% at the time of learning new information – this drops rapidly to 40% within the first few days. Thereafter, the decline in memory retention slows down again (Shrestha, 2017).

In order to retain information and set it to the long-term memory, we have to periodically revisit the information. Research concludes that a minimum of three reviews is necessary for obtaining the best results. Each subsequent repetition increases the time needed before the next one. This is called spaced learning. Repetitions have to be spaced for optimal effect (Shrestha, 2017).

Ebbinghaus (1885, cited in Growth Engineering, 2020) also discovered another phenomenon, called overlearning. The basic idea is that if you practise something more than is usually required to memorize it, the effect of overlearning takes place. This means that the information is now stored much more effectively and the effects of the forgetting curve are not as impactful. Eventually, this will lead to automaticity of recall (Shrestha, 2017).

There are various factors that can affect the rate of forgetting, including how meaningful the information is, how it is delivered and other external factors such as sleep and stress (ibid).

The rate of forgetting is not the same for everyone (ibid). Learners with dyslexia may forget more quickly due to their difficulties with memory. In addition, they may have abnormal difficulties in making skills automatic, despite extensive practice.

To explain this lack of automaticity further, Nicolson and Fawcett (2000) hypothesized the 'square root rule' – here, the amount of time needed for a learner with dyslexia to develop automaticity in a skill is proportional to the square root of the time taken by a non-dyslexic. For example, take the square root of repetitions normally needed to learn a task, such as recognizing sight words. If a non-dyslexic learner takes 25 consecutive repetitions to learn a word, the learner with dyslexia will need 125 consecutive repetitions to learn it. This is calculated by multiplying the number of repetitions by the square root. In this case, that would be 5 times 25, which equals 125 consecutive repetitions, and this is the number of repetitions needed for a learner with dyslexia to become automatic in recognizing the sight word.

Coupled with this extra time needed for learners with dyslexia, Nicolson and Fawcett (2008) also proposed the conscious compensation hypothesis. Here, more limited automaticity of skill means they have to concentrate harder to achieve the same level of performance as neurotypical learners. This is exacerbated if tasks involving reading and writing are demanded alongside factors such as tiredness, frustration, lack of motivation and low self-esteem.

The amount of overlearning required for a learner with dyslexia to achieve automaticity is difficult to know. However, the development of automatic responses is built into literacy programmes via multisensory routines and exposure to the teaching point (Kelly & Phillips, 2016). This then transfers information into the long-term memory to aid recall, as previously discussed.

Dehaene (2004, cited in Kelly & Phillips, 2016) suggests the use of drills and routines to help develop and strengthen neural pathways. Routines establish security for the learner – a consistent approach using multisensory strategies. They allow new concepts to be learnt by freeing up memory capacity. 'Familiarity and consistency facilitate automaticity' (Kelly & Phillips, 2016: 122).

Metacognitive strategies

Alongside the four pillars of specialist tuition, effective teaching interventions also aim to foster metacognition. Individuals with dyslexia learn best in effective teaching interventions where metacognition is fostered alongside multisensory principles. Learners with dyslexia learn best if they understand how their brains work. Metacognition refers to an awareness of how a person uses their own processes to solve problems and how to apply these to other areas of learning (ibid). This can help learners decipher which strategies works best for them (ibid.). Metacognitive awareness enables students to take more control of their own learning, building confidence and self-esteem.

Using metacognition can:

- encourage active learning and keep learners engaged
- build self-esteem, motivation and independence
- help identify skills or strengths that can be transferred to other situations/tasks.

Therefore, metacognition must be:

- taught (modelled) explicitly
- embedded into tasks or naturally occurring (not an 'extra' task).

Examples of metacognitive strategies are outlined in the table below.

	Metacognitive strategy	Example
PLAN	Encourage and model **'talk about thinking'** with students **BEFORE** you start a task.	Why am I doing this task? Have I done anything like this before? What's the best way for me to do/remember this?
	Model/scaffold tasks.	Demonstrate and/or give worked examples of different strategies that could be used.
	Offer a **wide range of learning methods.**	Use a multisensory classroom so the learner can experiment with what 'works best' for them.

cont.

	Metacognitive strategy	Example
MONITOR	Continue to model and encourage **metacognitive talk** while completing tasks.	Am I making good progress? Will I finish in time?
	Encourage shared teaching.	If a student can teach it, they are more likely to understand and remember it.
	Use **peer support ('buddies').**	Learners are more likely to talk and try ideas/strategies with peers.
EVALUATE	Give **feedback** on learners' use of strategies to guide them to become independent.	Why do you think that task went well? What did you do differently that made the task successful? What made it difficult? Would you use this approach again?
	Use **reflective assessment** approaches.	3Ws: What Went Well? Medals & Missions (Petty, 2021) (What have I done well? What do I need to do next?)

The strategies in the table above are especially effective for older learners from Key Stage 2. The ability to reflect on why a task went well or how particular strategies supported a learner's acquisition of knowledge or skills can serve to secure future learning approaches. For younger children, metacognition can be developed using simple visual systems, such as smiley/sad faces, thumbs up/down or a traffic light system in which a green dot shows they have understood something, orange indicates that something was difficult but they got there in the end, perhaps with some support or resources to help them, and then red means that they really did not understand something and will need to revisit.

We have examined the four pillars that underpin quality specialist teaching and that, when combined together, will form the foundations that ensure the best outcomes and progress for learners with dyslexia.

References

Adams, M.J. (1990) *Beginning to Read: Thinking and Learning About Print*. Cambridge, MA: MIT Press.

Adams-Gordon, B. (2010) *The Benefits of Multisensory Spelling Instruction*. Pomeroy: Castlemoyle Books.

Baddeley, A. (2000) The episodic buffer: a new component of working memory?. *Trends in cognitive sciences, 4* (11), pp.417–423.

Baddeley, A.D. & Hitch, G. (1974) Working Memory. In G.H. Bower (ed.), *Psychology of Learning and Motivation*, 8, pp.47–89. New York, NY: Elsevier.

Bastien-Toniazzo, M., Stroumza, A. & Cave, C. (2009) Audio-visual perception and integration in developmental dyslexia: An exploratory study using the McGurk Effect. *Current Psychology Letters: Behaviour, Brain and Cognition*, 25(3), 1–14.

Binder, C. (1996) Behavioral fluency: Evolution of a new paradigm. *The Behavior Analyst*, 19, 163–197.

Broadbent, H.J., White, H., Mareschal, D. & Kirkham, N. (2016) Incidental learning in a multisensory environment across childhood. *Wiley Development Science*. Available at: https://onlinelibrary.wiley.com/doi/epdf/10.1111/desc.12554?src=getftr [Accessed 27 May 2022].

Brooks, G. (2007) *What Works for Pupils with Literacy Difficulties?* London: Department for Children, Schools and Families.

Department for Education (2014) *Special Educational Needs and Disability Code of Practice, 0–25 Years.* Available at: www.gov.uk/government/publications/send-code-of-practice-0-to-25 [Accessed 27 May 2022].

Ehri, L.C. (2014) Orthographic mapping in the acquisition of sight word reading, spelling memory, and vocabulary learning. *Scientific Studies of Reading*, 18(1), 5–21.

Gathercole, S.E. & Packiam Alloway, T.P. (2007) *Understanding Working Memory: A Classroom Guide.* London: Harcourt.

Gillingham, A. & Stillman, B. (1956) *Remedial Training for Children with Specific Disability in Reading, Spelling and Penmanship*, fifth edition. Cambridge, MA: Educators Publishing Service.

Growth Engineering (2020) *What is the Ebbinghaus' Forgetting Curve (and How Do You Combat it)?* Available at: www.growthengineering.co.uk/what-is-the-forgetting-curve [Accessed 9 November 2021].

Kelly, K. & Phillips, S. (2016) *Teaching Literacy to Learners with Dyslexia: A Multisensory Approach*. London: Sage.

MacKay, N. (2012) *Removing Dyslexia as a Barrier to Achievement*, third edition. Wakefield: SEN Marketing.

Mortimore, T. (2008) *Dyslexia and Learning Style: A Practitioner's Handbook*. West Sussex: Wiley and Sons.

Nessy UK (2021) *Nessy Reading & Spelling Help for Children with Dyslexia*. Available at: www.nessy.com/uk/product/nessy-reading-spelling [Accessed 18 March 2021].

Nicolson, R. & Fawcett, A. (2000) Long-term learning in dyslexic children. *European Journal of Cognitive Psychology*, 12, 357–393.

Nicolson, R. & Fawcett, A. (2008) *Dyslexia, Learning and the Brain.* Cambridge, MA: MIT Press.

Petty, G. (2021) *Feedback: Medals and Missions*. Available at: https://geoffpetty.com/for-teachers/feedback-and-questions [Accessed 1 December 2021].

Piaget, J. (1969) *Science of Education and the Psychology of the Child.* New York, NY: Free Press.

Reid, G. (2009) *Dyslexia: A Practitioner's Handbook*, fourth edition. London: Wiley.

Rollett, S. (2019) *Education Inspection Framework 2019: Inspecting the Quality of Education*. Leicester: Association of School and College Leaders.

Rose, J. (2009) *Identifying and Teaching Children and Young People with Dyslexia and Literacy Difficulties: An Independent Report from Sir Jim Rose to the Secretary of State for Children, Schools and Families.* London: Department for Children, Schools and Families. Available at: www.thedyslexia-spldtrust.org.uk/media/downloads/inline/the-rose-report.1294933674.pdf [Accessed 17 November 2021].

Precision Teaching. https://www.structural-learning.com/post/precision-teaching-a-teachers-guide

Schlesinger, N.W. & Gray, S. (2017) The impact of multisensory instruction on learning letter names and sounds, word reading, and spelling. *Annals of Dyslexia*, 67(3), 219–258.

Shams, L. & Seitz, A. (2008) Benefits of multisensory learning. *Trends in Cognitive Sciences*, 721, 1–7.

Shrestha, P. (2017) *Ebbinghaus Forgetting Curve*. Available at: www.psychestudy.com/cognitive/memory/ebbinghaus-forgetting-curve [Accessed 9 November 2021].

Singleton, C.H. (2009) *Intervention for Dyslexia*. Bracknall: The Dyslexia-Specific Learning Difficulties Trust.

Snowling, M.J. & Hulme, C. (2011) Evidence-based interventions for reading and language difficulties: Creating a virtuous circle. *British Journal of Educational Psychology*, 81(1), 1–23.

Thomson, M. & Watkins, B. (2007) *Dyslexia: A Teaching Handbook*. London: John Wiley & Sons.

Toe by Toe (2021) Available at: https://toe-by-toe.co.uk [Accessed 18 March 2021].

Treichler, F.R. (1967) Reinforcer preference effects on probability learning by monkeys. *Journal of Comparative and Physiological Psychology*, 64(2), 339.

Vygotsky, L.S. (1978) *Mind in Society: The Development of Higher Psychological Processes*. Cambridge, MA: Harvard University Press.

Chapter 8

How to Support Learners with Dyslexia in the Classroom and During Intervention

LYNN LOVELL, LUCY FLETCHER, HUMARA ABIDI AND SARAH HAYMAN

This chapter aims to:

- discuss why learners with dyslexia may suffer low self-esteem and confidence, and the impact of this
- outline ways to improve affective skills, including the use of metacognition, learner voice, learner interests and learner strengths
- outline effective study skills for efficient independent learning and revision.

In Chapter 5, you learnt approaches to supporting learners with dyslexia in the classroom setting and during a one-to-one intervention. In this chapter, we will take this a step further and focus on tools that really empower the learner. A key factor to remember here is that while differentiation is hugely important for tackling individual tasks/activities, empowering learners will help them to tackle new and novel tasks in the classroom and beyond.

Learners with dyslexia can struggle with self-esteem in light of their difficulties (Humphrey & Mullins, 2002). This is not surprising if we bear in mind that they often need to work harder than their peers in order to carry out tasks. As an example, if asked to read a short section of text on the board, the learner with dyslexia may struggle to access single words, understand what they are reading or read at a good pace to keep up with others. This, in turn, can lead to frustration, lack of confidence and tiredness, all of which impact self-esteem.

Alexander-Passe (2006, 2015) suggests that learners with dyslexia can often exhibit low levels of engagement alongside an array of other coping mechanisms that have an overall effect on their motivation. This may further lead the child to hide their difficulties from the teacher and ultimately underachieve at school.

Due to this, learners can fall into a trap called 'learned helplessness', which is where students feel that success is beyond their control and therefore that they cannot change it (Humphrey & Mullins, 2002). This can be a particular difficulty for those with dyslexia in the classroom who may regularly be faced with tasks that they find difficult and who thus may feel that they have less chance of success than others. Subsequently, this can have long-term impacts on motivation into adulthood (Alexander-Passe, 2018).

In contrast, the concept of internal locus of control suggests that students with learning difficulties who believe that the ability to achieve is internal and comes from motivation and perseverance are more likely to achieve academic success (Galbraith & Alexander, 2005). This highlights a need to encourage students to view their chances of success as something that is malleable.

It is therefore important to support young people to develop positive attributes such as self-concept and self-esteem. In fact, Humphrey and Mullins (2002) outline a number of key suggestions to help counter negative attributes developing. These include making schools more 'dyslexia friendly', delivering self-concept and self-esteem enhancement programmes, early identification of dyslexia and better provision. It is worth noting that the British Dyslexia Association has since developed the Dyslexia Friendly Quality Mark (n.d.), providing schools with a framework for monitoring and developing good practice. The third standard of the Dyslexia Friendly Quality Mark considers the climate for learning, whereby pupils are encouraged to recognize and develop their own learning strategies, which will help develop their self-esteem as well as lifelong learning skills.

The good news is that those working in education can develop not only the academic skills of those with dyslexia but also their affective skills. This can lead to increased motivation, confidence and self-esteem. During interviews, adults with dyslexia have suggested that helping them manage their difficulties while they were in education would have been valuable (Nalvany *et al.*, 2011), and it has been suggested that improving attributes such as self-esteem may not only improve outcomes for learners with dyslexia in education but also after formal education (Raskind *et al.*, 2002).

In light of this, we are going to look at the following key approaches that may help to develop a pupil's sense of self-esteem, confidence and control over their learning:

- Metacognition
- Learner voice
- Learner interests
- Learner strengths.

Metacognition

As you saw in Chapter 7, metacognition is the awareness and understanding of one's own thought process. It is a method of self-regulated learning and is considered one of the most impactful intervention strategies, encouraging active learning and engagement (Education Endowment Foundation, 2011).

To develop awareness within learners, they are encouraged to think about their own learning explicitly, and specific strategies are taught for planning, self-monitoring and evaluation.

This learning can be broken down into three categories: cognition, metacognition and motivation. Cognition is the process involved in learning and understanding the relevant material; metacognition is the awareness of this learning, understanding one's own thought processes; motivation is where the learner engages with the cognition and metacognition processes for a particular outcome.

Metacognition is a taught skill that must be practised and nurtured. Lessons need to be planned to focus on the explicit teaching of these skills, encouraging the learner to apply this within the context of their learning need, actively moving away from tacit learning to reflective learning.

According to the guidance report by the Education Endowment Foundation (2011), teachers should understand which skills are required to develop their pupils' metacognitive knowledge and teach them the skills involved with this. To help with this process, the teacher needs to plan, monitor and evaluate learning, as well as teach the learner how and when to use a specific skill for a favourable outcome.

How can a teacher help with developing metacognition within their pupils?

- Model their own thinking, which helps to develop a learner's metacognition and cognitive skill set by opening opportunities to question and promote metacognitive talk within the learning environment.

- Ensure that work is set at an appropriate level that actively challenges the learner, encouraging them to use and develop these skills, but not so challenging as to deter the learner from wanting to try.
- Give effective feedback in a timely manner.
- Use strategies for the learner to judge for themselves whether they are learning effectively, and support learner motivation to tackle the task.

What are the skills that we want learners to develop?

- Self-questioning – to help check/edit the work.
- Meditation – clearing the mind for learning.
- Reflection – the action of pausing, reflecting, then improving.
- Awareness of strengths and weaknesses – in learning.
- Awareness of learning styles – visual, auditory, kinaesthetic, tactile.
- Writing down your work – including methodology to help the teacher to check.
- Thinking aloud – a method that is used before skills are embedded.
- Planning ahead.

There are many benefits to these approaches:

- They can foster independence and encourage learners to organize and manage their time effectively.
- These skills encourage resilience.
- They can help to develop the learner voice, self-esteem and autonomy.
- The skills learnt are transferable, effectively useable in all settings.
- They incorporate various multisensory strategies, which supports learners with SpLDs.

(Drew, 2022)

Here are some more ideas for teaching metacognition in the classroom or in a one-to-one setting:

- Ensure that learners understand that their ability is not 'fixed'. This concept is often called a 'growth mindset' (Dweck, 2008). This can be particularly important for those with dyslexia, who may be experiencing a lot of challenges in the classroom and need further opportunities for success. If they believe they can be successful, they may be more likely to persevere.
- Teach learners specifically to recognize what the challenges are and how to overcome

them. On the flip side of this, teach learners to recognize what success looks like and how it was achieved. This can be done by a simple review activity after larger tasks that asks these questions in a format suitable to the age of the learner. The aim then is to build this understanding and apply it across future tasks to enable success.

- Provide options and opportunities to discover them. For example, you could set a task, then give learners the option to write a response, create a storyboard, draw a poster, record a video, and so on. Then provide a review sheet: Was this approach successful? Why/why not? Would I use it again? How?
- Reflect on wider study skills and learning. As an example, a learner could keep a learning diary and reflect on questions such as: Which tasks did I enjoy this week? Why did I enjoy them? How could I use this when I find a task challenging? Questions could even be expanded to: What time of day do I learn best? How can I ensure I succeed at other times of the day? What tools do I have to succeed? In doing so, we empower the learner and help them feel in control of their learning.
- Encourage the idea that mistakes are not 'bad' but are a learning opportunity. This is a tool for everyday life. Encourage reflections such as: 'I tried this approach and I learnt that... Next time I will try...'
- Encourage learners to communicate and share what they have learnt. In this way, ideas are shared, and learners may want to try tools that have been successful for their peers. It also promotes the idea that everyone learns differently, everyone struggles with some things and everyone can find a way forward.
- Ask learners to set themselves goals. What do I want to achieve for myself? How might I do this? What tools and support can I access to help me succeed?
- For younger pupils, a simple smiley face or traffic light could be a useful way to get pupils starting to assess their own work and where they are in their learning journey (see Chapter 7 for more details).

Learner voice

In the section on metacognition above, we touched on ways to encourage learners to use their voice and to promote independence and empowerment. Giving learners opportunities to express themselves and their ideas has numerous benefits:

- It encourages reflection on learning.
- It promotes good expression of thoughts and feelings, which in turn can develop good vocabulary.
- It allows individuals to understand the views of others, and thus it can encourage the development of empathy.

- It can help the learner to realize that they are not the only one to find a task challenging.
- It may develop the use of approaches that the learner has not considered before.
- Learners feel valued when their views are listened to and are often therefore more likely to engage with what follows if they have a level of ownership and control.
- It also ensures that practitioners are fulfilling current legislation, as the SEND Code of Practice 0–25 (Department for Education, 2014) emphasizes the importance of pupil voice, as well as outlining the legal requirements for pupils to be an essential element of the graduated approach to learning.

Here are some ideas:

- Start the day by sharing news or checking in with pupils' emotional states, for example by asking them how they are.
- Involve learners in the graduated approach to learning, which includes taking time to find out what they feel they are good at or not so good at, as they are often right! This could be through a questionnaire or a simple 'out of 10' list of how they view different aspects of their learning. Then involve them in the goal-setting process, setting targets that they feel are both achievable and also aspirational.
- Design feedback sheets that cover things like what a good day looks like for me, what a not so good day looks like, what's working/not working for me with regard to classroom, work, support, intervention, and so on. This can link with pupil voice and with pupil-centred planning for annual reviews.
- Invite verbal feedback on learning activities.
- Undertake regular student surveys or votes.
- Have a show and tell – allow students to share an interest.
- In the student councils that represent learners across the school, ensure that there is a diverse representation across all abilities.
- Set up debates on topics being studied.
- Create learning mentors or buddies so that ideas can be shared between peers.
- Give immediate verbal feedback, creating a two-way dialogue, rather than a score of red marks and comments that learners may not be able to read or fully understand. This can then involve learners in the assessment process, encouraging them to be honest about how much they understand as well as how much effort they really put in.

In this way, learners with dyslexia may feel more able to express themselves when they feel something is challenging, and find a way forward through sharing ideas with peers. They may also feel their value in supporting peers with the activities that they find challenging. These approaches can be used with both the whole class and in one-to-one settings.

Using learners' strengths in teaching

Every learner has something they are good at. It might be that they are very able in sport, music or art. It could be that they have excellent interpersonal skills and communicate well with others. We can use this to promote confidence!

One way to utilize the skills of individuals is to allocate roles within a task. As an example, if you require learners to create a magazine article, you might set up a 'focus group' in which one person leads the discussion (the facilitator) and everyone shares ideas. You could have a scribe to record these ideas. When executing the task, you may pick someone with creative skills to design the layout, add images, and so on. In this way, learners work collaboratively to achieve an aim, with all skill sets being made use of.

Another way to celebrate and share individuals' interests is through the use of 'show and tell' activities. Pupils/participants take it in turns to share interests or skills, and these can be used to provide recognition to others that everyone has strengths. It can also be useful in showcasing diversity and may provide further learning opportunities for classmates, as well as promoting self-esteem and confidence for the individual.

In a one-to-one setting, you might ask the learner to use their strengths to aid learning. Those with good artistic skills might draw pictorial representations of words to aid recall of the spelling. Those with verbal strengths could describe a character, recording their thoughts before committing them to paper. Verbal and visual recording can be utilized, and so on.

Asking pupils to become reading buddies with pupils younger than themselves can give them a sense of purpose and empowerment as they are able to read at a level that they feel comfortable with but that also allows them to feel as though they are contributing to their peers' learning. This can also be mimicked with learning mentors such that older students with dyslexia become mentors for younger students with dyslexia. Connecting these students gives them an outlet for their voice with someone who may share similar difficulties. They may also be able to share experiences that have helped them with their learning journey.

Developing learners' strengths can be done in a variety of ways, one of which could be to lead a lesson like personal, social, health and economic (PSHE) education, for example on being healthy. The student can show their strengths by teaching a skill that they are good at and doing so in their own personal style. This enables them to contribute to their peers' learning while also giving them a sense of helping others to develop skills that maybe they aren't so strong in.

Including learners' interests

This also ties in with using learners' strengths in teaching as outlined above.

Example 1: A learner is into skateboarding and knows a range of 'stunts', which he practises at the skate park regularly. However, he struggles to understand the concept of angles. Students are asked to bring in scooters or skateboards for their maths lesson. In the playground, a demonstration shows them how to rotate their board/scooter 90°, 180° and so on. The learner who enjoys skateboarding gets the chance to show what he is good at and to develop an understanding of a concept he finds tricky using a medium he enjoys. This is also a novel task for other students, and as a physical activity, it provides memory hooks to help them retain this information. On return to the classroom, they can refer to the memory of the playground activity to inform more traditional written work.

Example 2: A young learner struggling to develop vocabulary may have more success with a practical task involving their interests. This could be building a Lego set, where the instructions are stated aloud throughout the process of the build, such as: 'Put the blue square with four bumps on top of the yellow rectangle with six bumps.' The vocabulary of colours, shapes and positional language can all be included, alongside sentence structure and questioning, often achieving the same result but with a more positive level of engagement and interest.

Here are other examples:

- Those who play football can use ball skills by kicking a football or similar into a goal with the correct letter pattern on a large card or into mini goals when choosing between two or more patterns, e.g. choosing whether a word has a lone 'e' sound in it (ee/ea).
- Those who love to sing can create a song to remember a spelling rule or put this to a song they already know.
- Gaming fans can create their own virtual character whom they describe in a writing activity.

- Those who like acting could dramatize a tricky spelling in actions, such as 'I will turn out the light when I go home tonight', where they act out getting up, turning off the light and leaving the room. The phrase also has a mnemonic to aid the spelling of the word: I turn out the Light when I Go Home Tonight: LIGHT.

The possibilities are endless. In doing such activities we show that we value their interests, we promote self-esteem because they are using their strengths and the learner is more likely to retain the information and enjoy the experience. Some of our learners may also have had negative experiences of learning and of specific subjects, so by re-engaging them in this way, we are hopefully making it fun and re-establishing the concept that learning can actually be fun!

The examples given do take something of a 'leap of faith' for educators. Trying new approaches can be challenging, time consuming and risky. There is a balance to be had between this and the outcome. The simplest ideas are usually the most effective, and the benefits can be numerous. When planning such tasks, think about the demands on you and your pupils, and then consider the outcomes. Involving the pupils in the planning process is also more likely to lead to a more positive result. Will it help to develop the self-esteem and confidence of a vulnerable student and others?

Effective study skills

It is unfortunate that sometimes learners spend a lot of time using study skills that are not effective. This can lead to wasted time, frustration, anger and low feelings. It also, of course, can lead to limitations in academic success.

Revision technique is one area where ineffective skills can be detrimental. Sometimes learners believe that the only effective way to revise is to study in blocks of time, reading content over and over. In fact, revision is more beneficial in short blocks of time. This is supported by research showing that learners are more likely to retain the first and the last things they learn, a phenomenon known as the primacy and recency effect (Ebbinghaus, 1913). This shows that if individuals study for long periods, they are unlikely to retain a good amount of that learning, whereas if they study in short chunks of time, there are more 'beginnings and ends' to information that they may recall.

For some learners, reading involves a high level of processing and can easily become overwhelming. Therefore, here are some alternatives to reading:

- Listening to podcasts about specific topics.
- Watching videos, such as those provided by BBC Bitesize.
- Creating mind maps of key concepts or vocabulary.
- Drawing timelines of key dates or events.
- Writing facts on post-its and putting them around the house so they are exposed to them regularly, for example on the fridge or bathroom mirror.

These approaches are also useful as everyday effective study skills. In addition, information is more likely to be remembered if revision is active. Learners could record summaries of what they know, and identify gaps to look up. They could discuss topics with peers or even act out key events, perhaps becoming a character from a key text they are studying. The important thing to remember is that words on a page can be hard to access and can lack meaning; what the learner needs to do is find ways to bring the words alive so that they have real meaning and thus are remembered more easily.

Other methodologies include SQ3R and PQ4R. SQ3R stands for survey, question, read, recite and review, as outlined below.

- Survey: Before reading, try to get an overview. Skim the headings and sections and read the final summary paragraph.
- Question: Next, read with purpose. Ask questions of the text based on what you need to know.
- Read: Read for purpose and detail. Actively search for the answers to your questions and develop an understanding of what the author is saying.
- Recite: Try to then recall the gist of the text without referring back. What has been retained and what needs further work?
- Review: Review your questions. Were they answered? Where does the work sit in wider reading and knowledge?

PQ4R is similar and stands for preview, question, read, reflect, recite and review. There are many other tools that can help an individual to study effectively, and these are based on the needs of the individual and where they struggle. Learners may need to be pre-taught vocabulary if they struggle with spellings or word meanings, they may need to learn touch-typing to get ideas on paper more efficiently or they may need IT tools such as text-to-speech and speech-to-text software. In taking time to teach effective study skills, we can save learners time and frustration and prevent them from using ineffective strategies that may limit success.

Summary of key points

Pupil voice is important for the learner and the teacher. It empowers the young person and gives them a clear channel for communication without fear of judgement. It allows them to reflect and consolidate learning and can also develop empathy. For the teacher, it is an effective tool that will help them assess progress for that pupil, what is working/not working for them, and adapt lessons to maximize success for them. It also aids to develop a deeper understanding between teacher and pupil and builds trust that worries or concerns are being valued and acted on.

Metacognition is a useful tool to help pupils understand how they learn. Thinking about how you think and how you learn can guide understanding and give the pupils a sense of control over their learning, where sometimes they can feel lost. It also helps to develop self-esteem and autonomy. Metacognition can help with developing personal skills such as organization and allows the pupil to feel in control of their learning. It can support the skill of time management and engage the pupil in a reflective process of evaluation of their learning.

Using learner strengths can be an important tool for empowering the pupil and giving them ownership of their learning and teaching skills. Allowing the pupil the opportunity to teach others, share their skills and take the lead role can give them a unique learning opportunity and the chance to highlight their strengths among peers. Peer teaching creates an excellent opportunity for the reciprocal teaching of skills that both learners need to develop. It also engages them in the reflective process of how they learn and how they can help others to learn.

Study skills can be a daunting topic for a learner with dyslexia, particularly one with memory difficulties. The volume of material to be learnt can be overwhelming and challenging and a great source of stress for the pupil. Learning the best way to study can be a fun and interactive process between teacher and pupil. Investigating different ways to study and finding out how to absorb information can be crucial to a learner's success. Creating opportunities to trial different study skills throughout the year reduces pressure on the pupil and allows them the time needed to evaluate and choose the method that best suits them. Studying can be an enjoyable experience and can give the pupil the opportunity to explore a variety of ways in which they can learn until they find one that they feel comfortable with. Creating time for active learning can be an enriching experience for the learner, using tools such as podcasts, video clips and mind mapping to explore revision methods. Pupils may also wish to use these methods as their own revision strategies.

References

Alexander-Passe, N. (2006) How dyslexic teenagers cope: An investigation of self-esteem, coping and depression. *Dyslexia*, 12(4), 256–275.

Alexander-Passe, N. (2015) *Dyslexia and Mental Health: Helping People Identify Destructive Behaviours and Find Positive Ways to Cope*. London: Jessica Kingsley Publishers.

Alexander-Passe, N. (2018) *Dyslexia, Traumatic Schooling and Career Success: Investigating the Motivations of Why Many Individuals with Developmental Dyslexia are Successful Despite Experiencing Traumatic Schooling*. Doctoral dissertation. University of Sunderland.

British Dyslexia Association (n.d) *Dyslexia Friendly Quality Mark*. Available at: https://www.bdadyslexia.org.uk/services/dyslexia-friendly-awards/dyslexia-friendly-quality-mark-awards [accessed 14 March 2023].

Department for Education (2014) *Special Educational Needs and Disability Code of Practice, 0–25 Years*. Available at: www.gov.uk/government/publications/send-code-of-practice-0-to-25 [Accessed 27 May 2022].

Drew, C. (2022) *Metacognitive Strategies*. The Helpful Professor. Available at: https://helpfulprofessor.com/metacognitive-strategies [Accessed 6 March 2022].

Dweck, C.S. (2008) *Mindset: The New Psychology of Success*. New York, NY: Random House Digital.

Ebbinghaus, H. (1913) *On Memory: A Contribution to Experimental Psychology*. New York, NY: Teachers College.

Education Endowment Foundation (EEF) (2011) *Metacognition and Self-Regulation*. Available at: https://educationendowmentfoundation.org.uk/education-evidence/teaching-learning-toolkit/metacognition-and-self-regulation?utm_source=/education-evidence/teaching-learning-toolkit/metacognition-and-self-regulation&utm_medium=search&utm_campaign=site_search&search_term=metacognition [Accessed 6 March 2022].

Galbraith, A. & Alexander, J. (2005) Literacy, self-esteem and locus of control. *Support for Learning*, 20(1), 28–35.

Humphrey, N. & Mullins, P. (2002) Personal constructs and attribution for academic success and failure in dyslexia. *British Journal of Special Education*, 29(4), 196–203.

Nalvany, B., Carawan, L. & Rennick, R. (2011) Psychosocial experiences associated with confirmed and self-identified dyslexia: A participant-driven concept map of adult perspectives. *Journal of Learning Disabilities*, 44, 63–79.

Raskind, M., Goldberg, R., Higgins, E. & Herman, K. (2002) Teaching life success to students with LD: Lessons learned from a 20-year study. *Intervention in School and Clinic*, 37(4), 201–208.

Chapter 9

Specialist Teaching

BRENDA FERRIE, SUZY SHEPPARD AND SARAH YOUNG

Phonics, as opposed to whole-word or whole-language approaches to teaching reading and spelling, has moved in and out of popularity over the years. The phonics approach came back into fashion in 1998 through the National Literacy Strategy but had limited success, partly because of the lack of teacher training in delivering phonics and the complexities of the English language. English is not a transparent language; it does not have single sound-to-letter correspondence, and it also contains letter groups that have their own sounds, multiple ways of spelling the same sound, phonically decodable words and phonically irregular words. Traditional approaches to phonics instruction – teaching the sounds that match letters and letter combinations – proved inefficient and often confusing because of the many hundreds of correspondences involved. The most effective phonics instruction teaches children to identify phonemes in spoken language first, then to understand how these are represented by letters and letter combinations (graphemes).

This approach was recommended by Sir Jim Rose in his report *Independent Review of the Teaching of Early Reading* (2006), which advocated the use of a systematic, synthetic programme built on a solid basis of blending and segmenting sounds.

While the structured teaching of synthetic phonics became recommended for all children after the Rose Report, structured, systematic, synthetic programmes of phonics have been used in the 'dyslexia world' for many years and are core to specialist teaching. In the early 1960s, Kathleen Hickey was called on to rescue boys and girls from the ignominy of failure in learning to read and write. Her solution was to provide a comprehensive multisensory approach, using reading and spelling cards, often referred to as 'Hickey' cards. These cards facilitated phonic units to be introduced in a specific order, cumulatively and in small steps, providing opportunity for multisensory learning in the form of 'see and say' when reading the graphemes on the cards and 'hear and write' to write the graphemes from the spelling cards. The cards also provided overlearning.

At about the same time, Sam Orton and Anna Gillingham were developing a remedial approach along the same lines to help children with reading difficulties. This was called the Orton Gillingham Approach, and it involved direct, explicit, multisensory, structured, sequential, diagnostic and prescriptive ways to teach literacy.

Today, most specialist programmes for teaching learners with dyslexia take their philosophy from the Hickey, Orton and Gillingham principles, including the one that is recommended for Level 5 specialist teachers, the Conquering Literacy Programme (Kelly & Phillips, 2016).

These intervention programmes are built on a firm understanding of the underlying deficits of learners with dyslexia. One of the core deficits is with phonological processing, involving difficulties with phonological awareness, phonological memory and rapid naming. The phonological deficit theory has been well researched by Franck Ramus (n.d.) and Margaret Snowling (2020), among others. This would suggest that any programme would need to include precise phonological awareness training beyond the age that typical learners acquire these skills, in recognition that learners with dyslexia have delayed and persistent difficulties with blending, segmenting and identifying sounds in words, syllables and rhymes, and that without a well-developed phonemic awareness, it is difficult for them to match sounds to letters and develop secure sound-to-symbol correspondence.

Another theory is magnocellular theory (Stein, 2008, cited in Kelly & Phillips, 2016), which suggests that the imbalance of magno and parvo cells causes disturbances in the clear transmission of visual and auditory information and that this could result in visual and auditory processing issues. Visual disturbances may include moving letters and other features of visual stress and make it very difficult for the learner to establish lexicons (word images) and to retrieve them easily for fluent reading. Auditory disturbances affect mishearing sounds or sound sequences in words. The implication of this is that learners with dyslexia need lots of opportunities to learn through different channels simultaneously to compensate for weak channels, with well-structured multisensory approaches.

Breznitz (2008) and others have found different activation speeds in the brains of learners with dyslexia compared to non-dyslexic learners, and this affects the speed of processing, especially between hemispheres. This is known as the 'asynchrony phenomenon'. The implication of this is that learners with dyslexia tend to take longer to complete tasks, and this needs to be reflected in any teaching programme.

Fawcett and Nicolson's (2004) research suggests that a dysfunction of the cerebellum can lead to a lack of automaticity, and further research by Norton *et al.* (2016, cited in Kelly & Phillips, 2016) relates similar dysfunctions affecting rapid automatized naming (RAN), the rapid retrieval of phonological information from long-term memory, which will affect reading and writing fluency and speed. The implication of this is that learners with dyslexia will generally need a great deal more overlearning than non-dyslexic learners. Fawcett and Nicolson (2008, cited in Kelly & Phillips, 2016) propose the square root rule, which suggests that if a non-dyslexic learner needs 900 repetitions to learn a task, the learner with dyslexia will need 27,000 repetitions. This is worked out by finding the square root of 900, which is 30, and then multiplying 30 by 900.

Learners with dyslexia also have difficulties with working memory. Working memory is the ability to hold on to information long enough to do something useful with it. The implication here is that there need to be lots of short and varied tasks that consolidate learning of a particular skill. For more information on the theories of dyslexia, refer back to Chapter 2.

The programme therefore needs to be structured, multisensory and cumulative and to provide overlearning. The use of reading and spelling cards forms the basis of introducing new phonic items in a multisensory way, providing cumulative structure and overlearning. The order for introducing the phonic units is of vital importance. Literacy acquisition is broken down into distinct skills with their own activities.

The overview of a specialist basic literacy lesson would include the following:

- Alphabet and/or dictionary work.
- Phonological awareness training.
- Review of previous reading and spelling cards.
- Discovery learning for the new phonic item.
- Introducing a new reading card and practising writing the grapheme.
- Making a new spelling card or adding to an existing one.
- Practising new phonic items such as dictation of words and sentences containing the new phonic item.
- Spelling rules and morphology.
- Irregular/whole word spelling.

- Regular word reading to promote reading fluency (non-words or deconstructing multisyllabic words).
- Irregular word reading.
- Prose reading.
- Writing skills – sentence level for punctuation, and so on, or text level for planning and story writing.
- Use of ICT to consolidate learning for teaching compensatory skills.
- Games to reinforce the lesson's learning.
- Plenary.

Alphabet work

Key terms

Alphabetic order: the sequencing of the 26 letters in the English language.

Alphabetic principle: knowing that letters (and groups of letters) represent the sounds of spoken language (phonemes).

A common characteristic of dyslexia is a difficulty with sequencing (Rose, 2009). Sequencing is the skill of being able to sort items in a specific order, like the days of the week, the months of the year, the letters of the alphabet, the sounds within spoken words or the letters within written words. For our learners, understanding sequencing and the permanence of many sequences is an important skill.

They may know how to sing the alphabet song, but when asked to place letters in order, inconsistencies become apparent. Letter names may not be known as well as the correct sequence of the alphabet.

Most specialist teaching programmes (Hornsby *et al.* (1999); Kelly & Phillips, 2016) recommend that time be given each lesson to teaching learners the alphabet. Learners are taught how to sequence the letters using letter names. They begin to realize that letters have one name although some make several sounds. It is recommended that upper-case letters are taught first as there is less confusion over correct orientation, and then lower-case letters are introduced subsequently.

Most teaching programmes suggest that the alphabet should be laid out in an arc. This allows the learner to see all the letters and takes up less space. For younger learners, a rainbow can be drawn, and there are many commercially available 'rainbows' for this purpose. Quartile markers can be used.

Once this is arranged, it is suggested that the learner points to and touches each letter in turn, saying its name. Touching the letter helps make links with the look and sound of the letter, and the learner is less likely to 'sing the alphabet'. When the learner is confident with upper-case letters, lower-case ones can be placed below.

Letter sounds tend to be introduced through reading and spelling cards. But once they start to know letter sounds, you can include them with the alphabet work. However, never ask the learner to recite the alphabet sequence using letter sounds. All sounds should be pure, without the schwa, for example 'mmmmm' not 'muh'.

Although wooden letters have been traditionally used, there are commercially available plastic letters and magnetic letters that have a clear front and back. Avoid using ones that are all different colours, although there is a brand that uses different colours for vowel letters and those letters with more than one sound. Learners can then be invited to make CVC words and change a letter to make a new word. This helps promote letter sound matching and emphasizes how the change of a letter changes the sound and word meaning. Joined digraph letters are useful as learners can build the word and then see which looks right, for example 'snail', 'snayl' or 'snale'. The digraph letters can also be colour coded to show if they have more than one sound. Specialist programmes tend to teach blends.

There are lots of games that can be played to help learners both learn and consolidate this knowledge, making it a fun activity (see Chapter 12 for ideas).

Some educational suppliers also provide vowel sound directories and cards that present the alternative spellings for a sound. Children can find it very useful to see the 'big picture' and all the different graphemes for a particular sound.

Phonological awareness training

Phonological awareness training is a hierarchical process and progresses through understanding syllables, onset and rimes and then individual sounds or phonemes. Phonological training includes exercises in tapping syllables, segmenting and blending sounds, onset and rimes into words and then phonemes, deleting and manipulating sounds and identifying and generating rhyme. The training is done orally or with the use of picture cards – no letters, flashcards or writing. Phonological training develops phoneme awareness, which is a fundamental skill for reading and spelling. If a child cannot identify the sounds in words, they will not be able to match the sounds to graphemes for spelling or blend sounds for reading (see Chapter 12 for ideas and resources).

Discovery learning and the reading and spelling cards

The order in which phonic units are introduced is very important. Most specialist programmes start with the letters 'i', 't', 'p', 'n' and 's'. This reflects the frequency of use and the number of rimes that can be generated, for example /in/, /ip/ and /it/, and consequently blended to make a good number of words such as 'pin', 'tip' and 'pit'. Specialist programmes also include blends, so 'st', 'sp' and 'sn' would be the next phonograms in the list, followed by 'a' and 'd'. After this point, different programmes may not follow exactly the same order.

A new phonogram is introduced by discovering a pattern visually or by sound. Discovery learning is the process of carefully structuring your teaching point and guiding your learner to 'discover' the learning for themselves. This is best done utilizing a different sense. For younger learners, this might mean using a feely bag containing objects or a series of pictures on flashcards that all begin with the chosen phonic element. For more experienced learners, the chosen phonic element may occur either within or at the end of the word to make learning more challenging. The questions to ask are 'What sound do these objects have in common?' and 'Where do you hear that sound?'

A list of words containing the chosen phonic element may also be read aloud to the learner, who is then asked to repeat them and again to try to identify the common sound. Riddles or questions may also be asked, the answer to which is a word containing the common sound. The learner has had to process this information more deeply, and so the common sound is recognized. Once it is clear that the common sound has been recognized, then the corresponding grapheme is introduced.

The learner may also be shown a list of printed words that correspond with the phonic element. The learner doesn't necessarily have to read these words, but the teacher should read each one, pointing along the word as it is being read to show where the sound is – beginning, middle or end. The learner is asked to identify the letters making the sound, thereby discovering the link between the phoneme and the grapheme. Then the reading card can be made.

The teacher can then make the new reading card by taking a card about the size of a credit card and writing the phonogram in the middle on the front of the card in lower-case letters and smaller upper-case letters in the bottom right corner. The learner is asked to identify a keyword that the teacher writes on the back, with the sound denoted by // or ( ), and then the learner draws a picture of a keyword that represents the sound. In most programmes, each new phonogram has a new reading card, although some programmes (Kelly & Phillips, 2016) ask you to share a card where the phonogram has more than one sound. For example, the phonogram 'ow' has two sounds: (ō) as in 'snow' and (ow) as in 'town'. In this case, there would be two keywords and drawings on the back. This also applies to the vowels, which have two sounds and thus two pictures. Some programmes have different coloured cards for the vowel cards; others draw a red square around the phonogram. The learner practises saying the sound at the front of the card, in the case below /st/, and then recalls the clue picture, 'star', before turning the card over to check that they are correct.

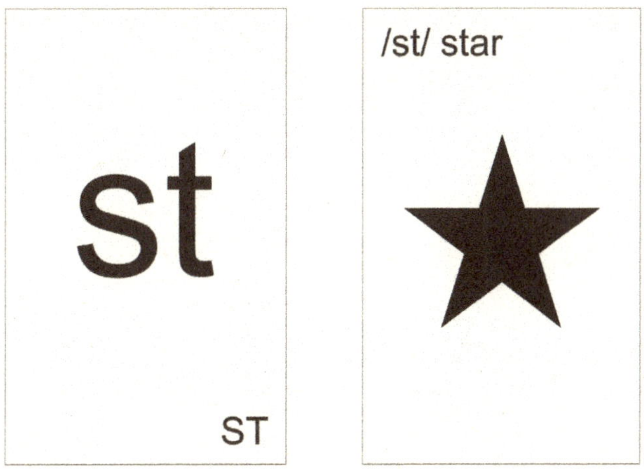

The learner should practise the reading cards regularly. This is called the reading card routine or review. The cards are shuffled, and the learner holds the pack, looks at the front of the card and says the sound, then turns over the card to name the keyword/picture. If incorrect, it is placed back in the pack for more rehearsal. This forms part of the multisensory approach 'see to say'.

In order to link the phoneme and grapheme for spelling, the learner is shown how to write the letter using a cursive script (more below about the importance of a cursive script). The letter is first printed in upper-case, with the lower-case next to it, and the teacher traces over this printed letter in cursive script, placing importance on starting on the line and talking the learner through what happens – for instance, 'Start on the line, draw all the way to the top, back down, along the same line to the bottom and a short flick.' The learner is encouraged to practise this, saying the letter sound and name – for instance "'l" is "/l/"' – as the letter is traced. Various methods to consolidate this include sky writing, writing in sand, tracing, writing on the whiteboard (always a favourite) and writing the grapheme with eyes closed. In Conquering Literacy (Kelly & Phillips, 2016), we are introduced to a superb handwriting grid to help the learner practise. Please do remember to ask your learner to say "'l" is "/l/"' without schwa while writing each grapheme, blend or digraph. It is always good to ask learners to put a tick next to their neatest or best-written letter. Your learner will now be ready to link the phoneme and grapheme to spelling, and a spelling card is made. Various teaching programmes have differing methods for this.

The spelling card is also shaped like a credit card and is usually a different colour. Some programmes ask that you use it horizontally and others vertically. The teacher writes the phoneme on the front and the grapheme on the back. To show that letters are a phoneme, we enclose them in // or ( ). Some programmes, for example Conquering Literacy (Kelly & Phillips, 2016), use a horizontal card with columns on the back for BME – beginning, middle, end – showing the position of the grapheme in the word.

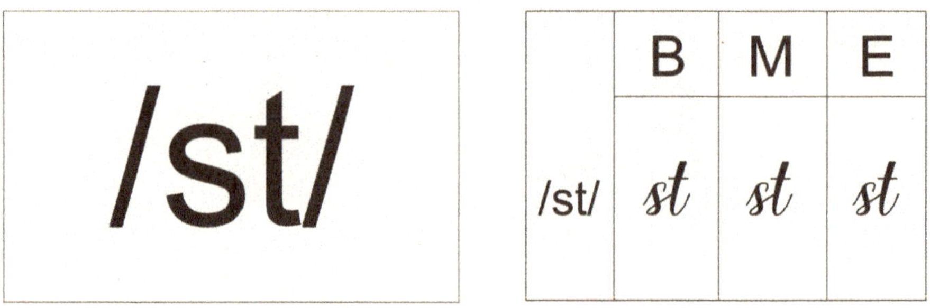

Where there is more than one grapheme for a sound, these are added to spelling cards in the order in which the learner encounters them in the programme. Vowel cards also have a breve to show that it is a short vowel and a macron to show that it is a long vowel. The learner also practises writing the phonograms as words or in dictated sentences.

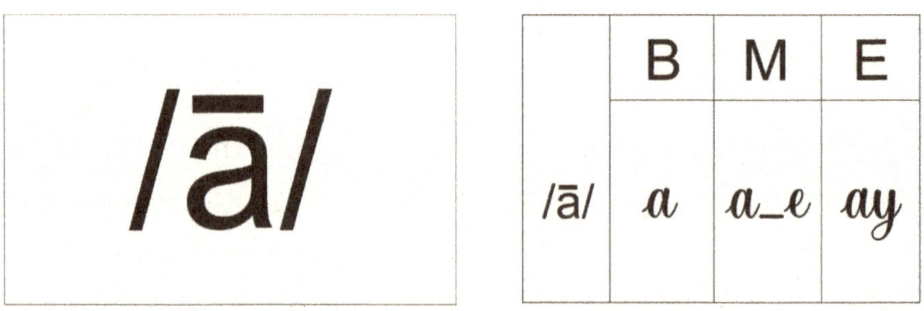

The spelling card routine is also practised in every lesson as part of the spelling card review or routine. There are different ways to do this, but they all share the same principle: the teacher dictates the sound and the learner repeats the sound and then says the letter names. The learner writes the grapheme in cursive form while saying the sound and name of the letter/s and the position that it can appear in a word (beginning, middle or end). The teacher then turns over the card so that the learner can check that it is correct. The learner also practises writing the phonograms as words or in dictated sentences. The Conquering Literacy Programme (Kelly & Phillips, 2016) has a short and long version of the spelling card routine, which forms part of the multisensory approach 'hear to write'.

It is important to note, though, that systematic, synthetic phonics does not work for all children, and the BDA has approached the government to discuss their latest guidance in *The Reading Framework: Teaching the Foundations of Literacy*, published July 2021 (Department for Education, 2021). Valerie Muter (2021), in her video presentation for the BDA, talks about the importance of analytic phonics, morphology and whole language. These should also be incorporated into a programme to support the development of literacy skills.

Spelling rules, syllables and morphology

Spelling rules can help learners understand some of the irregular conventions of the English language. There are a number of books with useful examples. For example, the 'flossy' or FLS rule. This states that after a short vowel in a single-syllable word, 'll', 'ff' or 'ss' are used at the end, as in 'mill', 'cuff' and 'kiss'. But single 'l', 'f' and 's' are used after a long vowel sound, as in 'heal' and 'loaf'. This concept can then be carried forward to 'ck'/'k' (as in 'back' and 'beak'), 'tch'/'ch' (as in 'match' and 'teach') and 'dge'/'ge' (as in 'judge' and 'cage').

The doubling rule is also useful. If you just add the suffix '-er' to 'run' without doubling the 'n' to protect the short vowel, you get 'runer', not 'runner'.

There are a number of different types of syllables, but the most useful are the closed syllable, which contains a short vowel and has the CVC pattern, and the open syllable containing a long vowel with the CV pattern.

Learning how to divide words into syllables is also very useful. Each syllable contains a vowel. For reading complex words, one starts by highlighting the vowels. The rule then is to divide between double consonants or after a vowel to make closed or open syllables. For example: ăc/cŏm/mō/dāte.

For spelling, we ask the learner to count the number of syllables they hear in the word. For example, 'romantic' has three syllables. The learner then draws three lines and listens for the open and closed syllables.

<u>Rō</u> <u>măn</u> <u>tĭc</u>

Morphology is about word derivatives and prefixes, root words and suffixes. There are many advantages to teaching even young learners about morphology. Not only does it help them to recognize groups of letters like 'ful' or 'ment', but it also helps them understand how word meanings change. For example, 'porto' in Latin is 'to carry', and words like 'import', 'export', 'deport' and 'portable' are all derivatives of 'porto'.

Teaching strategies also need to reflect the way a child learns to read and spell using either the upper, phonological circuit or the lower, orthographic circuit (Milne, 2005). Many words in English cannot be spelt using sounds, and therefore these words need to be learnt either as sight words or by developing motor memory. It is very important that children are taught both the names and sounds of letters simultaneously from a young age and that they know that there are some words that say their sounds and others that do not. Irregular words should be taught using letter names, and regular words with letter sounds. Sometimes these are referred to as 'sound' words and 'sight' words or as green words and red words. Phonically regular sound words can be broken down into their constituent sounds for spelling, but alternative methods need to be used for phonically irregular words. These include simultaneous oral spelling (where the letter names are recited, perhaps into a recorder), neurolinguistic programming (where the learner closes their eyes to visualize the word and note different features about the word), sand or sky writing, mnemonics, words within words and cartoons.

Reading

Reading should also be broken down into a variety of activities designed to develop discrete skills, as reflected in the two axes of the simple view of reading (Gough & Tunmer, 1986): word recognition and language comprehension. Word recognition should be further divided into phonically regular words and phonically irregular words. The variety of reading exercises therefore includes non-word reading exercises to promote reading fluency through the automatic recognition of letter groups and their corresponding sounds and being able to blend them easily into phonically regular non-words. Learners with dyslexia have difficulty recognizing groups of letters and tend to be reliant on single-sound correspondences, for example trying to read the word 'house' as single sounds /h/ /o/ /u/ /s/ /e/ instead of /h/ /ou/ /se/. Onset and rime tiles are a good resource and encourage learners to quickly recognize groups of letters in the onset and rime, such as 'sp' and 'oat'. Syllable division strategies and open and closed syllables should be taught to help with deconstructing multisyllabic words into their constituent syllables and reconstructing them through blending as described in the previous paragraph.

Flashcards or other sight strategies can be used for phonically irregular words, which should be learnt as whole words, and there needs to be complete clarity between the 'tricky' or high-frequency words that are phonically regular and those that are phonically irregular. Sometimes the phonically irregular words in the high-frequency lists are known as red words or sight words (with an eye drawn on the card, showing it has to be read as a whole word) and phonically regular ones as green words or sound words (with an ear drawn on the card, showing that they can be decoded using sound). 'Home', for example, is a phonically regular green word, but 'come' is an irregular red sight word.

The development of language comprehension can be promoted through prose reading and shared storybook reading (Hamilton *et al.*, 2021).

Questioning and sharing texts will improve awareness of sentence structure, use of punctuation, vocabulary and identification of genre, as well as developing skills to interpret and infer messages from the text, make predictions, form opinions and retell the story. Learners with dyslexia tend to have much better oral language and higher interest levels compared to their reading ability, and therefore shared and paired reading activities will allow them access to texts of greater interest. When supporting a learner with reading, do not interrupt the text by asking them to decode a word – instead, give it to them and come back later to teach decoding strategies as a distinct activity. Interrupting the reading disrupts fluency and comprehension and can be highly demotivating. It is important to read with learners with dyslexia at a higher level than they are able to access independently because of the 'Matthew effect' (Stanovich, 1986), whereby a learner's vocabulary and knowledge starts to decline over time because they are unable to learn from books in line with their peers. Audiobooks are also good for this reason. Of course, if a learner is to access a book independently, then it has to be within their reading level.

Writing skills

Again, when supporting learners with dyslexia, we must break tasks down to constituent parts. Producing a piece of written work involves many different skills that need to come together simultaneously. These include legible handwriting, sentence structure, spelling, vocabulary, getting ideas down on paper and structuring the text to respond to a question. To support writing skills, each of these has to develop distinctly. At first it may just be concentrating on handwriting, then short sentences, slowly building up the skills to writing short stories. However, some children's physical writing skills may never allow them to demonstrate what they know, and therefore assistive technologies such as laptops, planning software and speech-to-text should be considered.

Games

Games are an important part of a specialist programme for learners with dyslexia. They provide opportunities to practise skills and knowledge learnt in a forgiving way, and they can be rewarding. Be careful to incorporate games that are relevant to the learning objectives.

Plenary

It is sometimes surprising that what you think you have taught is not what the learner thinks they have learnt. It is therefore very important to allow sufficient time for the learner to 'teach back' to you what they think they have learnt in the session. This not only allows you to evaluate what skills and knowledge they have acquired, but also provides an opportunity for overlearning and transferring knowledge to long-term memory, as well as time to develop metacognition through careful discussion of useful strategies that can be applied to wider learning.

Conclusion

Phonics programmes that are designed for learners with dyslexia are distinct from regular phonics programmes because of their highly structured nature and the careful way that they have been designed to be cumulative and multisensory and to provide plenty of opportunities for overlearning. Development of skills is broken down into activities that promote distinct skills, and learning is delivered in small chunks. It is like putting lots of pieces of a jigsaw together to develop literacy. However, while phonics is very important, it must be set in a whole language context. There is no point in being able to decode words without understanding what they mean and how to use them.

Chapter summary

This chapter explored the requirements of a specialist programme for learners with dyslexia and literacy difficulties. It looked at systematic phonics programmes and how to deliver key elements of specialist programmes such as reading and spelling cards. It also introduced other elements of a specialist lesson, such as spelling rules, morphology and reading and writing techniques.

References

Breznitz, Z. (2008) The Origin of Dyslexia: The Asynchrony Phenomenon. In G. Reid, A. Fawcett, F. Manis & L. Siegel (eds), *The Sage Handbook of Dyslexia,* pp.11–30. London: Sage.

Department for Education (2021, updated 2022) The Reading Framework: *Teaching the Foundations of Literacy*. London: DfE.

Fawcett, A. & Nicolson, R. (2004) *Dyslexia: The Role of the Cerebellum*. Available at: http://repositorio.ual.es/bitstream/handle/10835/699/Art_4_45_eng.pdf?sequence=1 [Accessed 8 December 2022].

Gough, P.B. & Tunmer, W.E. (1986) Decoding, reading, and reading disability. *Remedial and Special Education*, 7, 6–10.

Hamilton, L.G., Hayiou-Thomas, M.E. & Snowling, M. (2021) Shared storybook reading with children at family risk of dyslexia. *Journal of Research in Reading*, 44(4), 859–881.

Hornsby, B., Shear, F. & Pool, J. (1999) *Alpha to Omega, fifth edition*. Oxford: Heinemann Educational Publishers.

Kelly, K. & Phillips, S. (2016) *Teaching Literacy to Learners with Dyslexia: A Multisensory Approach*, second edition. London: Sage.

Milne, D. (2005) *Teaching the Brain to Read*. Hungerford: Smart Kids Publishing.

Muter, V. (2021) *Phonics and Learning to Read*. Available at: www.youtube.com/watch?v=TAANo4iEYZ8 [Accessed 27 May 2022].

Ramus, F. (n.d.) Dyslexia, Phonological Processing. In H. Pashler (ed.), *Encyclopaedia of the Mind*, pp.1–3. Thousand Oaks, CA: Sage.

Rose, J. (2006) *Independent Review of the Teaching of Early Reading*. London: Department for Education and Skills.

Rose, J. (2009) *Identifying and Teaching Children and Young People with Dyslexia and Literacy Difficulties: An Independent Report from Sir Jim Rose to the Secretary of State for Children, Schools and Families.* London: Department for Children, Schools and Families.

Snowling, J. (2020) *Dyslexia: A Very Short Introduction*. Oxford: Oxford University Press.

Stanovich, K.E. (1986) Matthew effects in reading – some consequences of individual differences in the acquisition of literacy. *Reading Research Quarterly*, 21(4), 360–407.

Chapter 10

Specialist Teaching for Older Learners

ALISON FAIRFAX AND LYNN LOVELL

The Rose (2009) definition highlights dyslexia as a lifelong SpLD, and the underlying areas of difficulty continue into adulthood. Yet how this affects older learners and adults can change over time as each life stage brings with it new learning and experiences that influence us (International Dyslexia Association, 2008). Earlier in life, learning to read, spell and commit ideas and knowledge to paper in school would likely have been challenging, and difficulties with literacy will remain (Rice & Brooks, 2004). While many adults will have developed reading skills, their difficulties with phonology, verbal short-term memory, working memory and processing skills affect verbal and written communication, time management, planning and organization (McLoughlin & Leather, 2013; Moody, 2014).

Many people highlight spelling, writing and memory issues as their main concerns later in life, causing problems in practical ways. This might be through fearing spelling mistakes in sending text messages or emails, having difficulties ordering and expressing information in writing for a course or at work, planning time to meet deadlines, attending appointments and meetings or holding on to information. These difficulties and the consequences of them can be far-reaching, impacting on personal lives, study, work, self-esteem and self-efficacy (Reid & Kirk, 2001).

Many factors make a difference to the skills a person has acquired and the methods they have found to overcome challenges, including whether they have had appropriate support and the chance to focus on and develop their strengths. How each person responds to manage their daily demands can vary, whether it is avoiding certain tasks, having help from others, sharing roles according to strengths, discovering alternative ways to do things, learning a tricky skill through determination and practice, finding support strategies or technologies or choosing a path focused on their talents.

Older people with dyslexia are a distinct group. They will have moved through a variety of life experiences, whether at college, university or work or in everyday life, and their personalities, motivations and opportunities will all play a part in their achievements and challenges (Jamieson & Morgan, 2008). This means that when providing specialist support, we need to take into account the person's age, stage of learning or career, experiences and aspirations, as well as their solutions to the difficulties they have faced.

Considerations for assessment

Exploring a person's background and history is especially relevant with older learners as this provides a picture of their development, experiences throughout their educational career, any support they might have received both at school and at home and how their life choices might have been influenced by any difficulties (Reid & Kirk, 2001). When assessing a child for a programme of support, we usually have information from parents and teachers; as learners get older, this can be less easy to obtain. It is useful to explore what a learner remembers from their childhood and their school years, and they might be able to ask their parents about early developmental information. Tutors, lecturers, managers and support departments may be willing to provide information with the learner's consent. The learner themselves will be able to share a great deal, and we can help them explore this through the questions that we ask to gain an insight into previous learning experiences.

Developing a picture of a person's life so far can highlight important considerations. For example, the learner may have chosen to leave school, believing they were not capable of academic attainment, and moved into the workplace. They may have received early support and developed strong metacognition and a good range of strategies that have enabled success in education or a chosen career (Malpas, 2017). A learner may have done well in practical subjects at school and struggled in literacy-based subjects and chosen a course of study that draws on practical, creative and problem-solving skills and less on evidencing knowledge in writing (Wolf & Lundberg, 2002). These events and decisions are telling and help us to develop a picture on which to base our assessments for a programme of support.

It is equally important to identify an individual's strengths, to uncover talents, abilities and skills that can be used with ease. We need to explore what a person is good at, what they enjoy, what interests them and what motivates them in order to promote these skills and personalize teaching approaches. This initial sharing of the learner's story to this point, together with an understanding of the present areas of difficulty and the demands of the course or job role, will help with planning and preparing appropriate assessments to identify the learner's needs and strengths.

McLoughlin (2015) highlights the resilience learners with dyslexia have and the perseverance needed to keep going in the face of obstacles, finding alternative solutions and methods to overcome difficulties. These coping mechanisms and compensatory strategies can be consciously adopted from learnt strategies or drawn naturally from personal strengths and successful approaches. For example, a strong visual memory may have helped to develop a good bank of sight words or a well-developed vocabulary, enabling good use of contextual clues and supporting reading. In everyday life and at work, the use of routines, patterns and habits can be established to support memory and organization. A concentrated focus on learning particular skills and practising regularly can result in competence in an area of interest despite difficulties in the learning process.

However, areas of difficulty might have been avoided or hidden – for example, an individual might have sidestepped certain activities or made career choices less reliant on literacy skills. These strategies can, and often do, mask difficulties (Reid & Kirk, 2001). It is not uncommon for adults to only receive a diagnosis and seek specialist support later in life, and this could be as a result of a change of some sort. They may have been managing well, but new demands in the form of a change of job role or a next step up in education can make difficulties become more apparent. Being confronted with additional pressures can mean that developed literacy, organization skills and compensatory strategies are challenged in a new situation (Gerber & Price, 2008; Jamieson & Morgan, 2008; McLoughlin, 2015). This can be stressful and upsetting and may well bring back unpleasant memories.

It is important to listen to the person's story and to consider emotions as it is common for older learners to have had negative experiences that can stay with them (Moody, 2014). An older learner who was identified and diagnosed in childhood and received well-founded intervention will have different needs to someone newly diagnosed and only beginning to come to understand the reasons for the challenges they have experienced (Reid & Kirk, 2001).

Many older learners describe experiencing self-doubt in their childhood learning and questioning why something that appeared relatively easy for their peers was so difficult for them (Alexander-Passe, 2006). Memories of struggling to give an instant response to a question posed by a teacher, read aloud, keep up with note-taking or complete a piece of writing in a short amount of time can have a lasting and powerful effect. Even for those who have good strategies, this can continue to cause anxiety, and the effects of coping with dyslexia should not be overlooked (Alexander-Passe, 2006).

Undergraduates with dyslexia have been shown to have far higher levels of anxiety than those without (Carroll & Iles, 2006), and anxiety impacts on learning, impeding cognitive processes. Therefore, gaining an understanding of an individual's previous experiences and their emotional responses to them is essential in order to better understand the best teaching approaches for that person and to build confidence through success and meaningful strategies (Moody, 2014; Pavey *et al.*, 2010).

An older person's current situation will define their learning and support needs, whether they are studying functional skills courses, BTEC courses, A-levels or a university degree, or if they are in employment (Reid, 2016). Students will need to learn study skills such as note-taking, researching, higher reading skills, essay writing and proofreading skills. Some learners will still require support with basic literacy skills, which can include phonological awareness, phonics, reading, spelling and writing skills. Employees will need to develop workplace skills according to their role to help them reduce anxieties and increase efficiency. These can vary widely and could include time management, organization, reading reports and information, presenting information, managing others, attending meetings and minute taking, telephone calls, emails or text messages, and keeping records (Moody, 2006).

Specialist teachers will respond by identifying an individual's current difficulties in the light of the demands of a course or role and how these affect them in their studies, workplace and everyday life. By carefully considering these factors, an individualized programme that is aligned to the demands of the course or working environment can be developed to provide support to overcome any disadvantage and increase confidence.

The needs of older learners in a range of settings

Throughout their school years, learners with dyslexia will likely have experienced adversity and had to work harder than their peers to achieve the necessary grades to progress. It will have taken resilience and persistence throughout their educational career to achieve qualifications in curriculums based on text (McLoughlin *et al.*, 2002), and it will require continued determination to study at the next level.

As previously noted, times of transition often increase difficulties and anxieties

(McLoughlin, 2015). Specialist teaching, together with reasonable adjustments and good use of ICT and assistive technologies, can make an enormous difference and enable older learners to achieve their goals. Moody (2014) states that it could be the difference between passing a course or keeping a job and progressing. Specialist post-16 teachers can support a wide range of older learners at differing stages of life, study and career. Therefore, it is worth considering the range of requirements of courses and employers in order to align support.

Further education (FE) courses

When thinking of the variety of courses offered for post-16 learners in FE, the extent of the differences in the level of learning and type of support becomes apparent, as courses are varied, including functional skills, applied general qualifications (BTEC qualifications are best known), occupational (apprenticeships and T levels) and academic (A-levels), which encompass entry levels and Levels 1–3. Each study option will mean learners need to develop different skills and meet attainment standards, and teaching should focus on the skills the learner needs to achieve the qualification.

Functional skills

The difficulties caused by dyslexia can impede the process of attaining basic literacy skills, and those who have developed these skills can find themselves struggling to demonstrate them in tests. Examinations for GCSE students with dyslexia can be an immense pressure and a great cause of anxiety. Even with examination access arrangements in place, many learners struggle with these timed testing conditions as the method of evidencing their knowledge. As of 2016, a learner who has not achieved the necessary standards (grade 4) in English and mathematics in England is required to resit the qualification or achieve a Level 2 in a functional skills qualification (FSQ) (Department for Education, 2019). A learner working on a FSQ in English will need to demonstrate an understanding of written language and text and an ability to spell, punctuate and apply grammatical rules without aids such as spellcheck.

To support learners at this level of study, specialist teaching will need to focus on basic literacy skills of reading (decoding and comprehension), spelling patterns and rules, and sentence formation. For mathematics, learners must be able to use underpinning mathematical knowledge to solve problems and make calculations with and without a calculator.

Vocational and technical qualifications

Apprenticeships offer learners a route to employment, typically with 80% paid work experience and 20% classroom-based learning. The majority of these courses are practical and skills-based, although there are still required written elements.

Following a review of post-16 education opportunities, the government introduced a new qualification called the T level (Department for Education, 2020). T level courses are a mixture of classroom learning (80%) and industry placements (20%), where occupational, practical and technical skills are learnt.

Vocational courses are offered from entry level (e.g. BTEC firsts) to Level 3 (e.g. BTEC nationals) and apprenticeships up to Level 5, enabling learners to develop the knowledge, understanding and skills in a specific work-based sector (UCAS, 2020). Traditionally, these qualifications have been assessed through a series of unit assignments marked by tutors, and this approach to learning has attracted learners as an alternative to exam-based assessment because they find coursework more manageable. The criteria are often already 'chunked' into a series of elements to cover. More recently, there has been a reform to vocational courses such that some external marking by the awarding body is now required, which can be paper-based exams, onscreen tests or a set task for some subjects.

These routes highlight the differing expectations of skills. Some require far more independent learning and study skills that involve research, reading and coursework writing skills according to the level of the course. Work placements offer more opportunity to demonstrate skills and understanding, and this is often attractive to learners with dyslexia. There are still challenges involved with courses that place emphasis on workplace performance as this demands organization, time management, communication, working as part of a team, following instructions (often verbal), processes with a series of steps or analysis of complex information, feedback and record keeping.

A-levels

Advanced-level qualifications (A-levels) are considered the traditional academic route to employment or higher education. The academic research, reading and writing demands differ somewhat according to the A-level subject. For instance, English and history are heavily dependent on a volume of reading and the ability to write academic essays, whereas more practical subjects such as media studies may have more creative and experiential learning elements. Nevertheless, a range of study skills will be required, and A-levels are assessed through examinations to judge a learner's knowledge of the subject, which in turn demands effective revision and retention skills and the ability to recognize the requirements of a written question and respond in writing under timed conditions.

Access courses

Many adult learners return to education with maturity and experience and the desire to study at a higher level than might have been open to them when they were younger as the traditional entry routes to university in previous decades were far more rigid and did not offer the same opportunities (Jamieson & Morgan, 2008). Access courses offer a route to higher education. Studying in an FE environment can enable learning of 'stepping-stone' study skills, and build confidence.

Higher education (HE)

Undergraduate and postgraduate courses demand a new level of skills. While they are an extension of study skills that will have been required in previous levels of study, the level of complexity and independence is increased. Principally, there is an expectation of responsibility for the individual's own learning and participation, self-directed study, self-motivation and commitment, management of course requirements and a set of underpinning skills to enter education at this level.

It is a considerable shift for any learner, and more so for learners with dyslexia, as studying at this level is multifaceted in terms of academic abilities, social environment and day-to-day practicalities. The considerations of this new environment are vast when bearing in mind individuals' circumstances. There are 'younger' learners with dyslexia who have followed the 'usual' progression path of GCSEs to FE qualifications to HE, and there are adults who have returned maybe after completing access courses or who have had a significant gap in education. These may have experience in the subject or may be starting afresh. Some learners may be living independently for the first time; others may be juggling a family and/or employment with their studies. This means the adjustments and pressures of studying at HE level can be very different but no less challenging.

HE lectures tend to move at a fast pace. A topic is covered, and there is an expectation that students will supplement their learning with independent study. There is little or no opportunity for overlearning. The onus is on the learner to deepen their own understanding through a further exploration of the topic. Studying at this level requires getting to grips with university systems and language, accessing resources and carefully planning and managing time to meet deadlines. Students will need to develop study skills and confidence to participate in group discussions and collaborative activities, give presentations, take notes, read and analyse complex texts, write academically and reference accurately.

Work

To consider the needs of employees with dyslexia is to consider an even wider range of factors than those in FE or HE. This is because the range of job roles that an individual may have can vary greatly, from practical roles such as plumbing and care work to academic roles such as a university lecturer or civil engineer. Dyslexia does not have to create a barrier to any career, and thus those with dyslexia are seen in many diverse job roles (McLoughlin, 2015; Reid, 2021).

This requires specialist teachers working with adults to become familiar with the demands of their working role. These demands can change over time, and it may be that the individual has sought help as they have moved within their career, sometimes from a job that was practical to one that is office-based, or because they have progressed in their career to management level or similar. These changes may have highlighted difficulties that were less evident previously. It can also be the case that the individual has been struggling for some time and has decided to seek support.

Common areas of difficulty with study skills

It has been reiterated throughout this book that each learner is unique; they have individual strengths and challenges that must be identified and supported in a programme of specialist support. Yet there is a range of common areas of difficulty for learners with dyslexia that is helpful to consider in the light of studying at FE and HE (Jamieson & Morgan, 2008; Reid, 2021).

Reading

Although older learners studying at FE and HE will have developed reading skills, there are usually continued challenges. Those who have developed decoding skills can read text accurately, but this is often at the expense of speed if the focus is on word-by-word reading, causing a slow pace. Efficient reading requires both accuracy and good reading speed for fluency to take meaning from the text (Stuart & Stainthorp, 2015). It is common for learners with dyslexia to need to re-read, even if they have correctly read the words on the page; their efforts go into the reading process itself, which prevents them from taking in information. They are often further hindered by memory and processing speed difficulties, which affect their ability to hold on to the words in a sentence and the sentences in a paragraph. Re-reading is also caused by visual processing difficulties such as losing track of words or whole lines of text or mistaking a word with a similar letter pattern. This means that the reader needs to go back when they realize the sentence does not make sense.

Some learners with dyslexia can read at a good pace. They have strong lexical processes, which means known words are instantly recognized. Many whole-word shapes have been stored in memory, which enables good progress and reduces the interruptions of decoding. However, this can mean 'reading well' but not necessarily reading for meaning. It is often these readers who struggle when they meet unfamiliar words, and they need to break a word down into its component parts and blend sounds into a whole word to pronounce it. This is especially troublesome when starting a new subject, topic or level of learning (Pavey *et al.*, 2010). Some learners simply skip over the tricky word and keep reading, hoping to get the gist.

A common strategy is to use top-down processes of context and syntax clues to guess the word, and this can lead to misunderstandings if the guess is incorrect (Kelly & Phillips, 2016). This type of reading approach can still cause issues even when all the words are known but the reader does not pay close attention to each word in the sentence. They read what they think should be on the page rather than what is actually written, often in an attempt to read quickly (Jamieson & Morgan, 2008). The outcome is often grammatically correct in sentence structure (although not always), yet the meaning is changed, for example reading 'off' instead of 'on' or 'contact' instead of 'contract'.

Some learners may recognize errors and return to self-correcting and re-reading (which is time consuming); others may plough on having missed a key concept or technical word. All of these difficulties can be experienced in a quiet environment, but they are compounded by distractions and feelings of pressure. Anxiety creates further barriers. When a learner is faced with time pressures of reading, their concentration and ability to focus are further affected.

These challenges impact on a wide range of study skills and expectations in FE and HE. Reading matter becomes increasingly complex at each level of education as new vocabulary is added (often subject-specific or academic terminology) and the volume of reading also increases. In classrooms and lectures, information is often imparted through the written word in presentations, handouts, textbooks, articles, case studies and written procedures. This can be a barrier for learners who struggle to keep up with their peers and cannot complete the reading in the time allowed. Moreover, if the text contains new or complex vocabulary, this may mean the substance of the reading is not gained and the learner is unable to make sense of what they have read. Those who need to re-read to absorb information rarely have the opportunity in teaching time. This leaves the learner at a disadvantage when the next piece of information is presented, a question is asked about the content of the text or a task is set in the lesson.

Reading task instructions can be problematic if the vocabulary is unfamiliar. Academic language can be confusing in its complexity and formality. It can be difficult to decipher what is expected by the command words used in a title or question, for example 'apply', 'analyse', 'differentiate', 'justify', 'illustrate', 'evaluate' or 'critically discuss'. Moreover, there is often an expectation that a set of learning outcomes or assessment criteria are cross-referenced with the task and addressed in the response. Without the opportunity of an explanation or being able to check whether the interpretation of the task is correct, a learner with dyslexia can go off track at the outset.

Independent learning demands research, and there are a number of potential issues with this level of reading. Identifying and locating useful texts in libraries can be overwhelming and challenging if the sequence of the alphabet is not secure, which is common for learners with dyslexia.

Effective online search strategies require well-chosen keywords, and this can be impeded by spelling or word-finding difficulties or mismatched synonyms. The sheer quantity of results in an online search can be baffling and difficult to manage without skimming and scanning skills. Selecting appropriate information can be troublesome as this demands quick judgements of the content, appropriateness of the source and relevance of the information. The 'treasure hunt' nature of research, when one 'find' leads to another, can mean the original point being pursued is forgotten and the focus is shifted. Researching a topic can demand a considerable volume of reading, and if the selection process is not honed, this results in even greater burdens of reading when time is wasted reading whole chapters, articles or lengthy texts only to find there is nothing useful within them for the task at hand.

When pertinent information is found, the purpose of reading it is to capture the ideas and points contained within the text, and this poses further challenges of disregarding superfluous information, spotting the key points and using a method of retaining them (and where they were found). The research process can be laborious and very tiring for learners with dyslexia.

Writing

Writing in a range of learning activities requires efficient typing and handwriting skills. Some learners have not developed good handwriting due to poor motor coordination or a lack of automaticity. This places additional demands on concentration to form the letters in the written word in contrast to peers who perform this activity without conscious thought. Weak spelling skills further compound this and are often the main area of anxiety for older learners.

A lack of speed of writing and interruptions to spell a word make taking notes in the classroom extremely testing. Information conveyed verbally by the tutor and jotted down by the learner is often incomplete and difficult to read back. When copying information from a board, a learner may not be able to hold on to more than a couple of words at a time, which means they need to look up and down frequently and may need to look at one word several times to write it correctly. This may be even more challenging if they experience spelling difficulties.

While the use of a word processor reduces the need for handwriting, it is only helpful if typing skills are well developed, and even then, there is rarely time to use spelling tools, and misspelled words may not be later recognized for correction. These difficulties prevent listening and participation when efforts are focused on recording the information presented by the teacher. Older learners often report that their notes are not useful resources when they read them back. Many other classroom tasks require this type of recording skill such as creating group presentations, noting down findings in experiential learning and completing worksheets.

Writing at length, whether for a piece of coursework, a report, an essay or a dissertation, requires many skills that can be problematic for learners with dyslexia. Difficulties with spelling, grammar, processing information and working memory all impact on the complex process of presenting knowledge in writing according to the conventions required at FE and HE. Deciding on the order of information requires sequencing skills, memory and organization, which are all common areas of difficulty. Moreover, knowledge of how to form well-structured paragraphs with flow and connectivity is required, and learners who have struggled to develop literacy skills may not be confident in this level of writing skill.

Assignments need to be planned, but if there has not been explicit instruction on how to develop a meaningful, individualized planning system, this crucial stage is often missed out by learners with dyslexia, who set about writing immediately without a plan to follow. This may mean they struggle to stay on point and create logical discussions; the starting point is not followed through to the end, and as a result the assessment criteria may not be fully covered.

The writing process itself is demanding. Prior knowledge needs to be drawn from memory and new learning from notes together with research findings to present points clearly and succinctly and stay within set word counts. It is common for learners with dyslexia to 'lose their way' when writing (i.e. to forget what has and hasn't been included) and this may mean undeveloped points, lengthy descriptions or explanations, repetition of information or going off topic. It is often long sentences that are grammatically incorrect as syntax knowledge may not be secure or the learner may struggle to hold on to the whole sentence to work it through. Shorter sentences may be used without the necessary links to make clear how the points in each sentence relate to each other.

There is more emphasis on writing style in FE and HE, with the expectation of formality and academic language. Learning new vocabulary (especially multisyllabic words) and how to use them grammatically can be challenging. Spelling new vocabulary, even with the aid of spellcheck on a computer, can cause interruptions to thought and limit the choice of word to one that can be spelt or recognized by the software. All of this causes frustration and impedes progress when writing.

At undergraduate level, accurate referencing of sources of information is necessary. This poses difficulties with working to the correct style of referencing (there are many such styles – Harvard, for example), knowing where to find the key information, gathering it, ordering it and adding punctuation appropriately. The differences in the information needed for an in-text citation and that needed for a full reference can be confusing and difficult to remember, as can the details required in a prescribed sequence according to the type of information (book, journal article, website, etc.). Even once mastered, it can be tricky to be precise in this important element of HE study.

Writing for assessment requires proofreading skills. Learners with dyslexia often report great difficulty with spotting errors in their own work. They may read what they think they have written or not know that a word is spelt incorrectly or that a sentence is not grammatically correct. They may fail to notice repetition in their work, especially if the duplicate is further down in the writing. This can impact on the mark they receive, as the quality of the work will be reduced if it appears disorganized, contains errors or is difficult to read and follow.

Organization and memory

Learners are required to organize themselves and their studies to attend lessons on time, have all necessary equipment, follow instructions, plan out their independent study time to meet deadlines and, for many adults, juggle other commitments as well. Time management and planning are often skills learners with dyslexia find challenging. Working out how long something might take and allocating time to achieve it is not easy, and when many tasks take longer for learners with dyslexia than they do for others in their cohort, this puts further pressure on completing set work in time. Moreover, difficulties with sequencing and prioritizing can mean too much time is given to one task in favour of another, and the weighting of marks, complexity and nearness of completion date are not factored in.

Teaching approaches to support older learners

As you will have already read, the principles of specialist teaching are to plan an individualized, structured, sequential, cumulative, multisensory programme with opportunities for overlearning. While there are many programmes available to help create the structure in terms of early literacy skills for younger people, it is for the specialist teacher to create this for an older learner according to the needs that have been identified in the assessment and the priorities of the individual themselves. In the same way that a phonics or reading recovery programme begins with the earliest concepts and builds up knowledge, the skills that an older learner needs to learn are broken down into manageable steps and taught in a multisensory way. Plenty of practice is included to ensure skills are embedded and the learner is able to use them independently.

Teaching the use of learning strategies, technology and ICT is often a key element in this process to make sure the individual has the tools they need to complete the tasks that are difficult in the best way for them. Chapter 12 gives more detail about how to support reading and writing for all learners, including the use of technology and the development of study skills.

For an older learner embarking on a course of study, specialist lessons typically include:

- Review of previous learning objectives
- Spelling skills
- Academic reading skills
- Academic writing skills
- Study skills
- Metacognition
- Organization
- Management of stress
- Memory strategies.

Trainee specialist teachers often wish for a manual explaining how to teach these skills. The truth is that every person we support is an individual, and we need to create a personalized programme. There will be common areas of difficulty and particular skills, such as academic reading and writing skills, that need to be taught. A range of multisensory methods can be developed to teach the skills, and these can be selected and adapted according to the learner's preferred approach.

Multisensory approaches

It is important to maintain a multisensory approach and not water this down for older learners. Predominantly working on screens or on paper is not multisensory. Sometimes there can be a fear that older learners will not want to engage in certain activities that may be deemed patronizing, embarrassing or childish. We have to ensure that the way we present multisensory activities highlights the value of these approaches in ways that are age appropriate. Here are some examples of ways we can include varied activities for older learners:

- Visual – colour, images, videos, diagrams, drawing, visualization.
- Kinaesthetic – matching, sorting, working large scale (e.g. on large paper or on a board), movement, experiential learning.
- Auditory – verbalizing, recording, audio information (e.g. podcasts, shared thinking).
- Tactile – objects, manipulatives, concrete resources, cutting and pasting.

Common areas of difficulty in the workplace

For those in employment, programmes of support will include the following:

- Methods of overcoming difficulties, including adjustments.
- Resources and assistive technology.
- Skills required for the profession, e.g. reading, collating information, presenting information, reports, preparing written responses and communication.
- ICT.
- Workable routines.
- Time management and organization skills.

Reading

As we know, individuals with dyslexia can struggle with reading accuracy, comprehension and/or speed. This will affect their ability to access any written materials in the workplace, including documents, emails, signs, manuals and so on. Speed of reading can be a particular concern for adults, who have often mastered a level of reading appropriate to their role and home life but may not be able to execute this at a good speed.

As for those in education, software such as text-to-speech can be used to help adults access text more efficiently. This will be useful for all materials that are accessible on a computer, including emails and electronic documents. There are also additional software 'plug-ins' that can help present information from many sources at a speed and in a manner that suit the individual. In supporting adults, we will need to teach them how to use such software effectively. Changing the presentation of materials on a screen can make a lot of difference, from switching the background colour to adjusting font size and line spacing.

Spelling and writing

The presentation of an individual's writing can be a notable concern for many adults and a source of anxiety. This can impact on emails, texts and any other written communication. They may be self-conscious about their spelling and use of punctuation or grammar, both when handwriting and when typing. While spellcheck can ameliorate some of these difficulties, some adults have such severe difficulties that spellcheck cannot recognize the word, or the individual may not know if the suggested alternative spelling is correct. Many adults now use voice recognition software to manage this. Voice recognition can range from the use of a phone to identify the correct spelling of a word to speech-to-text software that can type verbally presented information. The effectiveness of such software is both increasingly accessible and user-friendly.

Again, there are also plug-ins that can help individuals in this area, such as software to help spot grammatical and punctuation errors. Some individuals may struggle to take notes in meetings, which is a requirement of some jobs. An option here is to use a smart pen that can record as the individual writes. Alternatively, meetings could be recorded, but this will depend on the confidential content of the meeting. In an ideal world, the individual would not be expected to take notes.

Time management

Difficulties with time management can affect many different areas of work. It can prevent individuals from getting to appointments on time, meeting deadlines and working effectively under pressure. Time is an abstract concept that works in blocks of 60 rather than 10 or 100, and this can be difficult for many individuals to manage. Adults may not be able to read an analogue clock or may not know how much time it will take to complete a job or get to a location. One simple solution is the use of a digital clock. However, individuals may still need to develop a sense of how long tasks may take in the workplace. Setting timers can help, as can using a calendar to allocate sufficient time to activities. Each of these skills will need to be taught if working one-to-one with an adult.

Organization

Organization can be challenging for adults for a number of reasons. One of these reasons is due to their possible difficulties with time management, as outlined above. Another contributing factor is difficulties with memory, which can cause the individual to forget key tasks, appointments, and so on. Difficulties with organization can also cause problems with the filing of records and with record keeping. There are a number of tools that can help with this, from paper-based 'to do' lists to online calendars and reminder apps. It is useful to explore the varying tools with adults to determine what will work best for them. Lists and paper diaries may be misplaced, so an online calendar may be better. Some individuals may not feel comfortable in using an online tool and prefer the paper option. The important thing is that they try various options. Adults often do not know what is available and what will work until they are shown these tools.

Verbal ability

Some individuals with dyslexia have what are called 'word-finding' difficulties. This means that they struggle to bring forth a word from memory to use in everyday speech. This can impact on job interviews, speaking in person or on the phone and if the individual is required to give a verbal presentation. While preparation and practice can help with any planned speech, this can be difficult to manage when the speech is unplanned and requires understanding from others. Individuals could also be taught breathing exercises to manage speech in everyday use.

When working with any adult, it is helpful if we can also develop a relationship with their setting so that organizational support can be put in place. This should start with guiding employers towards appropriate training around dyslexia. If organization-wide changes can be made, this can benefit a wide range of individuals. Simple actions such as adhering to the BDA style guide for good practice in the presentation of written materials can make a great difference. Other ideas include encouraging succinct presentation of documents or relaying information verbally, rather than/as well as in writing.

Conclusion

In summary, the process of supporting older learners should include the following:

- Getting to know the learner, including any historical factors that impact on current challenges and any compensatory tools they use.
- Getting to know their setting and the demands of their course or work.
- Determining the specific areas of challenge that are impacting on their ability to show their full potential.
- Looking for appropriate resources and methods that can help to manage these challenges.

- Planning how these will be used in lessons in a way that adheres to the principles of specialist teaching – that skills are taught in a structured, cumulative, multisensory way that allows opportunities for overlearning.

References

Alexander-Passe, N. (2006) How dyslexic teenagers cope: An investigation of self-esteem, coping and depression. *Dyslexia*, 12(4), 256–275.

Carroll, J.M. & Iles, J.E. (2006) An assessment of anxiety levels in dyslexic students in higher education. *British Journal of Educational Psychology*, 76(3), 651–662.

Department for Education (2019) *Functional Skills Qualifications*. Available at: www.gov.uk/government/collections/functional-skills-qualifications [Accessed 1 September 2020].

Department for Education (2020) *Introduction of T Levels*. Available at: www.gov.uk/government/publications/introduction-of-t-levels/introduction-of-t-levels [Accessed 1 September 2020].

Gerber, P.J. & Price, L.A. (2008) Self-disclosure and adults with learning disabilities: Practical ideas about a complex process. *Learning Disabilities*, 15, 21–23.

International Dyslexia Association (2008) *Dyslexia Basics*. Available at: https://dyslexiaida.org/dyslexia-basics [Accessed 19 November 2021].

Jamieson, C. & Morgan, E. (2008) *Managing Dyslexia at University: A Resource for Students, Academic and Support Staff*. London: Routledge.

Kelly, K. & Phillips, S. (2016) *Teaching Literacy to Learners with Dyslexia: A Multisensory Approach*, second edition. London: Sage.

Malpas, M.D. (2017) *Self Fulfilment with Dyslexia: A Blueprint for Success*. London: Jessica Kingsley Publishers.

McLoughlin, D. (2015) Career development and individuals with dyslexia. *The Career Planning and Adult Development Journal*, 31, 151–161.

McLoughlin, D. & Leather, C. (2013) *The Dyslexic Adult*. Chichester: John Wiley and Sons.

McLoughlin, D., Leather, C. & Stringer, P. (2002) *The Adult Dyslexic Interventions and Outcomes*. London: Whurr.

Moody, S. (2006) *Dyslexia: How to Survive and Succeed at Work*. London: Vermilion.

Moody, S. (2014) Dyslexia, dyspraxia, and ADHD in adults: What you need to know. *British Journal of General Practice*, 64(622), 252.

Pavey, B., Meehan, M. & Waugh, A. (2010) *Dyslexia-Friendly Further and Higher Education*. London: Sage.

Reid, G. (2016) *A Practitioner's Handbook*, fifth edition. London: Wiley.

Reid, G. (2021) *The Dyslexia Workbook for Adults*. Emeryville, CA: Rockridge Press.

Reid, G. & Kirk, J. (2001) *Dyslexia in Adults: Education and Employment*. Chichester: Wiley.

Rice, M. & Brooks, G. (2004) *Developmental Dyslexia in Adults: A Research Review*. London: National Research and Development Centre for Adult Literacy and Numeracy.

Rose, J. (2009) *Identifying and Teaching Children and Young People with Dyslexia and Literacy Difficulties: An Independent Report from Sir Jim Rose to the Secretary of State for Children, Schools and Families.* London: Department for Children, Schools and Families.

Stuart, M. & Stainthorp, R. (2015) *Reading Development and Teaching*. London: Sage.

UCAS (2020) *BTEC Diplomas*. Available at: www.ucas.com/further-education/post-16-qualifications/qualifications-you-can-take/btec-diplomas [Accessed 1 September 2020].

Wolf, U. & Lundberg, I. (2002) The prevalence of dyslexia among art students. *Dyslexia*, 8, 34–42.

Chapter 11

Planning a Specialist Teaching Programme

LYNN LOVELL AND SAMANTHA MAYLOR-WROUT

This chapter aims to enable you to:

- use results of screening to plan an individualized teaching programme, small group intervention and inform in-class support (pre- and post-16)
- create a scheme of work based on a learner's needs
- be able to write SMART targets.

From screening to teaching

Chapter 6 outlined how to identify strengths and limitations that individuals may face in learning. These were identified through the use of screening materials that can provide both qualitative and quantitative information. In the pre-16 age group, this included:

- Reading: accuracy, comprehension, high-frequency and irregular words, non-words
- Writing
- Spelling: high-frequency and irregular words
- Alphabet knowledge
- Phonological knowledge
- Memory.

This allows you to determine:

- the learner's reading, writing and spelling ability in comparison to their peers and to what is age appropriate
- any gaps in learning
- any particular error patterns that they are making
- the reasons why the learner may be struggling, including difficulties in alphabetical and/or phonological knowledge.

The results of this screening can be used to inform one-to-one support, small group work and classroom interventions. We will start by looking at one-to-one support.

One-to-one support for learners with dyslexia, and also any learners with literacy difficulties, will need to follow the principles of specialist teaching outlined in Chapter 7, and support is likely to follow a specialized teaching programme as outlined in Chapter 9. Such support will need to be planned using a scheme of work that follows a structured and cumulative format.

One-to-one work

A scheme of work is a document that acts as a guideline to the structure and content of a teaching programme. It will list the items you need to include in your teaching programme: the development of phonological awareness, phonic units to be taught, regular and irregular words you want the learner to be able to read and spell, reading and writing development over time, and so on. As such, it is likely to list the aims to be achieved in each lesson and thus to be divided by week/session. In creating a scheme of work, you are plotting the learner's intended progress over time.

It is essential when planning your scheme of work that you keep in mind the multisensory methods that are part of specialist teaching. You will also need to carry out the reading and spelling card routine each week, revising previous knowledge and building on this. You will need to include the other elements outlined previously, ensuring that they include the use of more than one modality at once. You will also need to ensure that your work is personalized and includes opportunities for metacognition and for the learner's voice to be heard. This is a lot to think about when planning your one-to-one work!

The scheme of work is not set in stone, and nor should it be. While you should aim to progress the learner through a scheme of work at a suitable pace, you will inevitably find that adjustments are needed as you start teaching. This may be because the learner makes faster progress than expected or because they struggle to master some concepts. It is essential that learning is secure and also that you keep the learner engaged by providing a suitable level of challenge. As such, changes to the scheme of work are likely over time.

Once the initial scheme of work is created, you should generate SMART targets using a graduated approach. SMART targets are essential if we are to monitor and ensure progress, as they clearly outline what we want the learner to achieve and by when. You are unlikely to be able to plan targets that cover a longer time span, as you will need to monitor the learner's progress and adjust their targets based on their individual achievement. You should therefore aim to plan such targets for a period of around five or six sessions. These may be adjusted after the bank of sessions, or you may need to review them more regularly. Either approach is acceptable and should be based on your monitoring of the learner and how they are progressing through the programme of teaching.

SMART TARGETS

There are variations on the exact words in the SMART acronym, though in general they are:

S – Specific
M – Measurable
A – Achievable
R – Realistic
T – Timely/time bound.

This means that you should:

- state exactly what you want the learner to achieve (specific)
- show how you are going to measure progress (measurable)
- create targets that the individual can meet or exceed (with some level of challenge) based on their ability (achievable)
- create targets that can be met (realistic)
- set a time period for when the learner will achieve this (timely/time bound).

SMART targets allow us to:

- know and understand exactly what it is that we want the learner to achieve
- give a time span in which we want them to achieve this
- ensure that we are moving them forward in their learning

- enable the learner to feel a sense of accomplishment, thus promoting self-esteem and confidence
- create a stepped progression that is achievable for the learner.

Writing SMART targets can prove to be somewhat tricky, and many teachers, tutors and support staff struggle to create targets that are truly SMART. The questions to bear in mind when writing SMART targets are: 'What will I see to show me that the learner has achieved that target?' and 'When would I expect to see this?'

Here is an example of a SMART target based on alphabet work: 'By session five, Learner 1 will be able to give the names and sounds of the letters A–M in the alphabet orally, with 100% accuracy.'

This is specific in that we have named exactly what the learner will be able to do. It is measurable because we outline how we will know that they have done so. In this case, they will verbally state the letters A–M with 100% accuracy. The time limit is by session five, and the target, we would assume, is achievable for the learner and thus realistic.

Another example of a SMART target, in this case for learning irregular word spelling, is: 'Learner 1 will be able to spell the words "said", "here", "there", "where" and "were", with four out of five correct by session five.'

Again, this states exactly what the learner will achieve, how we will know they have done so and by when. Achievability is based on knowledge of this learner gained from any background information we may have and our screening assessments.

Common pitfalls when writing SMART targets include:

- Use of the term 'understand'. As an example: 'Learner 1 will understand how to blend syllables to make words.' In this case, go back to the key questions: How will you know that the learner can do this? When should they be able to do this?
- Unachievable aims: 'Learner 1 will be able to read the five high-frequency words "come", "came", "you", "he" and "she" with 85% accuracy.' Eighty-five per cent of five words is 4.25 words and thus is not achievable. In this case, 80% accuracy or four out of five correct would be better.
- 'Wishy-washy' targets, such as 'Learner 1 will be able to read text fluently by session ten' or 'Learner 1 will develop confidence in their spelling skills by session five'. Again, how will you know that they have achieved this? Solutions will be specific, such as 'By session five, Learner 1 will read two

paragraphs within five minutes, making no more than five reading errors', or 'Each lesson, Learner 1 will orally name one strategy that he has developed to increase his spelling accuracy'.

- Being too wordy: 'By session five, Learner 1 will be able to segment words of four syllables or more, identify these on a phoneme frame, name the vowels in each sound and say if it is open or closed with 100% accuracy.' There are many parts to such a target, and the learner may not achieve them all. Thus it is useful to divide them into separate targets so that each achievement can be measured.

FROM SMART TARGETS TO LESSON PLANNING

Once SMART targets are accurate, these can then be carried across to a lesson plan and be used as the basis from which to plan activities and resources that can support the learner to achieve them over time.

Below are some examples of how to move from the creation of a SMART target to choosing resources and creating activities (more information on resources can be found in the next chapter):

Example 1:

Target: 'By session five, Learner 1 will be able to give the names and sounds of the letters A–M in the alphabet orally with 100% accuracy.'

Resources: Foam/plastic letters, alphabet arc template.

Activity: Learner 1 will place the letters A–M on the alphabet arc template, orally giving the letter name and sound as they do so.

Example 2:

Target: 'Learner 1 will be able to spell the words "said", "here", "there", "where" and "were", with four out of five correct by session five.'

Resources: Flashcards, coloured pens, handwriting book and writing pen.

Activity: Learner 1 will add the word 'said' to the back of a flashcard. They will highlight the tricky part of the word in one colour and write the rest in another colour. They will make a mnemonic to remember this part of the word or the whole word, such as 'Sally Ann Is Dancing'. They will add a picture to the front of the flashcard to represent the word, for example a speech bubble. Learner 1 will look at the picture and write the word, saying the word and then the letter names as they write. They will then check their spelling against the word on the back of the flashcard. They could rainbow write this word several times, saying the letter names each time.

Once you have created your activities and resources, the final step is to ensure that you have allowed time to introduce the lesson at the start and review learning through a final plenary or regular mini plenaries. Don't forget to ensure that tasks are multisensory and personalized and that they allow for metacognition.

Small group work

Planning for small group work will follow a similar format to one-to-one work but, of course, will include more than one learner. While some of the one-to-one methodology will need to be adapted, the general principles remain the same. The lessons should be structured, cumulative, multisensory, and so on. There are several ways to adapt one-to-one lessons to include more than one learner, as outlined below.

In the first instance, it can help to identify if there are any overlapping needs, that is, if more than one of your learners needs to work on the alphabet or the same high-frequency words. If so, they can work on these at the same time, while including an element of personalization, such as creating their own picture for reading cards. This is an ideal world, and, in many cases, you will need to adapt these to meet the differing needs of your learners. Some examples are given below:

- Learner 1 works on the alphabet arc, saying letter sounds and names. Learner 2 listens and can support with correction if needed. Learner 1 hides the arc and asks Learner 2 what the first/next letters are. In this case, Learner 2 knows the alphabet and can support Learner 1. Learner 2 is then challenged by Learner 1 to develop more confidence with the alphabet order. Peers support one another, and each has a role to play.
- During phonics work, learners could take it in turns answering questions on rhyme, differentiated by learner. So, Learner 1 may be asked to find a word that rhymes with 'cat' and Learner 2 to find a word that rhymes with 'train'.
- Learners pair up and complete the reading and spelling card routines with a peer. This would need to be securely modelled first. This could also apply to the irregular word reading and spelling.

Such work could be planned on one scheme of work/lesson plan, with each learner's targets colour coded.

Classroom

Planning specialist teaching within the classroom can be tricky, as there are a number of learners, all with varying needs. Grouping individuals will be a helpful first step, so you may want to place all those who need to learn the alphabet on one table. They could complete the alphabet arc, saying letter names and sounds as they go (this may be noisy) and self-checking afterwards against an example. Other groups could be quizzing one another on the next/previous letter. Others still could be working on a dictionary task, such as finding word meanings from a list given. As such, your scheme of work/lesson plan will show differentiation by group.

There are a number of things to consider here. One is that the learning needs to be planned so that learners can work as autonomously as possible and the teacher is free to monitor learning and address misconceptions and also so that the teacher's time is not entirely consumed with planning individual activities. This can be achieved if time is spent at the start of term creating a bank of resources that can be used over time. As an example, the alphabet arc, foam letters and self-check tool could all be ready to go and reused many times.

Another thing to bear in mind is that learning will still need to be as multisensory as possible. Learners should be seeing, saying, hearing and doing. This may result in a noisy classroom! For those who struggle with noise, this can be accommodated by allowing them to wear headphones, as long as instructions have been given and understood. Again, having a bank of resources can help. Sand trays allow learners to write spellings in a medium that gives them tactile feedback, as does sandpaper or even writing on the carpet. Establishing see-to-say/hear-to-write routines at the start of the year will ingrain this practice, which can be used continuously and requires no additional resourcing.

Whether carrying out one-to-one work, small group work or classroom teaching, you will need to regularly monitor and review progress against the targets set. You may find that the learner has not made as much progress as you may have expected, and this is not uncommon for those with dyslexia. The important thing to bear in mind is that small steps are okay and still indicate progress. A guide to reviewing teaching and next steps can be found in Chapter 13.

Additional considerations for secondary and post-16

In the secondary and post-16 age group, screening may include:

- Knowledge of subject words
- Academic reading
- Academic writing
- Speed of working
- Revision
- Organization.

As mentioned previously, the results of this screening can be used to inform one-to-one support, small group work and classroom interventions. We will again start by looking at one-to-one support.

One-to-one work

Older learners are most likely to require support because they are in some sort of training or education. They may need to develop some core literacy skills as outlined in the pre-16 section above. As such, a scheme of work for an older learner may include phonological awareness, phonic units, regular and irregular word reading and spelling, and reading and writing. These will reflect the age and stage of the learner. Individuals in a secondary setting or on a foundation learning course may require similar input to those in primary school, while those on a BTEC Level 2 or 3 course may need to focus on subject words and assignment writing.

It will be necessary therefore to adjust the scheme of work to acknowledge other skills that the learner will need to develop as part of an FE or HE course, such as:

- Time management strategies
- Filing notes
- Planning written assignments
- Question analysis
- Research skills
- Mind mapping
- Extended writing
- Paragraph openers and closers
- Genres for writing
- Connectives, grammar and punctuation
- Vocabulary extension

- Note-taking
- Note-making
- Advanced reading skills – SQ3R (survey, question, read, recite and review)
- Learning to read and spell polysyllabic technical words using syllable division
- Typing skills
- Using ICT – speech-to-text and text-to-speech
- Strategies for revision – review cycles, cue cards, posters
- Exam preparation.

In the lesson plan, this may take different formats:

- Personal targets
- Reading/spelling/concept/subject-specific cards
- Writing skills
- Study skills
- Organization, time management and planning
- Memory
- Managing stress
- Reflection and metacognition
- Developing confidence.

These skills will replace areas such as phonic knowledge, but the key principles of specialist teaching should continue to be a key feature of every lesson. The scheme of work should also be flexible and continue to be based on the needs of the learner and the progress they make. As for a pre-16 lesson, SMART targets will need to be created so that you know what you want the learner to achieve, how they will achieve this and by when.

Here is an example of a SMART target for a post-16 learner in an FE setting: 'Learner 1 will verbally define ten command words with 100% accuracy by session ten.' (NB: Command words often appear in assignment questions. These are words that define the task, such as 'evaluate' or 'compare'.)

An example of a SMART target for a post-16 learner in an HE setting: 'By session five, Learner 1 will have created an online timetable that includes every known assignment deadline and exam date in this academic year.'

Occasionally, it may be necessary to create targets that also help the learner to manage everyday tasks at home or at work. These will be taught in your sessions with a view to enabling the learner to use them independently.

An example of a SMART target for an adult in the workplace: 'Learner 1 will be able to use text-to-speech software to proofread one document of two or three paragraphs per session.'

An example of a SMART target for an adult to use at home: 'By session five, Learner 1 will have set a reminder in their online calendar for each appointment they have in the month of XX.'

An example of how to make some of these targets into teaching activities:

Target: 'Learner 1 will verbally define ten command words with 100% accuracy by session ten.'

Resources: Assignment question, highlighters, online dictionary, phone/recording software.

Activity: Learner 1 will highlight the command words in the assignment question, saying the words as they highlight. They will enter each word into the online search engine, saying the word as they type, to gain a definition. They will record the definition on their phone or voice record it in a computer file. The learner will revise by listening to each definition at least once a day for homework.

Or:

Target: 'Learner 1 will be able to use text-to-speech software to proofread one document of two or three paragraphs per session.'

Resources: Computer with text-to-speech enabled, or text-to-speech app.

Activity: Learner 1 will open the text-to-speech app/software and document. They will use the functions to read a document of two or three paragraphs aloud, following on the screen as it is read. Learner 1 will verbally summarize what they have learnt from the document, identifying at least one point per paragraph.

Again, while planning, ensure that the learning is personalized, is reviewed regularly and develops metacognition. Adults will come from a wide array of settings and will have a range of strengths. Art students may benefit from drawing reminders; those in the performing arts may like to act out key information. For example, a circus skills student might spell keywords while juggling!

Small group work

In some ways, it is easier to work with groups of older students, and in some ways, it is more challenging. Older learners are more independent and can be set tasks, but this makes it harder to ensure that they are using multisensory tools. Their course content and needs may vary. However, what you will usually find is that many learners struggle with the same types of activities, and thus these can be taught in small groups, though always with consideration of the individual.

As an example, imagine two learners, one on an animal care course and one on a photography course. The first learner needs to record what activities they carried out while on a veterinary placement; the other needs to annotate their photographs as part of a project. Both learners need to develop skills in structuring and extending self-reflection activities. As a group, you could brainstorm the questions to ask yourself during a self-reflection task and record these on a shared document. Each learner could record this verbally on their phone, perhaps personalizing it if not all questions are relevant, and then practise completing a response, playing the recording and responding to the questions. Responses could be recorded by text-to-speech software if needed.

Classroom

In the same way that the needs of learners may overlap in small group work, in the classroom it will be important to identify the skills that your class may need to develop and allow them to personalize this. Tutors and lecturers must not assume that learners have developed study skills, and these often need to be taught explicitly. Skills such as skimming and scanning may not develop or may not be possible for learners with reading difficulties, and therefore tools such as the 'find' function on documents can be used to locate key information, or text-to-speech software can read a document aloud. Both of these strategies may need to be demonstrated, explained and practised.

In the same way, learners often do not know that there are tools that can help them with a range of study activities they may find challenging. Examples include the following:

- Referencing tools.
- Text-to-speech software for proofreading written work.
- Mind maps, to plan work.
- Changing the background colour and font on documents to make these more accessible.
- Reminder apps.
- Online calendars.

All of these encourage the learner to engage with a range of multisensory tools, where they are seeing, saying and doing. Not only this, but in teaching these strategies and tools we are providing learners with tools for life. For more ideas, see Chapters 7, 8 and 12.

The next chapter will consider what resources are likely to be useful for learners of all ages to enable them to progress and gain the skills and knowledge they need.

Key takeaways

- Learning should always be structured, cumulative and multisensory, with opportunities for overlearning.
- Screening can be used to plan one-to-one support, small group work and classroom work that incorporate these key principles.
- SMART targets allow educators to plan appropriate tasks to ensure progress. These should be regularly monitored.

Chapter 12

Materials for Teaching

Resources and Methods for Specialist Teaching and Classroom Practice

ANNA SUTTON

Chapter aims

By this stage of specialist teaching practice, you will have acquired extensive knowledge, including the following:

- How to carry out an in-depth assessment of the learner's needs and generate a holistic profile of strengths and needs.
- The principles of specialist teaching.
- A range of strategies for supporting learners with dyslexia.
- How to prepare the reading and spelling programmes.
- The differences in teaching learners at different levels of education.

This chapter is designed to signpost the specialist teacher towards resources and methods for one-to-one sessions and quality-first teaching practice. It is filled with dyslexia-friendly approaches that have been gathered from experienced specialist teachers and organized into relevant skill-based sections for easy reference.

Where to start

Specialist teaching is customized specifically for the individual. The selection of teaching resources and materials will always be directed by the learner's strengths and needs. Planning the specialist lesson is like creating a recipe: the structured, multisensory, cumulative programme provides the framework, but specific skills and interests are interwoven to provide opportunities for overlearning in an interactive way. Active learning approaches are key, and the resources and materials selected are the 'icing on the cake' for the learner.

All of the ingredients are required to generate effective learning memories for the individual.

How to select appropriate materials and resources

You have placed your learner on the specialist programme.

You have identified the skills that require training, and it is time to select and create materials for the lesson.

Materials need to be:

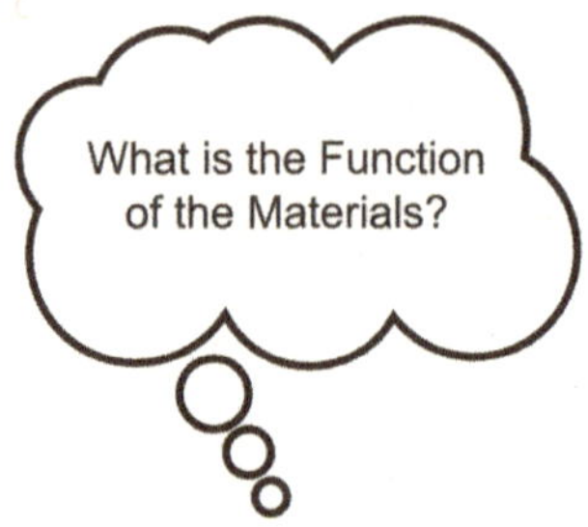

- multisensory
- interactive
- engaging
- memorable
- accessible
- appealing to the individual's learning style.

This is important to consider, as each learner will have their own preferences and learning styles. Assessment will have identified many factors relating to strengths and needs and will inform the selection of appropriate resources.

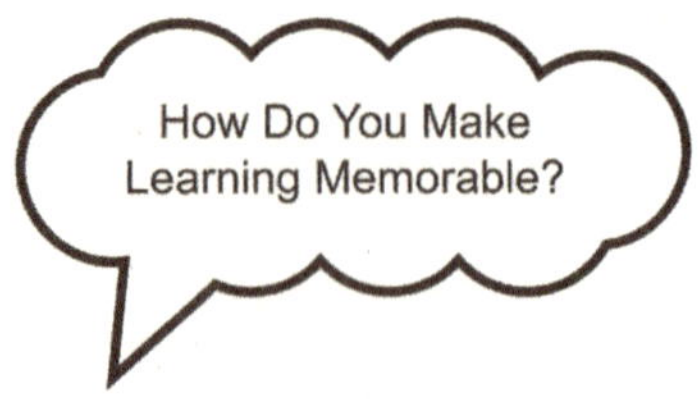

For example, a learner who enjoys dance and movement but has difficulty remembering how to form specific letter patterns may enjoy 'dancing out' the letter formation with ribbons, lightsabres or pom poms. Short videos can be made of the experience and replayed when the learner requires assistance with writing.

This is an interactive, multisensory and customized activity that provides a vivid learning memory.

Selecting materials relies on the skills identified in the learner's profile. This is the key difference with planning activities for an age-related or curriculum-oriented lesson.

Identify the skill to be taught first, which becomes the learning objective in the lesson plan. Then create the customized activity.

For example, a 14-year-old learner who experiences difficulty with sequencing the alphabet will require an age-appropriate task that targets the alphabet skill. In this situation, sensitivity is required. This could be achieved by generating image-based alphabet cards related to a special interest. Encouraging the learner to create these cards with the teacher and eventually to lead the project stimulates a sense of ownership over the materials. It also permits the learner to use a specialist interest and knowledge. An interest could be footballers' names (Lionel Messi), recipes, car logos (VW), animals, chemical symbols – whatever appeals most to the learner.

The cards can then be used in subsequent lessons and become a useful learning aid.

As an extension to this, the learner could teach a younger learner how to sequence the cards, thus sharing an interest, consolidating skills and gaining confidence.

A customized, interactive, engaging and useful material designed specifically for the learner provides an empowering learning experience.

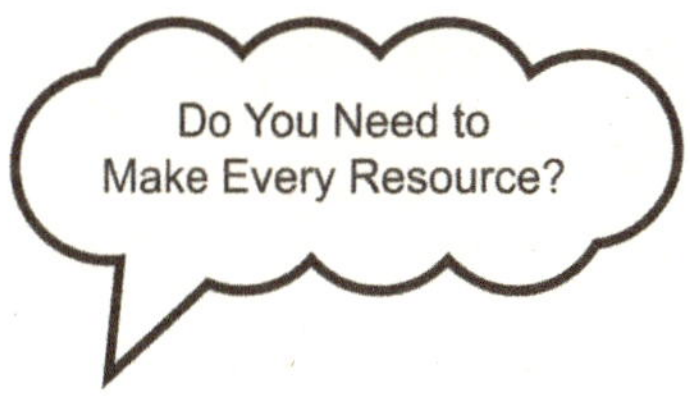

You do not need to make every resource. There are some great resources available commercially and on the internet.

Sharing ideas with colleagues and in networking groups is an ideal way to gain feedback about different resources. Encouraging the learner to make their own resources with your guidance as a facilitator is creative, self-directed, empowering and memorable. Learners love to have their own pack of customized activities and resources to dip into, and it can really make them feel valued to know that their teacher or tutor has designed an activity especially for them.

Eventually, you will develop the ability to customize and create a bank of resources specific to the learner.

The next part of the chapter is organized into skills-based sections with suggested resources, materials and links to stimulate your lesson planning and activities.

Checklist

Is the activity:

- skills-based
- multisensory
- interactive
- customized
- appealing
- engaging
- empowering
- transferable to other subjects?

Phonological awareness

Aim: Activities should train the development of sound processing skills, identifying and manipulating language at sound level. No association with the written word should be made.

Skill areas: Vowel and consonant discrimination, syllable detection, blending and segmenting of sounds and syllables, onset and rime building, detecting and generating rhyme and alliteration, listening skills.

Programmes, materials and approaches:

- Peter Hatcher's Sound Linkage Programme: https://books.google.co.uk/books?id=anjoAgAAQBAJ.
- STILE trays for phonological skills: www.ldalearning.com/product/cognition-and-learning/dyslexia-and-literacy/stile/stile-tray/acmt00705.
- Egon Publishers, *Learning Can Be Fun* series: www.egon.co.uk/page/learning-can-be-fun.
- Hertfordshire LA have produced a downloadable and printable pack for producing games: www.hertfordshire.gov.uk/microsites/local-offer/media-library/documents/resource-area-documents/spld-phonological-awareness-pack-pdf-6mb.pdf.
- Essex County Council, *Essex Ultimate Guide to Phonological Awareness*: https://leedsforlearningdirect.co.uk/Article/78042.

- Reading Rockets: www.readingrockets.org/article/development-phonological-skills.
- Carrie Hughes resources: https://carriehughes-slt.co.uk/resources.
- Roald Dahl's *Revolting Rhymes*, poems, song lyrics, performance poetry, poetry collections, role play and puppetry.
- Objects in a basket or magic box that rhyme.
- Syllable snap, rhyming lotto, phoneme bingo.
- A phoneme frame with counters and magnets.
- Phoneme jigsaws – generate your own pictures, cut into strips for the number of phonemes in a word.
- A pack of picture cards, created by you, that can be used for short/long vowel sound sorting, syllable detection, phoneme snap and with basic board games.
- Fishing games: use a magnetic fishing game and hook the picture cards associated with the sound.
- Syllable football, for active learners. Kicking a ball back and forth for each syllable in a selected word. If you miss a kick, it is passed to the other participant, and points are allocated.
- Drama workshop games: make the word a physical activity. Select a word, say it out loud, divide it into phonemes or syllables and add an action for each in the word. Literally 'act it out' while saying each sound/syllable. The participant watches and copies. This could develop into a game of 'guess the word' to facilitate blending. Drama exercises can be effective with older learners, too, especially for Shakespearean language and multisyllabic words.
- Vocal exercises: reciting tongue twisters and identifying the common sound; feeling the difference in voice production between voiced and unvoiced sounds; awareness of tongue, lips and teeth.

ICT:

- Nessy YouTube videos and apps: Chimp Fu – Syllable Division: www.nessy.com/en-us/shop/apps/chimp-fu.

Collaborate:

- Collaborate with other specialists, such as music and drama departments, speech and language therapists and early years specialists.

Alphabet skills

Aim: There is a range of skills to master in relation to alphabet and dictionary skills.

Skill areas: Upper-/lower-case letters; letter sounds and letter names; sequencing and ordering; visual and auditory skills; reciting; dictionary skills; vowels and consonants; rapid naming/automaticity.

Programmes, materials and approaches:

- Basic kit: 3D letters (wooden, plastic, magnetic); modelling materials; alphabet cards; picture cards; alphabet arc or rainbow mat; sensory letters; timer.
- Activities/games: sequencing and ordering picture cards and letters to match; recalling letter sound and letter; matching upper-case letters to lower-case letters; alphabet dominoes in groups of letters of two, three, four or five; sorting letters into quartiles; mnemonics for quartiles; timed exercises with sequencing the alphabet.
- Model alphabet letters out of pipe cleaners, clay, playdough.
- Print letters with stampers.
- Write in a tray of salt with a finger.
- Track for the alphabet sequence in a maze of letters.
- Alphabetical ordering exercises; washing line alphabet – peg the letters; identify missing letters.
- Alphabet yoga: https://kidsyogafun.com/yoga-theme-alphabet-yoga-for-kids.
- The active literacy kit: www.ldalearning.com/product/cognition-and-learning/dyslexia-and-literacy/beat-dyslexia/active-literacy-kit/acmt00569.
- Egon Publishers: a range of alphabet-themed books and sets of cards: www.egon.co.uk/product/learning-can-be-fun-book-1-alphabet-sequencing.
- Appeal to specific interests, such as making alphabet cards for musical composers, footballers, car logos, chemical symbols.
- Organize subject-specific vocabulary alphabetically and developing research and referencing skills.
- Inspire interests in orthography and different alphabet systems and codes from around the world.

ICT:

- Wordshark: alphabet games: www.wordshark.co.uk.

Collaborate:

- Collaborate with the local library and librarian or the school resource. Develop research skills and access online library catalogues.

Phonics

Aim: These resources and materials are intended to supplement the structured programme activities.

Skill areas: Sound/symbol correspondence; reading words containing the phonic unit; spelling words containing the phonic unit; cursive handwriting practice of the phonic unit.

Programme, materials and approaches:

- Multisensory activities are a key approach: modelling materials; different colours; coloured pens; chalk; shaving foam; glitter glue.
- Model with playdough, clay, pipe cleaners.
- Practise cursive letter formation with tracing activities, colour, large scale with paint, different sized pens.
- Word building with 3D letters, letter tiles and cubes.
- Games to practise sound/symbol correspondence: lotto, pelmanism, bingo, Go Fish, Trugs.
- Paired games to match similar words, words with same phonic unit, words to their meanings.
- Smart Chute or Postbox for practising reading card recall and sorting similar phonemes.
- Tracking activities and mazes for the phonic unit, individual or within words; letter mash up.
- Word puzzles: make your own word puzzles, jigsaws and board games.
- Read words with the phonic unit: generate wordsearches, crosswords, scan newspapers and magazines of interest, read series of short sentences.
- Use subject-specific words containing the relevant phonic unit and identify which links phonics with wider learning.
- Reading programmes that are based on phonic training: Phonic Books can be used with Catch-Up Readers (www.phonicbooks.co.uk) and has a very useful teacher resource book for making your own games and activities.

- Spelling words with the phonic unit: word-building games; spinner activities; crosswords; hangman. There are many websites that offer word game generators. SEN Teacher is useful: www.senteacher.org/printables/literacy.
- Resources produced for other structured programmes can be useful: Alpha to Omega card games; Beat Dyslexia; Smart Kids.

ICT:

- Nessy online videos and software: www.nessy.com/en-gb/recommendation?skills=Maths&age=6-11.
- Wordshark: phonic units can be selected and a programme customized for learners: www.wordshark.co.uk.
- Reading Eggs: https://readingeggs.co.uk/bing/phonicsgames.
- Phonics Bloom: www.phonicsbloom.com.
- BBC Bitesize videos: www.bbc.co.uk/bitesize/topics/zcqqtfr.
- Units of Sound literacy programme: www.nisai.com/unitsofsound.
- Free resources on the Letters and Sounds website: https://letters-and-sounds.com.
- BBC Skillswise: a collection of online resources and videos for developing literacy skills with adult learners: www.bbc.co.uk/teach/skillswise.

Collaborate:

- Collaborate with other learners. Older learners can create their own board games to practise different phonic units and teach younger learners.

Reading

Aim: Materials for developing reading fluency, comprehension and techniques. Language games and morphology.

Skill areas: Whole-word reading skills; non-word reading skills; reading comprehension; reading techniques for study skills; language skills.

Programmes, materials and approaches: Whole word reading skills/irregular word reading/sight words – these are words that rely heavily on sight word recognition.

Key approaches include plenty of opportunities for overlearning. These activities are also suitable as revision techniques for topic-based vocabulary.

- Lidia Stanton publications: *High Frequency Words in Cartoons*, with teacher workbook and flashcards: https://lidiastanton.com.
- SPLAT games: splat the sight words with flyswatters.
- Trugs for tricky words: www.thedyslexiashop.co.uk/teaching-aids/trugs.html.
- Flashcard games: matching pairs, bingo, lotto.
- Cloze passages: selecting the correct word to complete the sentence.
- Wordsearches and tracking activities.
- Traditional board games that can be adapted to include the reading of flashcards at certain points in the game. This can be used for irregular words and subject-specific vocabulary.
- SMART Chute: card packs include suffixes, prefixes, homophones, homonyms, and so on: www.smartkids.co.uk/collections/smart-chute?page=2.
- SNIP programme for reading sight words: www.snip-newsletter.co.uk/pdfs/downloads/literacy_programme_1.pdf.

Vocabulary and language skills: Language comprehension can be supported with vocabulary-based games and activities. Oral language games can be beneficial.

- Articulate board game. Junior and senior versions available. The game can be adapted to include topic-related vocabulary for an effective revision game.
- Headbands or Who Am I? games.
- Just a Minute and word association games.
- Oral language games, role play, storytelling and going to the theatre provide immediate access to the text.

Morphology and etymology: Breaking words down into components and showing how these components work; how words are formed and made up of morphemes (small word units that carry meaning or perform a grammatical function). This includes a focus on compound words, base/root words, prefixes and suffixes. This provides a concrete approach to reading and decoding words while developing vocabulary.

- Word puzzles and jigsaws; dominoes; spinner games; matching morphemes to build a word.
- Structured word inquiry: an approach that encourages the learner to discover words for themselves: www.wordworkskingston.com/WordWorks/Structured_Word_Inquiry.html.

- Word families and derivations that can be presented via word mapping and subject-specific vocabulary. For example, number-based words: bi-, tri-, quad-, oct-.
- Use a matrix or word web to create new words: www.neilramsden.co.uk/spelling/matrix/temp/index.html.
- Investigate the etymology of morphemes: Latin and Greek roots, prefixes and suffixes.
- Relates to dictionary skills and research skills or reading for meaning.

Non-word reading skills: Useful for application of phonics in blending and segmenting unfamiliar words.

- Onset and rime activities.
- Sort words into real and nonsense.
- Word-building and generator activities.
- Highlight phonic chunks in the word to sound them out.
- Books with flip flap pages for turning and creating own words for monsters, characters and minibeasts. Axel Scheffler's *Flip Flap Minibeasts* book. Alternatively, you can make your own flashcards for different word units (phonics/morphemes) for the learner to build and create their own words. The language used in the Harry Potter series and Roald Dahl books lends itself to word generation. This can also be applied to more advanced texts and vocabulary.
- Analytic phonics.

Reading comprehension and study skills:

- SQ3R technique: survey, question, read, recite, review.
- PQ4R is similar and stands for preview, question, read, reflect, recite and review.
- Proofreading techniques such as COPS.
- Use the six W questions for analysing a text and producing a summary: Who? What? Why? When? Where? How? This is especially useful for English literature questions and for analysing prose and poetry.
- Specific teaching of command words in questions and planning a response.
- Cloze passages and procedures.
- Barrington Stoke's *Target* book series for developing comprehension and decoding skills.
- Reading comprehension schemes, games and activities as published on leading educational websites. See the 'Additional links and resources' section for more.
- Shared and guided reading approaches.
- Accessing TV, media and film to develop understanding of key texts.

- Reading subtitles along with favourite TV shows.

ICT:

- Audiobooks: apps like *Audible* have a huge range of books for individuals to choose from, but they involve a monthly subscription and can be expensive.
- RNIB Bookshare: thousands of digital books are available, including exam papers and textbooks: www.rnibbookshare.org/cms.
- Listening Books: see www.listening-books.org.uk for access to a range of books, including GCSE and A-level textbooks, in audio form.

Collaborate:

- Develop links with English and drama teachers, media departments and librarians. Set up reading workshops to teach parents how to assist their children with reading. Generate links with study skills support departments.

Writing

Aim: Materials for developing spelling, creative writing, sentence level skills, handwriting, organizing and planning techniques.

Skill areas: Whole-word spelling skills; spelling strategies; creative writing; sentence construction; spelling; vocabulary; handwriting; writing techniques for study skills, including planning and organizing.

Programmes, materials and approaches:

Spelling materials:

- Multisensory ways of practising the spelling of words: pipe cleaners, chalk on the pavement, playdough/Plasticine, glitter glue, shaving foam, using a torch to write letters on the ceiling.
- Mnemonics: Big Elephants Can Always Understand Small Elephants (because).
- Dicey spelling: roll a dice and practise the spelling according to the instruction – this can be customized. It is a good activity for the pupil to practise independently. Choose the word you want to practise and write it on a card. Throw the dice and follow the instructions below for each number:

  - Write word with eyes shut.
  - Write word with opposite hand.
  - Spell word aloud backwards.
  - Write word in bubble writing.
  - Write each letter in a different colour.
  - Write a word with a similar meaning.
- Racetrack/board games with this week's spellings in a card pack. Word-based games such as Boggle, Bananagrams and Scrabble.
- Explicit teaching of suffix rules: teach specific spelling rules, for example for suffixes and plurals. BBC Bitesize provides free online teaching videos: www.bbc.co.uk/bitesize/topics/zqqsw6f/articles/zqjwcmn.
- Twinkl website: a range of teaching packs for teaching morphology and suffixing spelling rules: www.twinkl.co.uk/teaching-wiki/morphology?sign_in=1.
- A mini matrix maker for logically building words: www.neilramsden.co.uk/spelling/matrix/temp/index.html.
- *Morph Mastery: A Morphological Intervention for Reading, Spelling and Vocabulary* (2022) by Louise Selby (Speechmark).
- *200 Tricky Spellings in Cartoons – Visual Mnemonics for Everyone* and *First 130 High Frequency Words in Cartoons* by Lidia Stanton (independently published).
- *Spelling Rules, Riddles and Remedies* (2014) by Sally Raymond (Routledge).
- SEN Teacher has a range of features to create your own wordsearches, word building games and handwriting sheets: www.senteacher.org.
- Pinterest is a great resource for ideas of teaching and learning spellings in lots of different ways: www.pinterest.com.
- Generate a learning memory for tricky spellings. Create a short animation video, generate rhymes or songs, use sense of smell, a movement or rap for each letter name in the word, draw an image with the word. Appeal to the learner's strengths and preferences.
- The SNIP Literacy Programme for reading and spelling high-frequency words: www.snip-newsletter.co.uk/pdfs/downloads/literacy_programme_1.pdf.
- Target spellings/key vocabulary attached to the inside of the exercise book on a treasury tag. This can be discreetly flipped out as required to support the writing process.
- Helen Arkell's Spelling Windows: https://helenarkell.org.uk/product/spelling-window-pack-3.
- Dyslexia-friendly spelling dictionaries: *Barrington Stoke School Spelling Dictionary* or the *ACE Spelling Dictionary*.

Sentence level skills:

- *Tricky Punctuation in Cartoons* (2020) by Lidia Stanton (Jessica Kingsley Publishers).
- Make sentence-building games concrete and hands-on. Use coloured flashcards, Lego/Duplo blocks, sentence strips for the learner to manipulate to construct different types of sentences.
- Colourful semantics.
- Silly sentences games.
- Use the paragraph sandwich or burger for structuring: topic sentence, supporting sentences, concluding sentence.
- Kung fu punctuation for making punctuation physical. Available on YouTube videos and the TES resource website.
- Bloom's Taxonomy Verb Wheel: provides a list of action verbs for different levels of understanding. Useful for post-16 learners.

Creative writing materials:

- Literacy Shed contains a range of resources and video clips to stimulate all aspects of literacy: www.literacyshed.com.
- Pie Corbett publications and resources that promote talking and active learning to stimulate and support writing and grammar: www.talk4writing.com/train-with-us/pie-corbett.
- Drama and storytelling activities to generate creative writing. This could include going to the theatre, participating in drama workshops, role play or using drama as a learning medium. The Royal Shakespeare Company has a wide range of active learning resources available relating to plays and sonnets. Theatre companies often have educational resource packs and online videos or live-streamed performances available on their websites to accompany productions. Useful links include:
  - www.rsc.org.uk/support/your-help/education
  - www.nationaltheatre.org.uk/learning
  - www.littleangeltheatre.com
  - www.mantleoftheexpert.com/blog-post/using-drama-for-learning
  - https://dramaresource.com/about.

Handwriting:

- The National Handwriting Association: https://nha-handwriting.org.uk.
- The Left and Write Company: www.leftshoponline.co.uk.
- *Write from the Start* (1996) by Ion Teodorescu (LDA).
- *How to Identify and Overcome Handwriting Difficulties* (2016) by Lois Addy (LDA).

Planning and organizing:

- Graphic organizers integrate text and visuals for planning different text types of writing.
  - Mind mapping: publications and YouTube videos by Tony Buzan. An online tool for the creation of mind maps, such as Popplet: www.popplet.com.
- Storyboards and writing frames. This could include using cartoons or graphic novels as a stimulus.
- The PEEL technique for organizing ideas:
  - Point – make the point.
  - Example – use an example or provide evidence to back up the point.
  - Explain – explain how the evidence supports your point.
  - Link – link the point to the next idea in the following paragraph.
- Thinking maps for planning ideas through writing frameworks: www.thinkingmaps.com.
- Concept maps for note-taking, planning, creative writing and project work: www.lucidchart.com/pages/concept-map.
- Use the six W questions for planning a written response: Who? What? Why? Where? When? How?

ICT:

- See the assistive technology section below.
- There is a range of spelling apps and games available online. Some resources include Squeebles, ICT Games and WordWall.
- Programmes such as Wordshark and Nessy.

Collaborate:

- Collaborate with other departments and professionals to generate writing. This could be using drama, film and media as a stimulus. Working alongside professionals. Generating a project-based approach to writing to provide motivation. Artists and graphic designers may have their own visual ways of recording information that integrate visuals and text.
- Develop links with local occupational therapy services for support with handwriting strategies, ergonomics and motor skills.

Study skills

Aim: Dyslexia-friendly materials for developing access to learning.

Skill areas: Cross-curricular subjects, maths skills, academic skills.

Programmes, materials and approaches:

- Oaka Books produces dyslexia-friendly board games and visual resources for Key Stage 3 topics: www.oakabooks.co.uk.
- For creating and accessing online games for a range of skills: https://wordwall.net.
- Mathsbot: online resources for maths teaching: https://mathsbot.com.
- Mr Barton Maths: www.mrbartonmaths.com/index.html.
- Ronit Bird: a range of printable multisensory maths resources, online games and videos: www.ronitbird.com/resources.
- Twinkl has a range of visual resources, PowerPoint presentations and activities for maths development.
- For resources and materials for post-16 learners, access to functional skills websites can be useful: https://functionalskillsresources.co.uk and www.skillsworkshop.org.
- Active revision techniques: flashcards, post-it notes, large-scale mind maps, word association games linked to topic-based vocabulary, highlighting, colour coding information.
- Encourage links with study support departments at universities and colleges for access to direct teaching of specific skills. Many departments run helpful courses, drop-in sessions and tuition.

Publications:

- *The Dyslexia, ADHD and DCD-Friendly Study Skills Guide: Tips and Strategies for Exam Success* (2020), by Anne-Marie McNicholas (Jessica Kingsley Publishers).
- *Study Skills: The Complete Guide to Smart Learning* (2007), by Elizabeth Holtom (Galore Park).
- For advice on study skills for independent study and homework: *How to Study with Dyslexia: Rapid Study Skills for Students Pocketbook* (2018) (How2Become Ltd).
- *Study Skills for Students with Dyslexia: Support for Specific Learning Differences* (2016), by Sandra Hargreaves and Jamie Crabb (Sage Publications).
- *The Study Skills Handbook* (2019), by Stella Cottrell (Macmillan Study Skills).
- For explaining working memory to young adults, *How Can I Remember All That?*

Simple Stuff to Improve Your Working Memory (2019), by Tracy Packiam Alloway (Jessica Kingsley Publishers).

- *Working Memory and Learning: A Practical Guide for Teachers* (2008), by Tracy Packiam Alloway and Susan Gathercole (Paul Chapman Publishing).
- *Listening and Processing Auditory Instructions* (1995), by Jean Gillian DeGaetano (Great Ideas for Teaching). There is a range of publications available by this author for supporting auditory processing skills.
- *The Big Book of Dyslexia Activities for Kids and Teens: 100+ Creative, Fun, Multisensory and Inclusive Ideas for Successful Learning* (2018), by Gavin Reid, Nick Guise and Jennie Guise (Jessica Kingsley Publishers). This book contains a wide range of activities for supporting cross-curricular learning in addition to reading, writing and spelling skills.
- *Dyslexia in Secondary School: A Practical Handbook for Teachers, Parents and Students* (2004), by Jenny Cogan and Mary Flecker (Wiley).
- A practical guide to helping learners with numeracy difficulties: *The Trouble with Maths* (2020), by Steve Chinn (Routledge).

Being dyslexic:

- Take opportunities to share and talk about what it means to be dyslexic.
- *The Illustrated Guide to Dyslexia and Its Amazing People* (2018), by Kate Power and Kathy Iwanczak Forsyth (Jessica Kingsley Publishers).
- *Dyslexia is My Superpower (Most of the Time)* (2017) by Margaret Rooke (Jessica Kingsley Publishers).
- *The Self-Help Guide for Teens with Dyslexia* (2015), by Alais Winton (Jessica Kingsley Publishers).
- The British Dyslexia Association offers resources, support and advice to students and parents: www.bdadyslexia.org.uk/dyslexia.
- See online resource: https://thecodpast.org.

Fostering metacognition:

- Take opportunities to discuss how our brains work and how to learn. Many study skills publications incorporate this in specific chapters.
- *Blame My Brain: The Amazing Teenage Brain Revealed* (2013), by Nicola Morgan (Walker Books).

Access auditory and visual sources of information, such as podcasts, video clips and apps, as an accessible way of furthering interests:

- *You're Dead to Me* podcast from the makers of *Horrible Histories* – BBC Podcasts.
- BBC Bitesize videos available for different key stages: www.bbc.co.uk/bitesize and www.bbc.co.uk/teach/class-clips.
- BrainPop app and videos: www.brainpop.com.
- The British Library has a range of online teaching materials for primary and secondary learners: www.bl.uk/teaching-resources.
- *The Codpast* – for students and adults with dyslexia: https://thecodpast.org.
- The BDA has a range of videos, social media platforms and website resources for supporting young adults, parents and carers: www.youtube.com/watch?v=11r7CFlK2sc and www.bdadyslexia.org.uk.

Assistive technology and software

Accessibility options on the tablet or computer:

- Microsoft Word: there are a number of features built into Word. The most important are Dictate and Immersive Reader. Click the microphone labelled 'Dictate' in the top right-hand corner of the screen. It only works if wifi is on. It can type in English and other languages. Available in Office 365, 2016 and 2019: www.microsoft.com/en-gb/education/products/learning-tools. This has guidance and features for learners with dyslexia. For the Immersive Reader, select the view tab and then select 'Immersive Reader'. Ease of Access on Windows 10: www.thewindowsclub.com/ease-access-settings-windows-10. This will provide options such as making text larger, changing the background colour, and so on.
- Natural Reader App has a speech reader and is free.
- Google Drive: having a Google account provides access to a range of useful apps and organization tools, such as Google Docs, Sheets, Classroom and Calendar. Google Docs contains free voice typing software, a read aloud function and other accessibility functions. It can be accessed across mobile devices and PCs.
- Apple apps: Claro Scan Pen: a text-to-speech tool. It takes a picture of the text, and it reads it all back to you. More cost effective than a reading pen. You can highlight different parts of the text, and it will be read aloud.
- Other Claro apps are helpful, including Claro Speak Plus and Claro PDF.
  - Voice Dream: a text-to-speech reader for e-readers and PDF documents.
  - Glean Notes: can replay spoken notes. You can use this function to record homework tasks orally and play back sections of a lesson.
  - WordTalk: a free app that includes a talking spellchecker.

Further software and apps to help with writing:

- Voice recorder apps are useful for recording verbal ideas for a written task so that it can be replayed to help with planning and writing. Talking Tins.
- Speech-to-text software: Dragon Dictate – available on iPad, iPhone and computer.
- Crick Software: Clicker 8 and ClickerDocs Plus.
- Popplet: A mind mapping app.

Touch-typing programmes:

- BBC Dance Mat – free.
- Touch Type Read and Spell.
- English Type Junior/Senior: https://englishtype.com.
- Nessy Fingers: www.nessy.com/en-gb/product/nessy-fingers-home.

Further links to dyslexia-friendly ICT, software and apps:

- CALL Scotland: an excellent resource of dyslexia-friendly technology, accessibility functions and apps: www.callscotland.org.uk.
- AccessAbility Solutions – Myles Pilling: https://aas123.com.
- British Dyslexia Association Technology: https://bdatech.org.

Collaborate:

- Form links with the ICT department to develop use of assistive technology and software. Workshops and support with different approaches can benefit learners, teachers and parents with using assistive technology effectively and keeping up to date with new programmes.

Please note that the resources and materials presented in this chapter complement the materials on the Level 5 e-learning site, and materials are constantly being updated. Accessing short courses, conferences and online webinars and discussion forums can be a great way to remain current and find new resources and ideas for specialist teaching.

Additional links and resources

Useful companies:

- Crossbow Education for a range of dyslexia resources: www.crossboweducation.com.
- SMARTKids for multisensory resources and programmes for all aspects of literacy development: www.smartkids.co.uk.
- LDA Learning: www.ldalearning.com.
- ROMPA for sensory-based resources: www.rompa.com.
- Jessica Kingsley Publishers: https://uk.jkp.com.
- Links to resources to support speech and language development: https://ican.org.uk/i-cans-talking-point/professionals/tct-resources.
- *Brooks's What Works for Literacy Difficulties? The Effectiveness of Intervention Schemes*, sixth edition (2020), by Gary Lavan and Joel Talcott (The School Psychology Service). This is a reference text where you can look up specific intervention programmes and access evidence of their effectiveness.

Useful websites:

- The BDA: www.bdadyslexia.org.uk. The BDA has an online shop with free webinars and books.
- Dyslexia Action/Guild has a useful online shop, and membership with the Dyslexia Guild provides access to a library of dyslexia reading material: https://dyslexiaguild.org.uk and https://dyslexiaaction.org.uk.
- SpLD Trust: www.thedyslexia-spldtrust.org.uk.
- Reading Rockets: www.readingrockets.org.
- PATOSS has a resources section: www.patoss-dyslexia.org/Resources.
- Helen Arkell has an online shop: https://helenarkell.org.uk/shop.

BDA publications:

- *Dyslexia in Education: A Guide for Teachers and Teaching Assistants* (2012), by Sue Thurtle.
- *Dyslexia and Useful Technology* (2012), edited by E.A. Draffan.
- *The Dyslexia Friendly Schools Good Practice Guide* (2018), second edition, by Linda Eastapp and Joanne Gregory.

Chapter 13

Evaluation of Teaching

LYNN LOVELL

This chapter aims to enable you to:

- know when and how to evaluate learning
- understand the benefits of reflective practice
- plan next steps to ensure learner progress
- plan next steps for yourself as an educator.

The duration of one-to-one or small group teaching can depend on many factors, including the learner's needs, timetabling and resources. Regardless of this, at regular intervals and at the end of teaching, you will want to review the learner's development to see how far they have progressed and what support they may need next. Teachers and support staff should also reflect on their own practice, identifying good practice and any gaps in their knowledge that they may like to develop.

Throughout the sessions, it is likely that you will have been monitoring the learner's progress against the SMART targets set. For one-to-one work, you will want to evaluate this each lesson, halfway through teaching and at the end of teaching. Group and class work may be evaluated less frequently than every lesson (and less formally), but educators should always be informally monitoring learning and adjusting teaching and resources as appropriate.

When completing any regular evaluation, the following questions should be addressed:

- Did they achieve the target? This may include the degree to which the target was achieved, such as three out of five words spelt correctly.
- Why/why not? The reasons for success or otherwise. These reasons may be

complex and wide ranging, from concentration difficulties to inability to access the tools required and lack of practice at home. Alternatively, they may have been successful due to good effort, as an example.

- What would you do differently? This leads on from the previous question and asks you to evaluate your practice. You may need to change your teaching approach, change class groupings or provide assistive tools. You may need to use different multisensory approaches, such as including out-of-seat activities for those who struggle with concentration.
- How will you change the target to ensure it is met or to create further challenge? You may need to make the target more achievable if they are struggling, as we do not want to damage confidence. Alternatively, you may want to make it more challenging if they are succeeding with little effort.

This is the case where we are continuing teaching and thus can continue to plan next steps for our learners. Where the evaluation comes at the end of teaching sessions, you will want to consider what needs to be done to ensure continued success within the classroom setting.

Sometimes evaluations can seem like a chore, and the value of them can be hard to recognize. However, they are essential in many settings. Evaluations form part of a reflective cycle, both on the progress of your learners and your own progress as a practitioner. They are a celebration of success, a chance to recognize the causes of this success and to continue to grow and develop. They are an important part of teaching and learning and crucial for a learner's achievement. If we do not recognize that one approach is not working or that a target is not appropriate, we risk restricting the learner's progress, which is the opposite of what we want to achieve. Evaluations, therefore, are always worth the time and effort.

Evaluations can also be used to inform future teaching. If we recognize that an approach, strategy or resource has been successful for some learners, we may want to use this again. We may also want to consider any factors that affected the teaching session overall and plan how to avoid or reduce the impact of these as far as possible.

From evaluation of progress, there are several ways forward:

- Continue the intervention to achieve the set targets.
- Continue with new targets.
- Discontinue the intervention.

If continuing the intervention with the same targets, you will need to make sure that you have considered why the learner did not achieve the targets and if the current approach is working. Self-reflection and listening to the learner's views will help you to determine which methods are useful and which may need adjusting to be more useful. For example:

- The learner is still unable to spell a range of high-frequency words. In discussion with the learner, you discover that they can retain them in the short term but not in the long term. You therefore decide to plan activities every three sessions to review this in detail. It would help if this were through a fun activity, such as an online game. You may also decide to contact the teacher or parent for additional revision opportunities to be shared.

If you choose to continue with new targets, you will need to ensure that you are clear about which targets have been mastered and the next steps to build on these skills using a cumulative approach. We should not teach skills in isolation – we need to consider how the learner can use what they have already learnt and continue from there, linking previous learning to new learning. Learners with dyslexia often do not automatically identify links between information. For example, if a learner can spell the suffix '-ing', this will help them to spell words with that suffix, such as 'meeting' and 'helping'. They may need to be explicitly taught to make these links. For example:

- The learner knows the suffix '-ing', which they write on a card. They may write on a whiteboard all the words they have currently learnt with the suffix '-ing'. The next step is to introduce a new root word through multisensory teaching and then ask the learner to place this on a card. This card can then be matched to their '-ing' card to create further words. Such approaches help links to be made without overwhelming the learner. They know part of the word already and thus only need to learn the root, reducing the demand on memory.

At the end of teaching, you may want to carry out a session where you check whether the targets have indeed been met. This may involve asking the learner to spell the regular and irregular words learnt, name sounds, create a mind map, and so on. It is important that you have a really clear picture of the individual's progress, against what you planned/expected them to gain, so you will want to match such assessment to their SMART targets.

It is also advisable to carry out tests of single-word reading and spelling to see if these skills have improved since the intervention began, as it is likely that the overall aim of your support was to improve literacy skills (and sometimes numeracy skills). Depending on the needs of the learner at the start of the programme, you may want to see how many sounds and letters they are able to name securely or what their reading fluency or writing is like – it really depends on the individual.

If the learner has made suitable progress and the decision is to discontinue the intervention, it will be important to ensure continuity of support for them. You will ideally have already planned the intervention so that the learner is gaining transferable skills and all learning is linked to the classroom and to wider life. You will have liaised with the class teacher to ensure that learning in the intervention allows for teaching of key skills and consolidation of knowledge. The step at the end of the intervention then is to liaise with the teacher again to share information and ideas for the ongoing support of that learner. This may include discussing effective approaches that benefit the learner or going over the key targets and the extent to which they were met.

You will need to plan how these can be adjusted to be accommodated within the classroom setting and tap into any good practice shared.

The teacher or support staff who carried out the intervention may want to provide some tools to support the learner in using the skills they have learnt. For example, they could:

- provide keywords on a keyring or bookmark and encourage the learner to ensure they spell them correctly at every opportunity
- create resources in one-to-one time to support learning back in the classroom, such as a mind map or pictorial representations to help remember formulas in maths
- ensure that the learner is confident in using strategies and tools in the classroom, such as a spellchecker or scanning pen
- discuss how the learner learns best and show them how they can apply this independently in the classroom.

It is also important to ensure that the results of intervention and next steps are discussed and planned with parents. Ideally, as you have liaised with teachers throughout the intervention process, you should also have been in close contact with parents. Learners with dyslexia need as much repetition and overlearning as possible, and parents will often be key partners in ensuring that skills are practised outside the classroom and that this is ongoing. As such, they will be fully involved in the continued support of the learner in the home setting and will want to know of any strategies and approaches that may be helpful at home or they may share other ideas that can support the learner at school.

It is a good idea, where possible, for all parties to review how the learner is getting on in the classroom after a period of time and to determine if any additional support is required and what form this support may take. Again, this is part of a reflective cycle that aims to ensure the most positive outcome possible.

Even if the above practices have taken place, there will still be key things that teachers may want to consider following intervention:

- The learner may lack confidence in applying the skills they have gained in the classroom, particularly where this may be different from their peers. The teacher may need to encourage the use of the skill, teaching it to others in the classroom so that it becomes part of normal practice. As an example, they may want all pupils to start a personal dictionary of words that they struggle with so that these can be referred to when writing.
- Do not assume that the individual will retain the skills learnt. This is something that learners with dyslexia struggle with due to poor memory, difficulty with automaticity and so on. Skills are likely to need continuous revision. It can help to ask the individual to recall how they learnt these skills as this can prompt memory.
- The learner may revert to previous habits, such as over-relying on in-class support or trying to 'hide' within the classroom so that difficulties are not as evident. In this case, they should be encouraged to use the tools they have gained and work towards greater independence.
- The learner may lack confidence in continuing without the support they had previously and may need reminding of their strengths and how to utilize these. Our eventual aim is for the learner to develop strong metacognitive skills and a sense of autonomy.

As practitioners, we want the best for all of our students and need to manage these against the numerous competing demands on our time and practice. Supporting learners before, during and after intervention is an important aspect of what we do and is part of our overall role of ensuring the progress of all pupils. As part of this, we may need to develop our practice, and it is likely that we will need to do so regularly throughout our time working with learners. There are a number of options to facilitate this:

- Formal training: You may choose to take a short course in person or online, or you may want to gain more formal qualifications such as a Level 3/4/5/7 course in dyslexia.
- Informal training: You may want to shadow a colleague or have a one-to-one session with the school SENCO or equivalent. The SENCO or equivalent could also provide whole-school/college training.

- Sharing good practice: The most accessible people will be colleagues within your settings or in a wider network such as a federation of schools. In-service training days can be an opportunity for professionals to get together and discuss key topics. Alternatively, consider setting up a forum for staff to share ideas.
- Webinars: You could attend a free or paid-for webinar on a topic of interest or one that addresses a gap in your knowledge. Many charities and other organizations run such webinars.
- Forums: There are also online forums that can be joined in order to ask questions of others and to share best practice.
- Books/online sources: There are many books on the topic of teaching and learning and dyslexia that you may want to read to develop your knowledge. There are also online sources such as web pages or video platforms where professionals share good practice and where experts in the field often share their knowledge and experience for no cost.

The next chapter will consider a whole-school approach to supporting those with dyslexia and literacy difficulties by outlining dyslexia-friendly schools good practice and how to achieve this.

Transition from one-to-one work to classroom

The best one-to-one work follows the following principles:

- Uses a well-founded intervention that targets needs.
- Focuses on SMART targets in their IEP/provision map.
- Is multisensory, cumulative and structured, with opportunities for overlearning.
- Ensures the learning is applied back into the classroom.
- Focuses on pre-teaching/consolidation from classwork.

Examples of ensuring learning is linked to work in the classroom

- Work alongside the class teacher to agree areas that require pre-teaching, such as technical vocabulary that is going to come up in a science lesson or pre-teaching a maths concept.
- Consolidate classwork with additional skill practice using concrete/pictorial resources to support and deepen understanding.
- Ensure that any high-frequency words being targeted in one-to-one spelling work

are focused on in the classroom. Provide these on a keyring or bookmark and encourage learners to ensure they spell them correctly at every opportunity.

- Create resources in one-to-one time to support learning back in the classroom, such as a mind map and pictorial representations to help remember formulas in maths.
- Discuss how the learner learns best and show them how they can apply this independently in the classroom.

Key takeaways from this chapter

- Evaluation is key to ensuring the progress of learners and educators.
- Learners are more likely to continue to progress if all parties work together to practise and consolidate key skills and to encourage independence.
- Support for learners will require us to maintain our ongoing professional development, and this can be achieved through a range of channels.

Chapter 14

Dyslexia-Friendly Practice

ALISON FAIRFAX

A dyslexia-friendly organization is one that has developed strategies to support those with dyslexia and put in place strategies to support their learning. Becoming a dyslexia-friendly organization requires the involvement and commitment of all those working there. It requires a review of the organization's approaches to teaching and learning, monitoring and assessment, differentiation and inclusion across the range of ability and need.

Organizations can be dyslexia friendly without working towards an award. However, many choose the award route as recognition and celebration of their practice. This can be done via the BDA, or alternatively there are some local authorities who run their own awards. Local authorities will usually hold the BDA award themselves to ensure they are promoting best practice.

The BDA Dyslexia Friendly Quality Mark provides a framework of support and understanding to ensure that everyone within an organization understands the needs of the dyslexic individual and that they provide appropriate support strategies and resources. The Quality Mark philosophy is that changing practice to accommodate dyslexic individuals results in good practice for everyone.

This award is only issued to organizations that can demonstrate that they provide high-quality education and/or practice for dyslexic individuals. Above all, holding the BDA Dyslexia Friendly Quality Mark is a positive statement that lets everyone know that the organization is a good place for dyslexic individuals.

In addition, the BDA Dyslexia Friendly Quality Mark may help to demonstrate a setting's commitment to criteria that are part of the Education Inspection Framework, such as the need for school leaders to demonstrate that they are actively promoting the welfare of learners (OFSTED, 2019). The Quality Mark can also help to demonstrate that a school adheres to the SENDCO vision that all teaching and support staff should be trained and have awareness of quality teaching for students with special educational needs (The Dyslexia-SpLD Trust, n.d.).

The BDA Dyslexia Friendly Quality Mark is offered to the following organizations and institutions:

- Organizations (including organizations in Northern Ireland)
- Further education (FE)
- Higher education (HE)
- Children and young people's services
- Post-16 training providers
- Youth offending teams and institutions.

All organizations that have achieved the BDA Dyslexia Friendly Quality Mark are included on the register of maintained sector organizations at CReSTeD (Council for the Registration of Schools Teaching Dyslexic Pupils). CReSTeD maintains a register of schools and teaching centres that meet its criteria for the teaching of pupils with SpLDs. It acts as a source of names for educational establishments that parents can use as their first step towards making a placement decision. The majority of schools on the register are mainstream schools that are also able to give excellent help to pupils with SpLDs – dyslexia and also, when combined with dyslexia, dyscalculia, dyspraxia, ADD and pragmatic and semantic language difficulties. In addition, it includes teaching centres where children can find additional support outside and/or in addition to their day-to-day schooling.

Why dyslexia friendly?

We know through research that at least 10% of the UK population carries the genetic background that makes them predisposed to SpLDs. Typically, we see about 4% with very serious issues and another 6% with mild to moderate difficulties. When placing this in the organization context, that will equate to approximately three individuals in a class of 30. A dyslexia-friendly approach meets the needs of legislative obligations to support the needs of SEND learners and other stakeholders in ensuring we are making 'reasonable adjustments' to support learners with dyslexia (British Dyslexia Association, 2020).

The BDA Dyslexia Friendly Quality Mark for educational settings has been in existence for approximately 15 years. It first came into being through the work of the BDA alongside

Neil MacKay, a dyslexia specialist with extensive teaching experience and knowledge of working with dyslexic individuals (British Dyslexia Association, 2018).

A 'wish list' of standards was constructed, and once agreed, they were issued out to 'pilot' organizations across the country. The key questions are: did they present a challenge, did they achieve the required changes to working practice and were they realistic and achievable? Feedback from the pilot was collated before a final, polished version of the standards was published and issued to organizations across the country.

The mission statement of the Quality Mark is for organizations 'to promote excellent practice by the organization as it carries out its role of supporting and challenging its staff to improve accessibility for more learners'. There are four standards to evidence. Under the leadership and management standard, organizations need to evidence that pupils with dyslexia are considered and catered for within whole-organization documents and policies so that everyone in the organization knows how to provide effective support. As well as updating policies, organizations will often tackle this by producing a dyslexia handbook or information sheet giving useful information such as a definition of dyslexia, signs and indicators, what to do if you suspect a child in your class is dyslexic and useful strategies to support teaching and learning.

The second area to consider is the learner's experience with regard to the quality of learning within the organization or institution. Staff ask learners if the way they are being taught helps their dyslexia or if there are other strategies that could be employed to support the individual more effectively. Supportive strategies for learners with dyslexia include the following:

- Multisensory teaching and learning.
- Pupils being taught using a range of learning methods such as mind mapping.
- Recording learning using a range of formats such as bullet points, storyboards and flow charts.
- Provision for one-to-one and small group teaching.
- Opportunities to use a scribe to record written work.
- Use made of recording devices such as dictaphones, Talking Tins and other such software.

The next area to consider is whether the climate for learning is dyslexia friendly. Is diversity valued throughout the organization via assemblies and displays? What reward systems are in place? Is praise for effort and achievement given in all areas, not simply academic ones? Does the organization or institution promote strengths, and what does the organization do to promote self-esteem? Does the organization provide opportunities for success away from academic activities and opportunities for individuals to share their successes beyond the organization?

The final area to reflect on is the organization's relationship with parents, carers, governors and any other stakeholders. How does the organization involve parents in planning provision for the child?

What meetings are arranged with parents, and how often do they take place? What information is sent home to parents? What is the format? Is it dyslexia friendly? Have any workshops been run for parents to understand how to support their dyslexic child/young person at home? What are the procedures for parents to raise a concern? Is there an open-door policy?

Organizations begin their journey to achieving dyslexia-friendly status by carrying out an audit of their current practice. Course providers who wish their candidates to develop a well-rounded and detailed knowledge of dyslexia and good practice may ask you to carry out such an audit in order to recognize dyslexia-friendly practice in your own setting with the aim of developing this if necessary. For the BDA award, organizations complete an audit document that assesses whether they meet the standards or whether more development needs to take place in a particular area.

They will need to assess which of the following categories they fit into for each standard:

- Focusing – recognizing areas for development.
- Developing – work is taking place in this area.
- Established – this is happening (standard has been achieved).
- Enhancing – additional work is being done above that is required by the standard.

Some organizations have found it useful to issue the audit to each department or year group as an activity during staff training days, asking staff members to give their opinions as to where they feel they score against the audit and to explain why. This demonstrates a 'whole organization' approach to achieving the award; becoming dyslexia friendly is not the responsibility of just one person in the organization – everyone has a part to play in achieving it.

Following the audit, the Action Plan has to be completed to address those areas in the 'Focusing' or 'Developing' categories, ensuring that targets are SMART: specific, measurable, achievable, relevant and time bound.

The BDA is able to offer a full support service in areas identified as needing development. This can include training for teachers in inclusive classroom strategies, for parents and governors on basic dyslexia awareness, specialist training in screening and identification, and teaching literacy to dyslexic individuals. Training can be tailored to meet individual organizations' needs. Alternatively, training delivered by the SENCO, a local authority or another approved training provider will be accepted as part of the award.

The organization will then work on areas of the Action Plan to ensure that by the end of the two years their practice is established or enhanced. They will then be ready to become a dyslexia-friendly organization and be verified to be considered for the award if they are working towards it.

A typical journey over the two-year completion period would include the following:

- Completing the Audit and Action Plan.
- Ensuring that the Organization Development Plan shows dyslexia as a focus.
- Ensuring that the SEN Action Plan shows the specific actions towards dyslexia-friendly provision.
- Providing training to whole-organization staff, and a staff handbook outlining strategies for identification and support.
- Carrying out assemblies focusing on dyslexia awareness.
- Holding parents' information evenings, coffee mornings, presentations.
- The SENCO working alongside the SEN governor to ensure that they are aware of the organization's desire to become dyslexia friendly.
- Making the SEN information report available on the organization website, outlining how the organization assesses and identifies pupils with dyslexia and how it meets their needs.
- Making organization policies available online and showing how learners with dyslexia are supported via the SEN policy, separate dyslexia policy, teaching and learning and marking policies.
- Working on at least two case studies to show the learning journey for those pupils over at least a year and how the organization has responded and supported their needs.

These are the standards (British Dyslexia Association, 2019) that require evidencing in order to become a BDA dyslexia-friendly organization and achieve the award, as well as the suggested evidence that should be provided:

<table>
<tr><th colspan="2">Standard 1: Leadership and management</th></tr>
<tr><td>1.1</td><td>The organization conducts a self-audit of its provision for dyslexic pupils and uses this to inform the Organization Development Plan and SEN Action Plan.

These plans should show that:

• supporting dyslexic pupils is a priority area for the organization
• there are clear targets for support for dyslexic pupils
• the senior leadership team supports dyslexia-related continuous professional development (CPD) for all staff
• resources (financial, staffing, time) are allocated to dyslexia and managed effectively
• there are clear roles and responsibilities for provision, and accountabilities are understood.

Evidence:

• Completed Organization Audit and Action Plan
• Organization Development Plan
• SEN Action Plan</td></tr>
<tr><td>1.2</td><td>Whole-organization policies show how the organization meets the needs of pupils with dyslexia. The key principles of the SEND Policy are known to all staff.

Evidence – key policies should be available on the organization website, including:

• SEND Policy consistent with the SEND Code of Practice 2014
• Dyslexia Friendly Policy
• Teaching and Learning Policy
• Marking Policy
• Exam Access Arrangements Policy</td></tr>
<tr><td>1.3</td><td>The board of governors encourages a culture of high aspirations for all learners. All governors are aware of the challenges faced by dyslexic pupils. The governor with responsibility for SEND has enhanced knowledge and understanding of dyslexia and meets SENCO regularly to review dyslexia-friendly provision and monitor progress.

Evidence:

• Annual SEND Report to Governors
• Discussion with governor with responsibility for SEND during verification visit</td></tr>
<tr><td>1.4</td><td>Quantitative and qualitative data indicates the impact of dyslexia-friendly practice.

Evidence:

• Data presented in e.g. Annual SEND Report to Governors indicates attainment and progress levels of pupils with dyslexia and wider outcomes such as attendance and improvement in self-esteem of pupils. Internal data is compared with external sources of information to challenge improvements to provision.</td></tr>
</table>

<table>
<tr><th colspan="2">Standard 2: Quality of learning</th></tr>
<tr><td>2.1</td><td>A plan of ongoing in-service training is in place, including:

• Whole-organization awareness – all staff have a working knowledge of indicators of dyslexia, classroom strategies, evidence-based programmes of support and when to refer for extra support
• New staff receive awareness training and guidance
• Supply staff are provided with guidelines on dyslexia-friendly teaching

Evidence:

• PowerPoint slides of training delivered or notes from training provider
• Interviews with members of teaching staff during visit</td></tr>
<tr><td>2.2</td><td>Staff with specific responsibilities (e.g. SENCO) have dyslexia expertise gained through appropriate training, e.g. Level 5 (specialist teacher) or Level 7 (specialist teacher and assessor), or evidence of how this expertise is available within an academy or local authority.

Evidence:

• Certificates of appropriate qualifications or enrolment on suitable training</td></tr>
<tr><td>2.3</td><td>Systems of assessment are in place to identify pupils with literacy difficulties. Information is shared to all staff, including supply teachers, through pupil profiles or similar, which include individual teaching and learning strategies. Pupils' progress and targets are closely monitored and evaluated regularly. Adjustments are made to support provision where necessary.

Evidence:

• Anonymized case studies/pupil profiles of two pupils showing how needs have been identified and supported and the success of interventions evaluated</td></tr>
<tr><td>2.4</td><td>Classrooms conform to the BDA Dyslexia Friendly Classroom Checklist.

Evidence:

• SENCO has completed BDA Dyslexia Friendly Classroom Checklist with teachers and made changes where necessary
• Lesson observation during verification visit</td></tr>
<tr><td>2.5</td><td>Teachers across all curriculum subjects use multisensory teaching approaches; teaching assistants use multisensory strategies to support pupils in the classroom. There are opportunities for collaborative learning and peer support.

Evidence:

• Completed BDA Dyslexia Friendly Classroom Checklist
• Lesson observation during verification visit</td></tr>
</table>

2.6	Pupils are taught a range of planning methods, e.g. mind mapping, and can record their work in a variety of ways (e.g. bullet points, storyboard, flow chart, scribed, using a laptop or speech recognition software). Evidence: • Work scrutiny during verification visit
2.7	The marking policy ensures pupils are assessed on the basis of their knowledge (rather than spelling). Marking should be for success and for identifying development and improvement points. Evidence: • Marking policy on website • Work scrutiny during verification visit
2.8	There is provision for one-to-one and small group teaching and specialist support using multisensory teaching methods. Appropriate, evidence-based intervention programmes are implemented and their success evaluated. Evidence: • Small group observation during verification visit • The effectiveness of interventions is evaluated in SEN Action Plan
2.9	Homework is provided on separate sheets, scribed into homework diaries or recorded on a phone. Pupils are offered a choice of recording method. Evidence: • Discussion with pupils and parents during verification visit
2.10	Appropriate systems are in place to make reasonable adjustments in examinations and organization tests. Assessment and application to the Joint Council for Qualifications (JCQ) is made in good time so that pupils are taught how to use the time and any resources appropriately. Evidence: • Examination Access Arrangements Policy on website

<table>
<tr><th colspan="2">Standard 3: Creating a climate for learning</th></tr>
<tr><td>3.1</td><td>The organization works in partnership with pupils to:

• help pupils to understand their dyslexia and value their achievements
• promote a ‘can do’ culture
• assist pupils in identifying their own learning strategies
• involve pupils in planning their own learning targets
• support with emotional and behavioural issues.

Evidence:

• Discussion with pupils during verification visit</td></tr>
<tr><td>3.2</td><td>Pupils’ self-esteem is promoted through:

• valuing the individual and their diversity
• praise for effort and achievement in all areas
• having high expectations for those with dyslexia
• developing resilience and resourcefulness
• promoting strengths and providing opportunities for success
• providing a stress-free learning environment.

Evidence:

• Discussion with pupils during verification visit</td></tr>
<tr><td>3.3</td><td>Effective measures are in place to deal with harassment or bullying related to SEND. The organization actively raises awareness of dyslexia and SEND among peers and promotes positive attitudes towards diversity.

Evidence:

• PowerPoint of assembly to raise awareness
• Discussion with pupils during verification visit</td></tr>
</table>

Standard 4: Partnership with parents/carers	
4.1	Governors and senior leadership team seek meaningful involvement from stakeholders, including learners with SEND and their families and carers, and use this to reflect critically on progress and outcomes. Evidence: • Organization Development Plan shows involvement from stakeholders
4.2	Parents are aware of how the organization meets the SEN of their children. They are aware of the ways in which they can contact the organization and are aware of complaints procedures. Evidence: • SEN Information Report is on organization website and is regularly updated
4.3	The organization has a process in place for notifying parents of concerns at an early stage and listens actively to the concerns of parents. The organization actively involves parents in planning provision for their child, which is regularly reviewed with parents. Evidence: • SEN Information Report • Discussion with parents during verification visit
4.4	The organization runs parents' workshops for parents to understand dyslexia and the way in which the organization supports their child's learning and how they can support their child at home. Evidence: • PowerPoint slides of training offered
4.5	The organization makes parents aware of the community-based support available in the local offer. Evidence: • SEN Information Report on organization website

In summary, dyslexia-friendly organizations are effective, proactive, empowering, inclusive and value-adding organizations that promote excellent practice in supporting and challenging their staff to improve accessibility for learners. Dyslexia-friendly practice is essentially good teaching practice, and any adjustments that are put in place for this group of learners are unlikely to affect any other learner.

References

BDA (n.d.) *Dyslexia Friendly Quality Mark for Individual Organizations.* Available at: www.bdadyslexia.org.uk/services/dyslexia-friendly-awards/dyslexia-friendly-quality-mark-awards [Accessed 30 May 2022].

BDA (2018) *Dyslexia Friendly Good Practice,* second edition. Dartford: Diamond Colour Print Limited.

BDA (2020) *British Dyslexia Association.* Available at: www.bdadyslexia.org.uk [Accessed 9 November 2020].

OFSTED (2019) *The Education Inspection Framework.* Available at: www.gov.uk/government/publications/education-inspection-framework [Accessed 13 November 2020].

The Dyslexia-SpLD Trust (n.d.) *Every Teacher is a Teacher of SEN Resources.* Available at: www.thedyslexia-spldtrust.org.uk/4/resources/2/schools-and-local-authorities/381/every-teacher-is-a-teacher-of-sen-resources/#:~:text=%27Every%20Teacher%20is%20a%20Teacher%20of%20SEN%27%20resources,support%20staff%20in%20working%20with%20students%20with%20SEN [Accessed 13 November 2020].

Subject Index

A-levels 166
access courses 167
additions (in reading) 68
adjustments *see* classroom adjustments
affixes 76
alphabet
  resources for teaching 196–7
  skills 75, 99–100, 117
  teaching the 150–1
alphabetic principle 60
amplitude modulations 36
anxiety 45
assessment/screening
  baseline setting 107–8, 109
  building picture of learner from 110–3
  classroom observation 112–3
  individual learners 113–4
  older learners' history of 162–4
  parent/carer information 109, 111–2
  of phonics skills 115
  pupil voice in 112
  purpose of 106–7
  questionnaire design 111
  of reading 115–8
  recommendations from 118–9
  reporting results 118–21
  of spelling 116
  strengths identification 118–9
  teacher information 111
  timeframe for 113
  of whole classes 107–10
  of writing 116–7
assistive technology/software 207–8
asynchrony phenomenon 148–9
attention deficit hyperactivity
    disorder (ADHD) 46–8
auditory processing difficulties 22–3
autism spectrum disorder (ASD) 48–50

behavioural indicators (of anxiety) 45
Berlin, Rudolf 29
'bottom-up' approach 61

central executive 37, 125–6
cerebellar theory 33–5, 149
chunking information 127
classroom adjustments
  alphabet skills 99–100
  focus and concentration 96–7
  giving instructions 93–4
  memory 97
  one-to-one targeted intervention
      98–9, 180–4, 186–8
  oral language learning environment 93–4
  organization skills 98
  overview 90–3
  phonics programmes 100–1
  phonological skills development 96
  quality-first teaching guidelines 92
  reading 94
  reading comprehension 101
  spelling 94–5
  study skills 101
  teaching methodology 102, 185
  writing 95–6, 101
classroom observation 112–3
co-occurring developmental disorders 43–5
components/composites 126–7
concentration difficulties
  classroom adjustments 96–7
  overview 23
connectionist model of reading 62
Conquering Literacy Programme 148
conscious compensation hypothesis 130

context processor 62
continuity of support 214
CReSTeD register 220
cumulative approach to teaching 126–8

definitions of dyslexia
  BDA 20
  Rose Report 19
development coordination disorder (DCD) 55–7
developmental language disorder (DLD) 50–3
Dispel Project 24
double deficit theory 33
doubling rule 155
dual cascaded model of reading 62–3
dyscalculia 53–5
dyslexia (definitions) 19–20
Dyslexia Friendly Quality Mark
  Action Plan 222–3
  audit for 222
  history of 220–1
  mission statement 221
  overview 219–20
  register of organizations 220
  standards of 221–2, 224–8
Dyslexia Friendly Schools Good Practice Guide 91
dyspraxia 55–7

echolalia 49
employment *see* workplace
English written system (history) 60
environmental factors 31
episodic buffer 37–8, 126
etymology 199–200
evaluation of teaching 211–7
evolutionary advantage (dyslexia as) 25
executive function 46

feedback from learners 112, 139–41
'flossy' (FLS) rule 155
fluency 20
focus 96–7
forgetting (rate of) 130, 143
functional skills 165
further education (FE)
  expectations of 165–6
  reading requirements 169–70
  referencing sources 172
  time management 172
  writing in 171–2

games *see* resources
genetic factors 38–9
graphemes 71, 72–3
grapheme–phoneme correspondence
    see phonics (GPC)
grapho/phonic cueing system 67–8
group work 184–5, 189
guessing (while reading) 61–2, 169

handwriting 203–4
hereditary factors 38–9
hesitations 68
'Hickey' cards 147–8
higher education (HE)
  expectations at 167
  reading requirements 169–70
  referencing sources 172
  time management at 172
  writing in 171–2
history of dyslexia 29–30
hyper-/hypo-sensitivity 49–50

ICT
  alphabet skills 196
  overview 207–8
  phonics 198
  phonological awareness 195
  reading 201
  writing 204
instructions (giving) 93–4
intellectual ability (definition) 21–2
interests (learners') 66, 142–3

Kussmaul, Adolf 29

language comprehension 64
learned helplessness 136
learner voice 112, 139–41
lesson overview 149–50
lexical routes 62–3
lexical-semantic process 63
locus of control 136
lower (orthographic) circuit 60

magnocellular theory 35–6, 148
maths difficulties 53–5
Matthew effect 65, 157
meaning processor 62
memory
  classroom adjustments 97
  forgetting (rate of) 130
  verbal 21
  see also working memory
mental calculation difficulties 23

mental health difficulties 45
mentors 141
metacognition
  importance of 98
  teaching 131–2, 137–9
miscue analysis 66, 67
mispronunciation 63–4
morpheme 71
morphemic awareness 71, 76
morphology 156, 199–200
morphonology 64
motor coordination difficulties 23
multiple deficit model 39–40
multisensory teaching 123–6

Neurodiverse Voices: Opening Doors to Employment report 24–5
neurodiversity (concept of) 44
non-lexical route 63

observation (classroom) 112–3
offending behaviour link 24, 25
older learners
  access courses 167
  assessment history 162–4
  in the classroom 189–90
  issues for 161–2
  multisensory approaches 174
  needs of 164–5
  one-to-one work 186–8
  reading 168–70
  small group work 189
  study skills issues 168–72
  teaching approaches 173
  understanding the experiences of 163–4
  writing 170–2
  see also further education (FE); higher education (HE)
omissions (while reading) 68
one-to-one targeted intervention 98–9, 180–4, 186–8
online searching (effective) 170
oral language
  learning environment 93–4
  testing 117–8
organization difficulties 23–4, 98, 175–6
orthographic awareness 71
orthographic (lower) circuit 60
orthographic processor 62
orthography 71
Orton Gillingham Approach 148
overlearning 129–31

parents/carers
  information from 109, 111–2
  involvement of 214
phonemes 71, 72–3
phonic cueing system 67–8
phonically irregular words 157
phonics (GPC)
  assessment/screening 115
  'bottom-up' approach 61
  definition 71
  order of introducing 152–5
  resources for 197–8
  rules 63–4
phonics programmes 100–1
phonological awareness
  definition 20–1, 71
  difficulties 66, 81–2
  importance of 74
  resources for 194–5
  skills 100
  testing 117
  training in 151–5
phonological deficit theory 31–3, 148
phonological loop 37, 126
phonological skills 75, 96
phonological (upper) circuit 60
plenary 158
prevalence of dyslexia 24, 25, 220
prison system population 24–5
pronunciation 63–4
proofreading skills 172
prosody 36
pupil voice 112, 139–41

Quality Mark *see* Dyslexia Friendly Quality Mark
quality-first teaching *see* classroom adjustments
questionnaire design 111

rapid automatized naming (RAN) 149
reading
  assessment/screening of 115–8
  classroom adjustments 94
  comprehension (vs. language comprehension) 64
  connectionist model 62
  definition 59
  dual cascaded model 62–3
  enjoyment of 65
  further/higher education 169–70
  ICT 201
  Matthew effect 65
  neurology of 59

reading *cont.*
  older learners 168–70
  phases of development 64
  phonics ('bottom-up') approach 61
  resources for 198–201
  rope model 61
  teaching 65–6, 156–7
  upper/lower (simple) model 60–1
  whole language ('top down')
    approach 61–2, 169
  in workplace 174–5
reading buddies 141
reading cards 152–4
reading pens 66
'reading wars' 61
referencing sources 172
register of DFQM organizations 220
repetitions 68
report writing 119–21
resources
  for alphabet skills 196–7
  for phonics 197–8
  for phonological awareness 194–5
  for reading 198–201
  selecting appropriate 192–3
  study skills 205–7
  for writing 201–4
reversals 68
revision technique 143
rhythmic timing 36
rise time 36
rope model of reading 61
Rose Report (commissioning of) 19

scaffolding learning 129
scheme of work 180
screening *see* assessment/screening
secondary age learners
  in the classroom 189–90
  one-to-one work 186–8
  small group work 189
self-correction 68
self-esteem 135–6
semantic cueing system 67–8
sight words 60
signal intensity 36
small group work 184–5, 189
SMART targets 181–3, 187–8
spaced learning 129
speech energy 36
spelling
  classroom adjustments 94–5
  definition 72
  difficulties (overview) 80–1
  'layers of spellings' 74
  learning 74–6
  in National Curriculum 79–80
  phonemes/graphemes 72–3
  phonics learning difficulties 82–4
  phonological awareness difficulties 81–2
  rules 155–6
  stages of development (models) 76–9
  strategies to help with 84–5
  testing 116
  in workplace 175
spelling cards 154–5
SQ3R 144
'square root rule' 130
statistics 24, 25, 220
strengths identification/
    development 118–9, 141–2
structured teaching 128–9
study skills 101, 143–4, 168–72, 205–7
substitutions 68
syllables 155–6
syntactic cueing system 67–8
synthetic phonics 147

teaching
  evaluation of 211–7
  methodology 102
technical qualifications 166
temporal sampling theory 36–7
terminology 20–4
three-level framework 30–1
time management 172, 175
'top-down' whole language
    approach 61–2, 169

upper (phonological) circuit 60

verbal ability 176
verbal memory (definition) 21
verbal processing speed 21
visual processing
  definition 22
  difficulties 66
'visual stress' 22
visual-spatial sketchpad 37, 126
vocabulary development 93, 142, 199
vocational qualifications 166

whole language ('top-down')
    approach 61–2, 169
Wide Range Intelligence Test 21–2

working memory
definition 21
model of 37–8, 125–6
workplace
difficulties faced 24–5
dyslexia not barrier in 168
organization skills in 175–6
reading 174–5
spelling 175
time management 175
verbal ability 176
writing 175
writing
assessing 116–7
classroom adjustments 95–6, 101
ICT 204
older learners 170–2
resources for 201–4
teaching 157–8
in workplace 175

zone of proximity 129

Author Index

AchieveAbility 25
Adams, M.J. 99, 128
Adams, W. 21
Adams-Gordon, B. 126
ADHD Foundation 46, 47
Alexander, J. 136
Alexander-Passe, N. 13, 136, 163, 164
Alloway, R.G. 91
Alloway, T.P. 91
Armstrong, T. 25
Augur, J. 34

Baddeley, A.D. 13, 37, 125, 126
Barkley, R. 46, 47
Bastien-Toniazzo, M. 126
Bielby, N. 62
Binder, C. 127
Bird, R. 53
Bissex, G.L. 75
Boudreau, D. 81
Bourassa, D. 75, 76, 77
Bowers, P.G. 10, 33
Bowers, P.N. 12, 76
Bradley, L. 10, 32, 74
Braun, E.M. 25
Breznitz, Z. 148
Briggs, S. 99
Brilliant Reading Comprehension 101
British Dyslexia Association (BDA) 10, 15, 20, 24, 25, 44, 45, 48, 51, 54, 55, 91, 221, 223
Broadbent, H.J. 124
Brooks, G. 83, 85, 128, 129, 161
Broomfield, H. 100
Bruck, M. 100
Bryant, P.E. 10, 32, 74, 76

Cambridge Dictionary 21
Caplan, M. 75
Carroll, J.M. 164
Cassar, M. 76
Chall, J.S. 75
Chinn, S. 53
Clifford, V. 100
Coltheart, M. 11, 62
Combley, M. 99, 100
Cowling, H. 100
Cowling, K. 100
Crystal, D. 74
Curran, A. 44

Davis, C. 74
Davis, R.D. 25
Deacon, S.H. 76
DeFries, J.C. 39
Department for Children, Schools and Families 92
Department for Education (DfE) 12, 25, 75, 79, 80, 92, 127, 140, 155, 165, 166
Department for Education and Skills 83, 96
Devonshire, V. 81
Drew, C. 138
Dweck, C.S. 138
Dyslexia Gold 101
Dyslexia-SpLD Trust 220

Ebbinghaus, H. 129
Education Endowment Foundation (EEF) 13, 25, 137
Ehri, L.C. 12, 64, 74, 75, 77, 78, 84, 128

Fawcett, A.J. 10, 23, 34, 91, 124, 130, 149
Fisher, S.E. 39
Flanagan, B. 25
Fletcher, H. 75
Frith, U. 11, 30, 31, 39, 74, 77, 78
Fulbright, R.K. 33

Galbraith, A. 136
Gathercole, S.E. 128
Gentry, J.R. 11, 77, 78
Gerber, P.J. 163
Gibbon, H. 55
Gilchrist, J. 22
Gillingham, A. 124
Glutting, J. 21
Gooch, D. 43
Goodman, K. 61
Goswami, U. 10, 36, 81, 100
Gough, P.B. 11, 61, 156
Gray, S. 128
Green, L. 76
Growth Engineering 129
Guardiola, J.G. 30

Hall, K. 71
Hamilton, L.G. 157
Hatcher, P. 100
Hayes, H. 76
Henry, M. 74
Hermann, K. 30
Hickey, K. 99
Hinshelwood, J. 29
Hitch, G. 13, 37, 125
Hornsby, B. 100
Hulme, C. 33, 44, 128
Humphrey, N. 135, 136

ICAN 52
Iles, J.E. 164
International Dyslexia Association 161

Jamieson, C. 162, 163, 167, 168, 169
Jarrett, P. 53
Jolly Learning Ltd 83, 96

Kaplan, B. 23, 44
Kelly, K. 12, 13, 81, 83, 85, 91, 92, 99, 100, 115, 124, 126, 130, 131, 148, 149, 150, 153, 154, 155, 169
Khalid, S. 56
Kirby, A. 55
Kirby, P. 29
Kirk, J. 24, 161, 162, 163
Klein, C. 24

Leather, C. 161
Lexia Learning 101
Li, J.J. 33
Liberman, I.Y. 10, 32
Livingstone, M.S. 35
Lovegrove, W.J. 35
Lundberg, I. 81, 162

McClelland, J.L. 11, 62
MacKay, N. 129
McLoughlin, D. 161, 163, 164, 165, 168
McMurray, S. 81
McVeigh, C. 81
Malpas, M.D. 162
Maxwell, C. 95
Miles, M. 100
Milne, D. 11, 12, 60, 74, 77, 84, 156
Moody, S. 161, 163, 164, 165
Morgan, E. 162, 163, 167, 168, 169
Morgan, W.P. 29, 38
Mortimore, T. 123, 128
Morton, J. 30, 39
Moseley, D. 95
Mullins, P. 135, 136
Muter, V. 13, 32, 43, 44, 155

Nalvany, B. 136
National Autistic Society 48
National Human Genome Research Institute 38
Nessy Learning Ltd 83, 85, 100, 127
Nicolson, R. 10, 23, 34, 91, 124, 130, 149
Nicolson, T. 75

Office for National Statistics (ONS) 24
OFSTED 220
O'Hare, A. 56
One Minute Reader 101
Orton, S.T. 30

Packiam Alloway, T.P. 128
Pam, N. 35
Pavey, B. 164, 169
Pennington, B.F. 10, 11, 38, 39, 43, 44, 56
Peterson, R.L. 38
Petty, G. 132
Phillips, S. 12, 13, 81, 83, 85, 91, 92, 99, 100, 115, 124, 126, 130, 131, 148, 149, 150, 153, 154, 155, 169
Piaget, J. 123
Pop, H.M. 75
Price, L.A. 163

Rack, J.P. 32
RADLD (Raising Awareness of Developmental Language Disorder) 51
Rae, C. 34
Ramus, F. 10, 91, 148

Raskind, M. 136
Read Naturally 101
Read Successfully 100
Read Theory 101
Reece, C. 75
Reid, G. 14, 24, 82, 83, 128, 161, 162, 163, 164, 168
Rice, M. 161
Richards, T.L. 76
Rising Stars 101
Rollett, S. 126
Rose, J. 10, 13, 14, 19, 20, 21, 22, 23, 31, 32, 33, 34, 37, 43, 60, 61, 89, 91, 99, 128, 147, 150
Rose, S.J. 11
Rowe, D.W. 71
Rowlandson, J. 95

Scarborough, H. 61
Scerri, T.S. 38
Schlesinger, N.W. 128
Schreiber, L. 81, 84
Schuele, C.M. 81
Schulte-Körne, G. 38
Seidenberg, M.S. 11, 62
Seitz, A. 123, 126
Shams, L. 123, 126
Sheslow, D. 21
Shrestha, P. 129, 130
Sinclair, J. 25
Singleton, C.H. 128
Snowling, M.J. 10, 11, 32, 44, 64, 74, 75, 91, 128, 148
Stainthorp, R. 63, 168
Stanovich, K.E. 10, 32, 65, 157
Stein, J. 10, 35, 36, 91, 148
Stevenson, J. 47
Stillman, B. 124
Stone, L. 75
Stuart, M. 63, 168
Sumner, E. 81

Talking Products 97
Tallal, P. 35
Think 2 Read 101
Thomson, M. 124
Toe by Toe 127
Treichler, F.R. 123
Treiman, R. 75, 76, 77, 84, 100
Tunmer, W.E. 10, 61, 156

UCAS 166
United Nations 24
Units of Sound 100

Vellutino, F.R. 10, 31, 32
Vygotsky, L.S. 129

Wagner, R.K. 32
Walker, J. 74
Walsh, V. 35, 36
Watkins, B. 124
Willcutt, E.G. 43
Wolf, M. 10, 33, 162
Wolf, U. 178
Wordshark 83, 85, 100